A Little Noticed Revolution

A Little Noticed Revolution:
An Oral History of the Model Cities Program and Its Transition to the Community Development Block Grant Program

John Sasso and Priscilla Foley

National Community Development Association
Community Development Training Institute

With Chapters by
Mark Tigan and Madeline Landau

Community Development Training Institute
Berkeley Public Policy Press
Institute of Governmental Studies
University of California, Berkeley
2005

Library of Congress Cataloging-in-Publication Data

Sasso, John, 1938-

A little noticed revolution : an oral history of the Model Cities Program and it transition to the Community Development Block Grant Program / John Sasso and Priscilla Foley, with chapters by Mark Tigan and Madeline Landau.
     p. cm.
     ISBN 0-87772-418-0
1. United States. Model Cities Administration. 2. Community Development Block Grant Program (U.S.) 3. Community development, Urban—United States. I. Foley, Priscilla, 1943- II. Title

HN90.C6S26 2005
307.1'416'097309045—dc22   2005001281

In memory of
Audrey Nelson, Luther Roberts, Jr., Erwin France, Paul Poulos, Don Slater,
Goldie Watson, Logan Delaney, and Thomas Foley

Acknowledgments

In the years I directed the Model Cities Program Directors Association and the National Community Development Association, I had the privilege of working with many able, imaginative, and often selfless individuals. We believed that Model Cities was something special and rare in government and perhaps the most exciting idea ever to be applied to the problems of poverty. Remembering these former colleagues was the inspiration for this book.

For their tireless work in transcribing the interviews and for keeping the process going, thank you to Dorothy Allen, Sandra Paton, Linda Nilsson, and Cameron Moore. For offering good sense and timely advice, thank you to Cheryl Lander and Lynda Tisdell. For their financial support, thank you to the National Community Development Association and the Community Development Training Institute.

For their time and candor, thank you to all those interviewed. And for those with whom I have had the honor to work and who continue toiling in our communities, I have the deepest appreciation.

Contents

Preface

In 1968, the United States Congress passed legislation authorizing the Model Cities Program (MCP). The program was, arguably, the most ambitious nationally funded effort to date to reverse the debilitating effects of prejudice and studied neglect on urban communities. In all, 151 cities across the United States were selected as participants. A modest number, but funding was generous. The program was to be a demonstration, and, hinging on its perceived merits, further legislation to help impoverished communities might or might not be proposed. Targeted communities might include neighborhoods pocketed in vast industrialized cities or a designated quadrant in a small regional city whose urban edges quickly give way to farmland.

Model Cities was a field study for democratic experimentation, the trial-and-error moment of truth for many social theories. It captured and focused the energy of people ready to entertain a new standard for social justice. It attracted and empowered individuals previously disenfranchised from exercising control in matters affecting their own destinies. For nearly every participant in the program, whether city official, program staff member, neighborhood resident, congressional aide, or government appointee, it was an experience that altered attitudes. The program provided career opportunities to minorities and expanded expectations of city government for services relating to health, transportation, education, daycare, housing, recreation, employment, infrastructure, and sanitation.

Drawing both praise and criticism while still in progress and long after its conclusion, Model Cities could not guarantee complete success, particularly as it moved in the direction of innovation—creativity is sometimes messy. The ability to experiment resulted in impressive successes, and some embarrassing excesses. Lasting but five years, it was a brief moment in time demarcated by a confluence of conditions—urban riots, the war in Vietnam, the zealous idealism of the 1960s and, ultimately, a challenge to act. People from diverse backgrounds came together, eager to right social and economic wrongs, eager to test the institutions of city government.

I was one of those people, drawn to the Model Cities Program by its promise, at its most elemental, to help people help themselves. Many others, of every social and economic caste, seemed to find themselves in the same place.

An earlier Johnson administration initiative in the "War on Poverty," the Office of Economic Opportunity (OEO), had created a climate of distrust between city government and citizen participation groups. Funding was one of the divisive issues since federal funds went directly to the Community Action Agency, whose citizen participation group functioned independently of city government.

In contrast, the Model Cities Program adhered to the "three-legged stool" theory. The program emphasized a structure of shared power between a citizen participation group and the city government under the guidance of the program's professional staff. The program would bring an arsenal of federal resources to bear on the causes of poverty and attempt to bring local opposing factions together in a cooperative effort.

The first step to becoming a Model City was the application process, which required a city to document need. Once selected, a combination of MCP staff, resident citizen participants, and city officials prepared a comprehensive plan that addressed the needs of a targeted neighborhood. The planning process could take as long as a year. Although approval by the U.S Department of Housing and Urban Development (HUD) was required before a plan could be implemented, federal regulations could not dictate the specific components in a plan. Each program model was different. For example, San Francisco had two Model Neighborhoods, each with a different structure and plan (see Richardson, chapter 3). Variation and flexibility underscored the Model Cities concept: address as many problems as can be identified in a specific area . . . not just one or two, because the underlying causes of poverty are complex and may differ from one location to another. And within a location, treat those causes as interconnected.

No matter how good the plan, it had to be tweaked as things went along. Citizen participation groups had to learn to establish a working relationship since members of groups were often new to the exercise of power. They often had to learn to diagnose problems and recommend solutions in cooperation with city officials. In fact, the National Citizen Participation Council (NCPC) provided training for citizen participants. (see Hyde, chapter 1) Just the timing of a vote—allowing all the information and opinions to be heard and getting past the emotion of the moment—could be a problem. For example, as director of the Pawtucket Model Cities Program in Rhode Island, the citizen participation group typically took a vote at one meeting and reversed it at the next. This indecision went on for months until, finally, all participants agreed to rules governing the voting process.

Despite the bureaucratic attitudes of some elected officials and the unrealistic demands of some citizen participation groups, the Model Cities Program left its mark on cities across the country. Tucson, Arizona, dramatically improved sanitation for residents living in substandard housing (see Lander, chapter 6). Alma, Alabama, initiated the cultivation of blueberries as a cash crop for the surrounding region (see Walden, chapter 9). Seattle, Washington, turned a crumbling downtown district known as Pioneer Square into a thriving tourist attraction. (see Hundley, chapter 6) Gainesville, Georgia, was so successful in attracting industrial enterprises that the city itself became a successful enterprise (see Cox, chapter 4). Housing, education, health, employment opportunities, employment training, recreation, parks, and transportation, to name a few, were all within the purview of the Model Cities Program.

In conducting the interviews that are the basis for this oral history, I have revisited many friends and colleagues from the Model Cities Program. Invariably, we continue to debate what did or did not work, what has changed in today's political climate, what we would have done differently given what we know today.

The tone of our discussion is friendly—from the outset of the program, we had established a pattern of shared ideas and information. In the recounting, we relive the felt conditions of our experience: relishing the dynamics of face-to-face problem solving; challenging the bureaucracy; actualizing citizen participation; inviting controversy and experimentation; and believing we could succeed.

John Sasso

Abbreviations

ARA: Area Redevelopment Administration
CAA: Community Action Agency
CAP: Community Action Program
CDBG: Community Development Block Grant Program
CETA: Comprehensive Employment and Training Act
EDA: Economic Development Administration, U.S. Department of Commerce
FANNIE MAE: Federal National Mortgage Association (FNMA)
FHA: Federal Housing Administration
FREDDIE MAC: Federal Home Loan Mortgage Corporation (FHLMC)
GAO: General Accounting Office
GINNIE MAE: Government National Mortgage Association (GNMA)
GSE: Government Sponsored Enterprise
HDR: Housing and Redevelopment Reporter
HEW: U.S. Department of Health, Education Welfare
HHFA: U.S. Housing and Home Finance Agency
HHS: U.S. Department of Health and Human Services
HPD: Department or Housing, Preservation and Development, New York, New York
HRA: Housing and Redevelopment Authority
HRA: Human Resources Administration, New York, New York
HUD: U.S. Department of Housing and Urban Development
LRMCP: Little Rock Model Cities Program
MCO: Mission Coalition Organization
MCP: Model Cities Program, HUD
MMNC: Mission Model Neighborhood Corporation
MSHDA: Michigan State Housing Development Authority
NACO: National Association of Counties
NAHRO: National Association of Housing and Redevelopment Officials
NCDA: National Community Development Association
NCPC: National Citizen Participation Council
NDP: Neighborhood Development Program
NLC: National League of Cities
NLIHC: National Low-Income Housing Coalition
NMCDA: National Model Cities Directors Association
NMCP: Newark Model Cities Program
NSA: Neighborhood Strategy Area
OEO: U.S. Office of Economic Opportunity
OMB: U.S. Office of Management and Budget
REMIC: Real Estate Mortgage Investment Conduit
RICC: Regional Interagency Coordination Committee

RLA: Redevelopment Land Agency, Washington, D.C.
SMCP: Seattle Model Cities Program
TVA: Tennessee Valley Authority
UDAG: Urban Development Action Grants
URA: Urban Renewal Administration
USCM: U.S. Conference of Mayors
VISTA: Volunteers in Service to America
WCDC: Winooski Community Development Corporation, Winooski, Vermont

List of Photographs

Part One

A Laboratory for Social Change

"What President Johnson probably said is, 'Look, we need a goddamn program for the cities. You guys put it together.'"

George Gross

By design, the Model Cities Program engaged in an experimental, often controversial effort to counter the causes of poverty. HUD encouraged flexible planning and strategies that would allow each community to identify and address its own distinct problems. Among the 151 cities participating no two plans were the same. And the perceived success or failure of a program was subject to debate by detractors outside the program as well as opposing factions within the program. Of Model Cities, Warren Butler (chapter 2) would say, it "resists definition."

Part One focuses on administrators from HUD who formulated and oversaw the Model Cities Program, legislative counselors who were instrumental in bringing the program to fruition, and representatives of public interest groups whose experience and input gave it definition. They also speak to issues that affected the program including support from, and rivalries among, federal agencies; citizen participation and empowerment; cooperation between citizens and local government; and the critical necessity for balanced, encompassing planning.

1

HUD, the Hill, and the Public Interest Groups

Tom Cochran, a young southern lawyer, describes the Kennedy administration's sense of commitment as "almost religious." He moves to Washington, D.C., during the Johnson administration and becomes Office of Economic Opportunity (OEO) chief lobbyist for Jobs Corps and Head Start. After Nixon takes office, Cochran joins the U.S Conference of Mayors (USCM). He views the MCP as the federal government's agent for change, in part, by bringing disenfranchised people into leadership positions thereby forcing mayors—at first resistant to the MCP—to recognize the program as a political force.

To H. Ralph Taylor, 1966 HUD assistant secretary for the MCP, falls the task of setting a politically acceptable direction for the program. He believes that Model Cities should not be cast in the mold of Urban Renewal—focusing on physical development only—but should also address "social boundaries." Further, because HUD cannot audit the many smaller programs included under the MCP, Taylor wants to simplify the administrative process. To demonstrate the quirks in the Model City selection process, Taylor, a Red Sox fan, relates a humorous anecdote in which Winston-Salem, N.C.—home to a Boston Red Sox farm team—is rejected for the MCP; however, later on, the application quietly reappears and is accepted.

When President Nixon takes office in 1968, the National League of Cities (NLC) recognizes the political potential of Republican Mayor Floyd Hyde of

3

Fresno, Calif., and places him in a leadership position. Soon, he attracts the notice of President Nixon and becomes the Republican appointee to replace Ralph Taylor. When told that his task is to end the MCP, he is surprised; however, the program is politically too well established. Hyde convinces the Nixon administration of the program's worth and makes it more acceptable to Republicans. He emphasizes the program's cooperative relationship between citizens and government and urges that, for efficiency, money be funneled through one agency rather than many separate agencies. Long before the end of the five-year MCP, Hyde is already considering how to preserve and transition the program's best ideas to a larger, more encompassing successor program in community development.

In the mid-1960s, parish priest John Tuite, attracted by the antibureaucratic nature of the MCP, leaves the church to work at HUD in Washington, D.C. Tuite, having learned community organization on the South Side of Chicago, Ill., has seen neighborhoods self-destruct. At HUD, the Saul Alinsky philosophy—bring people together by treating government as a common enemy—is the subject of debate and perceived by many as self-defeating. With the advent of the Nixon administration, Republicans attempt to reorganize and control HUD, however the result is chaos. Also, there is rivalry within HUD between the functional people and the operational people because each group believes it is doing the more important work.

In California, Don Dodge investigates problems of juvenile delinquency. Because he designs a data system to track offenders that attracts the notice of OEO, he is soon working in Washington, D.C., as a consultant on problems at Job Corps centers. This leads to work with the MCP. He compares the premise of the MCP—if the causes of poverty are interrelated, then remedies must be across the board—to earlier programs that operated in narrow categorical terms. To Dodge, the evolution of the MCP beyond OEO is in devolving power to cities to remedy problems.

A teacher in Bogota, Columbia, Don Patch makes a career change to become the administrative officer for the Inter-American Housing Center. In 1959, he returns to Washington, D.C. He becomes a HUD intern; learns about renewal and public housing; joins the Urban Renewal Administration; and before long, is earmarking HUD programs for the MCP. Patch believes that if separate agencies can be made to work together in support of the MCP, the program will be more effective, but the agencies are resistant. One problem he cites is that money from Renewal and Housing Programs and earmarked for the MCP is instead used to finish Renewal projects that serve the broader interests of the city but do not provide housing for the poor. Another problem is that neighborhoods in the program are too big with populations so diverse that the desired impact cannot be achieved.

Pat Henry helps manage OEO funded, antipoverty programs in New York City. The programs are weak, he believes, because they fail to foster economic development and do not run "in sync" with City Hall. Also, he thinks that "maximum feasible citizen participation" ought to be fine-tuned. Henry becomes lead-man in the MCP Regional Office in NYC but soon accepts a job at HUD as Federal Response Coordinator for the MCP. The difficulty, he discovers, is that other federal agencies do not want to support the program. HUD loans Henry to the city of Cleveland, Ohio, to oversee the transition of that city's MCP to a CDBG Program. The Cleveland MCP has lost four years of funding owing to the citizen participation group's veto power and the group's inconsistent planning and priority setting process.

J. Thomas Cochran
Executive Director, United States Conference of Mayors

In the early 1960s, the conviction that the time had come to break the gridlock of poverty seemed to carom through the offices of government. For Thomas Cochran, a young lawyer from Butler, Georgia, caught up in the building momentum, Washington, D.C., was the place to be. After Lyndon Johnson took office following the assassination of President Kennedy, Cochran became chief lobbyist for Head Start and Jobs Corps, programs initiated through President Johnson's creation of the Office of Economic Opportunity (OEO). With the advent of the Nixon administration in 1968, and needing a new job, Cochran began a career with the United States Conference of Mayors (USCM) that continues today.

Pride and Optimism

I had grown up in a segregationist area of the South, a rural agrarian area. School was segregated. Everything was segregated. We didn't think there would ever be a southern president of the United States.

I was 14 years old when I first saw President Kennedy on TV during the 1956 convention. That same year, I saw Elvis Presley for the first time. We'd gone through the Eisenhower years and *Que Sera Sera* with Doris Day. There was something about Kennedy and Elvis that stirred me. It was almost religious. I [expected] to go into political life in Georgia because my grandfather had been

Photo 1: Ed Somers, U.S. Conference of Mayors; Thomas Cochran, U.S. Conference of Mayors, John A. Sasso; and Eugene Lowe, U.S. Conference of Mayors

a state senator. At age 18, I went to the University of Georgia and was head of the Young Democrats, [and] even though challenges about race were inside [me], something about Kennedy touched me. Washington, D.C., was about doing something for people; it was about fighting poverty.

We [felt] a strong commitment with President Kennedy. It had nothing to do with money; it had something to do with being proud of our country, feeling patriotic. Kennedy was a war hero. We were proud of the American flag; we felt wonderful, and we were optimistic.

It's still there . . . in those of us in our mid-50s and early 60s. America changed when President Kennedy was shot. We'd never seen television like that. Television moved into our lives, became our synagogue, our church, and our temple. Now, when [the country] has trouble, [we] don't go to church; [we] go to the TV.

Johnson took [up Kennedy's commitment] and transformed the whole onslaught of civil rights legislation. Political leadership came right out of the streets [with Community Action Programs] and slid right into the Model Cities Program (MCP). People became involved; these programs were their lives. Once the mayors recognized that the program was a political force, the U.S. Conference of Mayors changed, city hall changed, and cities changed.

At first, mayors were resistant, [but, at a USCM meeting] in Chicago, Mayor Richard Daley advised, "Do this Model Cities Program. [Make] it work." So, rather than let the program [operate] outside their political systems, the mayors adopted it . . . and became activists at an early stage. The 1950s [had been] a dormant period [for social action]. Writers such as Michael Harrington wrote about poverty [in *The Other America*]. From such writings came the recognition that the country needed to bring everyone into the mainstream. In the 1960s, the Model Cities Program became the federal government's agent for change.

Tom Cochran lives in Fairfax, Virginia, and is executive director of the U.S Conference of Mayors.

H. Ralph Taylor
HUD Assistant Secretary, Model Cities Program

In 1939, Ralph Taylor was a teacher of Elementary Government at Louisiana State University in New Orleans. In 1940, he was the 11th pick out of 9,200 for the draft. For Taylor, the logical response was to enlist early. He served for almost five years, got discharged, got married, and used the GI Bill to study at Harvard's graduate school of Public Administration. And, he was a Red Sox fan.

Although jobs were scarce after World War II, he was able to secure a position with the Boston Housing Authority. By 1949, Taylor, now the State House expert on urban redevelopment, had prepared a program budget for the Boston Board of Aldermen, won their approval, and was appointed the program's director. However, owing to the board's lack of follow-through, when the city of New Haven, Connecticut, asked him to direct its redevelopment agency in 1955, he accepted.

In 1966, Bob Wood, undersecretary of the U.S. Department of Housing and Urban Development (HUD), invited Taylor, now in private development, to Washington, D.C., and his choice of two available positions. Taylor chose assistant secretary for Demonstration Cities—soon renamed the Model Cities Program because the word "demonstration" was too politically volatile. When puzzled colleagues asked why he chose Model Cities, he answered, "In a man's lifetime . . . it's rare he has the opportunity to start something from scratch."

From Scratch

I knew little about the program, but I did understand that it put together social and physical development. My experience in Boston taught me that public housing was not succeeding. After conducting a series of interviews as follow-up to several projects, I knew that [to be effective], Urban Renewal had to [address] social boundaries as well as physical urban development. Urban redevelopment just didn't have all the tools it needed.

[For my staff], I wanted people with urban dirt on their hands, people who were not academics. Some of my new staff members were people I had worked with in New Haven, who now worked for the Agency for International Development (AID) in Europe. They convinced me that the attributes and skills needed to assist development overseas were the same basic skills needed [for the Model Cities Program].

What was the internal political situation at HUD?

It was a mixed bag. For example, Robert Weaver, secretary of HUD, was supportive of the planning process for cities. It was clear that the funding resources were now available, but we wanted to know the full extent of a city's problems. Revealing that information would violate the [unwritten] rule never to expose the full amount of funding required for [fear of alarming] Congress. I called this issue to Weaver's attention. After giving it careful consideration, he gave me the "go ahead." He supported me [despite] my background in Urban Renewal and his concern that I would tend to the old-line urban redevelopment position, [which focused on physical development only].

That the Housing and Redevelopment Authority (HRA) couldn't be [the model] for the Model Cities Program, was a decision I made on my own. When I told Bob Weaver, he was enthusiastic. I [aired] that decision publicly in, of all places, New Haven, Connecticut. My old companions thought I had betrayed them. Their attitude was so ingrained in respect to real citizen participation that change would have been a major problem. The roots of my position went back to 1946—when a court decision had ruled that the federal government could not be directly involved in the construction of public housing. This led to the mechanism of [local quasi]-independent housing authorities constructing public housing with federal money. What was clear was that the federal government's power, although legally taken away, was still retained.

The initial number of cities in the Model Cities Program was small. The program could not operate like OEO—with funds from the federal government going directly to a community; there had to be a mechanism for funding the cities. A good chunk of the resources going into the neighborhoods was under city control. For example, the program couldn't create an alternative board of education or a sanitary waste system or the other things that were part of city government. [And yet], in slum areas, these functions of city government had been neglected. So I considered Model Cities Program funding as "glue money," money that could be used to [coax the city into putting more of its resources into a Model Neighborhood]. It was leverage money.

You have a story about Winston-Salem, North Carolina, and the importance of being a Red Sox fan?

It's a story that I enjoy telling. Winston-Salem was home to a Red Sox farm team in the 1960s and also, one of 75 second-round cities being considered for the Model Cities Program. However, the White House killed Winston-Salem's approval because the congressman who represented Winston-Salem during the Johnson administration had voted against the war in Vietnam.

Winston-Salem was a [deserving] city, and I wanted it approved. So I waited until the names of the next half dozen cities were to be sent to the White House and slipped Winston-Salem back in with that group. This time the city was approved. While attending a convention a year or so later, I saw a man wearing a Winton-Salem badge. I innocently inquired if he knew why Winston-Salem was in the Model Cities Program. [After listening] to two or three paragraphs of rhetoric [about] how great the city was, I said, "Want to know the real reason? I forwarded the grant because I'm a Red Sox fan."

Under the Nixon administration, Floyd Hyde became the next HUD assistant secretary for Model Cities, and you were in charge of the transition. Did you have any parting concerns?

I had complete faith in Floyd Hyde. However, at the time he came to HUD, I had recently seen the plans for Seattle, Washington, and Atlanta, Georgia. It was clear to me that these plans could not be administered in Washington, D.C. There were too many details, too many separate programs that would require audit controls. I directed the staff to simplify the process. We needed a solution that said to the city, "Use your share [of Model Cities funding] to set objectives for the city. Show how you will meet the statutory [requirements] such as citizen participation and equal opportunity provisions." But [HUD] should not be required to keep the audits straight for a whole series of small projects. [Later], when the Community Development Block Grant Program (CDBG) came out, it seemed the solution that I [had] been headed for.

In 1968, Ralph Taylor returned to private development. He currently lives in Chevy Chase, Maryland.

Floyd Hyde
HUD Assistant Secretary, Model Cities Program

One day in 1964, Floyd Hyde was driving home, "listening to the radio go on about all this squabbling on the City council." His hometown, Fresno, Cali-

fornia, "had gone to hell in a hand basket—terrible local government . . . no relationship between government and people." He got home and announced, "'I'm
going to run for mayor; that's what I'm going to do.'" Hyde, who had been a
Marine in the South Pacific during World War II, was 42 years old, owned a
summerhouse in Monterey, and had a successful career as a lawyer. Although he
had never entertained the idea of a career in politics and had no campaign committee, Hyde stepped into California's exotic mix of political ideologies to become the newly elected, more-liberal-than-moderate, Republican mayor of
Fresno, California.

In November of 1968, Hyde, nearing the end of his term as mayor, attended
a National League of Cities (NLC) meeting. The NLC saw an opportunity in
Hyde: a Republican in the White House required a Republican in the Democrat-
dominated NLC leadership; however, the NLC already had a president. The solution: elect Floyd Hyde as vice president and incoming president for the following year.

Within days he was summoned to New York, along with Pat Healy, executive director of the National League of Cities, and John Gunther, executive director of the U.S Conference of Mayors, to meet with President Nixon and
Nixon's domestic advisor, Pat Moynihan. The issues being presented had been
well prepared the evening before. At the meeting, Nixon just listened. Later,
while waiting for a flight home out of Kennedy Airport, Floyd heard his name
being paged. It was a call from Pat Moynihan, who said, "Mayor Hyde, the
president wants you to come back and serve in his administration."

Floyd Hyde wasn't sure. George Romney, former governor of Michigan,
and now secretary of HUD, executed a wily pursuit for several weeks. At first
Romney said, "Give us some ideas; will you do that?" Days later, he reminded
Hyde about "patriotic duty," before ending abruptly with, "You've had enough
time."

"All right! I'll come," said Hyde.

A Liberal Republican at HUD

H. Ralph Taylor, the previous assistant secretary for Model Cities under
President Johnson, put together his team. They briefed me day and night saying,
"This is a new program; you understand cities. Here's something 'demonstrate'
and you can find out how to do it better." These were Democratic appointees!
They were only interested in good government and hoping this scary Republican
from California might not ruin things.

Two weeks later, Secretary Romney said, "We've got to go to the White
House for a meeting" . . . with Erlichman and a couple of other staff people. The
purpose of the meeting was to figure out how we should get rid of the Model
Cities Program. I was stunned!

Erlichman said, "We've got to take a hard look at it." Some cities had already been announced for planning grants—it was a good move by the Democrats. Erlichman said, "We have to be careful politically."

Now, I'm a little country mayor from Fresno. And here's the task force I'm heading up: George Romney; George Schultz, Secretary of Labor; Elliot Richardson, Secretary of Health, Education, and Welfare (HEW); John Volpe, Secretary of Transportation; someone from OMB [U.S. Office of Management and Budget]; John Erlichman; and Patrick Moynihan, [advisor to Nixon on urban affairs]. We met once a week for about three or four months. The burden was on me to justify, improve, or get rid of the program.

When we'd agreed on basic recommendations, we had a cabinet meeting. Nixon asked each of the cabinet officers what they thought. Romney was supportive of course. Elliot Richardson said, "This makes so much sense to me. If the program is abandoned, I'm going to try to construct something like this at HEW."

Then Nixon got to George Schultz, who said, "I don't really understand what this program is about"; I never really figured him out.

Nixon said, "Well, let me think about this."

I said, "Mr. President, if you have any questions or reservations, I suggest we put together a task force . . . and look at several of the cities underway in their planning." He didn't say anything.

Outside in the parking lot, Romney blew a fuse. "Why did you say that?"

I said, "Governor, I didn't sense the votes were there."

The next morning, Erlichman called and said, "The President likes your idea."

We visited Seattle, Denver, and Hartford. The [departments and offices] represented on the task force were HEW, Labor, Commerce, Transportation, and Budget. One of the highlights was Seattle—a great staff and a great program. We got to Hartford . . . into a citizen participation meeting. Talk about confrontation! I was eating it up. This is the way it has got to be.

We made a nice report—I'd worked in how to massage the program to be more like republicanism. And we were off and running. I'm going into detail because, if the Model Cities Program had not gone forward, the transition to the Community Development Block Grant Program could not have taken place, there would be no program today.

What were your thoughts on the Model Cities Program?

I saw Model Cities as a vehicle for creating a relationship of meaningful citizen involvement with the mayor's office, the "power structure." Up to that time, I saw federal programs as being at arm's length—the Office of Economic Opportunity became adversarial because it functioned apart from city government. My thought was; it isn't going to work that way. Federal programs provide maybe five percent at most, of a city's budget. That's not going to change things. But if five percent can impact the reallocation of resources for the other 95 percent, to meet the needs of the more disadvantaged citizens, we have something.

And something else, we wanted all federal aid to cities to follow the same funnel, to go through one coordinating agency, as opposed to funding through separate grants [from] different federal agencies. The local government could then put the pieces together—employment training, housing, economic development, and social services assistance, the whole range. But that effort failed. In fact when the CDBG Program came along, I tried without success to get an interagency component in, and it was shot down at OMB [U.S. Office of Management and Budget]—"too complicated, doesn't work."

Interagency coordination at the federal level never came to fruition. However, citizen participation gave people a voice.

Yes, I'm proud of the citizen participation part. I had to do some battle to keep that component in the Community Development Block Grant Program. The attitude was, give the money to the mayor, he's held accountable by the citizens. Well, that's garbage. He's held accountable by the powerful citizens.

On one occasion, Secretary Romney came to say a few words to the National Citizen Participation Council (NCPC) leadership. They were meeting in HUD's main conference room . . . blacks, Mexican Americans, Native Americans, and low-income whites, the typical mix we really appreciate. He asked, "Now Floyd, tell me, what group is this?" I told him. "You mean you've been spending money to teach these people how to participate in local government?" He paused, and started laughing. And then he said, "Okay."

Not only to participate, but at a level previously unimagined.

I've seen it all over the country. When I was mayor of Fresno, there weren't two blacks in city government. I chose a black, Jim Aldridge, as director of the Fresno Model Cities Program. Not many years later, he was the city manager at $100,000 a year. Time after time, when I was called before Congress, I'd relate some of these anecdotes. The members only wanted to know how many streets had been paved, how many schools built. I'd say, "We're building something better." But the concept just didn't get through.

I saw the handwriting on the wall for the Model Cities Program. Everybody kept saying "demonstration, five-year demonstration." Long before the five-year period ended, I was asking, "Where do we go from here, how do we preserve what's best about Model Cities?"

Floyd Hyde resigned from HUD in 1975.

John Tuite
HUD Region One Desk Officer, Model Cities Program

In 1958, newly ordained Catholic priest John Tuite learned community organization while assigned to a parish on Chicago's South Side. There, for the first time, the Industrial Areas Foundation (IAF)—using the theories of Saul Alinsky—organized in the black community. Several years later, after reassignment to another parish, he trained and organized a group of doctors, priests, married couples, and psychologists into a faculty of educators on matters of family life. By 1968, Tuite, disaffected with the church, owing in part to the changes effected by the Vatican Council, left the priesthood. Tuite then headed for Washington, D.C., where he began working in the Model Cities Administration during the remaining months of the Johnson administration. Tuite, pleased because the program was antibureaucratic, also found the Model Cities staff an "interesting group of folks, many of whom had come out of [the] Office of Economic Opportunity."

They were different in character than the rest of the people I saw in HUD—old Federal Housing Authority folks and Water and Sewer Program folks. This was a completely different ilk. Anyone can now perhaps recognize what excitement there was in working with this group. They were always thinking ahead and looking to the next program.

"A Different Ilk"

I had lived close to, and was involved with, neighborhoods in the slums of Chicago. The disorganization and lack of any sense of belonging characterizing the people I saw, seemed so beyond the ability of the parishes and priests to do anything about. That these neighborhoods were self-destroying was obvious. Something bigger was needed, something that gave a sense of ownership in those neighborhoods. The parishes did provide a sense of belonging for some groups, but something larger was needed, and it was seeing this "something" in terms of government that I hoped Model Cities might be able to create.

The key debate, as a matter of fact, [was] . . . whether Model Cities would be a program for local governments or for neighborhoods. The narrow focus—really a Saul Alinsky strategy—that OEO had taken was: organize people against the enemy—government at all levels—and create confrontational situations from which people would get this sense of belonging and unity among themselves.

In 1968, we saw that it created a situation in which the people, who made key allocation and resource decisions, were just turned off. In some minds, there was something self-defeating about a philosophy [that created an enemy]. However, others thought that you still had to continue some level of antagonism [to] get any place because government—the bureaucracy—was going to continue to do its own thing and nobody was going to gain. The attempt was to come down somewhere in the middle, to organize around neighborhoods, to create alliances within the neighborhood itself. Government [had] to go ahead and cooperate. The tension, always there, tailored [each city's] program differently.

Local government had to be brought to the table at a time when government generally didn't feel it had to sit down with people in the neighborhoods. There was always that sense of paternalism. And remember that OEO hadn't died; it was still going on and moving into the areas of health, health reform, health clinics, and getting hospitals to deal with issues. That movement was an important part of the organization of Model Cities at the federal level. The line-up of staff in Washington was divided between the operational and the functional sides. The functional folks, people with expertise in labor, health, and education, thought they were doing the important work. The operations folks thought that the functional folks were absolutely irrelevant.

Floyd Hyde, director of Model Cities during the Nixon administration, felt the one thing he just couldn't accomplish was coordination at the federal level.

Well, once the Nixon administration got over the early battle to get rid of the Model Cities Program, the next important stage was the reorganization within HUD. The reorganization was an attempt to capture HUD by the Republicans, who felt they had been out of office for so long that the only thing to do was throw the place into chaos in order to grab control. All the various parts of the department were brought in under community development. A lot of programs [suddenly] lost the autonomy they had had for years, including Urban Renewal, which had been a dominant program and had disdained programs like Model Cities—"that bunch of socialists."

Pulling all the various strings together was just the drastic kind of change that eventually led to the block grant program. Even with H. Ralph Taylor, who had [preceded] Floyd Hyde, the attempt was made to get coordination of all [HUD] programs and the resources from all departments [such as Labor, Transportation, HEW, etc.], into those 151 relatively small neighborhoods. The Model Cities Program was so small and untested; it was a small growth on the body of government . . . and it was never really taken seriously because no one knew whether the program was going to last through another appropriation or not. So those in other departments, who considered themselves so much more important, couldn't even entertain the idea of throwing their major resources into Model Cities neighborhoods.

That was 1968. Thirty-one years later, the Community Development Block Grant Program, [successor to Model Cities] not only continues, but is also one of the longest lasting, largest programs in government.

Why was the Community Development Block Grant Program so successful?

It was a change in relationship: federal and local governments were incorporated into one team. That was the excitement of the whole thing in the1970s, when the program really began to succeed. Before that, the feds wrote the rules and everyone else kept them . . . the disdain for social programs was deeply imbedded in the Urban Renewal Program. That's why, I think, that reorganization within HUD did things that no one anticipated or intended. And that was to wed the social programs and the hardware programs. That marriage became the genius of the Model Cities program, but even more, the genius of the Community Development Block Grant Program.

Following the Model Cities Program, John Tuite became HUD director of the Office of Community Development Block Grants, and next, HUD Area Director in Los Angeles, California. Currently, he is retired and lives in Rancho Mirage, California.

Don Dodge
Director of Program Development, Model Cities Program

In 1953, following several years of military service in Korea, Colorado-born Don Dodge chose California as the place to pursue his education. After attending several schools within the California State University System, Dodge became a Co-principal investigator and research director into the problem of juvenile delinquency at the University of Southern California. In 1964, while working in the city of Santa Monica, Dodge attended a conference sponsored by the National Council of Crime and Delinquency in Las Vegas, Nevada, where he presented a paper on a data system that he had designed to track offenders. As a result, the Office of Economic Opportunity asked him to come to Washington, D.C., to work as a consultant on problems at Job Corps centers. With his acceptance, Dodge began a 35-year career that would progress from director of recruitment and selection for Job Corps trainees, to special assistant to the director of Job Corps, and, in 1967, to the Model Cities Program.

"The Driving Force"

The program was based on the premise that problems were interrelated, therefore remedies—physical, economic, and social—[had to be] across the board. The concept gave rise to legislation that created the [Model Cities] Program. Bob Wood—later the undersecretary of HUD—chaired the committee that began thinking this thing through. Before that time, programs were very narrowly defined in categorical terms . . . including OEO, which was supposed to be the solution to poverty and the salvation [of the poor]. But it turned out that OEO was categorical too. Several OEO programs—Job Corps, Head Start, and the Community Action Agency—still remain, but they were not based on the premise of interrelationships.

I'm making this point because some part of the [Model Cities] Program had its origin in OEO. The evolution [in the MCP]: if problems are in cities, the power to remedy those problems should be in cities . . . and controlled by cities. Previously, power was centralized in Washington, D.C., and, to some extent, in states. The transforming notion was to devolve power and authority to localities because localities would be most aware of their distinct problems and the distinct solutions to those problems . . . keeping in mind the triumvirate of social, economic and physical remedies. Model Cities was an experiment, a demonstration . . . and all good. To me, it was a great adventure.

For five years, instead of "Gotcha," HUD brought federal and local government together to achieve a common good.

Even though there were people at HUD who were cavalier, who thought they were the very best—and I hate to say that I was in that category—we had extraordinary commitment to the program. We had all these specialists as guiding lights for problem resolution. But the real spirit was that we were providing assistance to localities so they could make their own decisions, good or bad.

The constant debate in the early years of the program centered on who was in charge. There was a debate about who was in control, citizens or cities. [More than] one person thought that CP [citizen participation] was the key to everything and that was the banner . . . the driving force. As it turned out, HUD was in control because HUD, as mandated by Congress, had ultimate responsibility.

The program had "lead men", people assigned to cities to be a helping hand. Instead, some were too directorial—"Do it the way I want it done." Lead men fashioned their position with regard to the cities in their region and were quite powerful.

Ideally, the lead man was supposed to blend in, to function as part of a program's staff.

But they set themselves apart. With 15[1] cities, differences in behavior were huge. We had conferences to bring to the fore the idea of citizen participation as the motive power behind the program. However, for citizen participation to be the model of political decision making was foolish because the way we exert political decision-making is through elected officials. We were doing this hybrid thing that was outside the traditional political process.

Citizen participation was like water; it reached its own level and was different in each community.

Yes! Let me tell you about consequences in citizen participation. Let's say six people are on a city council. Each wants one sixth of the pie, but neighborhood groups say, "We are more pressed. We need more resources than the guy next door."

Well, that's why there are means tests . . . and someone has to be at the throttle. However at the local level, government's role dissipates. But that doesn't diminish the idea that government has a role.

As an aside, when I left HUD there were approximately 17,000 people who tracked where money was going. We had plenty of scandals over the years, so everybody beat themselves on the chest to minimize government. But if nobody is tracking the money, people misuse money. So the minimizing of federal government angers me because there is a point where you can no longer get the job done. Not a single dollar is spent that is not appropriated by Congress . . . someone has to be responsible for the use of that money as Congress intended.

From your perspective, what conditions hindered achieving program goals?

I want to talk about the benefits of coordination. Coordination just does not happen. Cooperation does . . . but coordination requires a superior supportive effort.

The expectation was that other federal agencies would produce and deliver monies and resources to Model Neighborhoods. My belief . . . the money and resources that went into the Model Neighborhoods would have gone to them without being earmarked by Model Cities.

The intra-agency idea, coordination of agencies within HUD, was doomed. People resented Model Cities because we attempted to put the arm on them. I'm talking about HUD, Urban Renewal, Water and Sewer, and Housing. These agencies didn't like us trying to maneuver them. They had their own system and wanted to remain within their own process and their own regulations.

In 1970, I wrote a paper that argued for streamlining regulations and requirements . . . however, the HUD leadership did not want to do anything that would rock the boat. And what happened in 1974—[The Community Development Act of 1974]. Rules and regulations could be modified. They could be streamlined and were!

In the Pawtucket MCP, we had the ear of an exceptionally strong mayor, who could command the attention of non-Civil Service department heads. Their jobs were not secure, but the same leverage with agency leadership at the federal level is not possible since the Civil Service system is so tight that agency heads run their own ship.

Yes, at the federal level, all the words are there, but not the delivery system. Except that determination is also a key word. I call it motive power . . . and if you can infect other people with it, and you have access to the political leadership, things can happen.

If you could repeat the Model Cities experience, would you make any changes to the program's philosophy and design?

Philosophy changes? I would not. But I would make one change. I would lodge a supreme power, a single agency. It could be corrupted and I understand that perfectly. But, in terms of cooperation and coordination . . . in terms of stroking, one agency could accomplish a lot.

Don Dodge lives in Arlington, Virginia. He was HUD Deputy Assistant Secretary for Program Management, Community Planning, and Development until his retirement.

Don Patch
HUD Director, Office of Block Grant Assistance

His parents and his mother's parents were ministers. Still, Don Patch knew that the ministry was not for him. Instead, he went to Mexico to earn a master's degree and learn Spanish in preparation for the Foreign Service. Time in Mexico gave way to time in the army. More time followed in Washington, D.C., until Patch, realizing that "things weren't progressing very well on Foreign Service career opportunities," accepted a teaching post with the Colombian/American Institute in Bogota, Columbia, followed in 1955, by an administrative position with the Inter-American Housing Center

After returning to Washington in 1959, Patch spent the next year in the HUD Intern Program learning about renewal and public housing. By 1963, rather than transfer with his field office to Philadelphia, Patch joined the Urban Renewal Administration (URA) to handle the Section 314 Demonstration Grant Program. There, he learned categories of renewal assistance, planning and urban planning programs, how housing programs worked in conjunction with existing programs in community development, Urban Renewal, and eventually, how to earmark HUD programs for the Model Cities Program.

Coordinating the Fiefdoms

The White House [wanted] to make this War on Poverty effort work. We had strong support with [Joseph] Califano, [President Johnson's chief domestic aide], but there was some reticence. [HUD, formerly the U.S. Housing and Home Finance Agency (HHFA)], had just gone through the transition to a cabinet level department.] The Federal Housing Administration (FHA) still felt it wasn't part of HUD. And, except for enlightened souls, getting FHA staff to realize that, as far as the program was concerned, participating in ongoing efforts to assist Model Cities would help FHA's image to serve poor neighborhoods. And help strengthen HUD's ability to assist cities if it could be shown that public housing programs, Federal Housing Administration programs, and community development programs could be tied together in better ways.

With very strong support from [HUD] Secretary Robert Weaver, we sent out a series of memos earmarking community development programs out of the Communities Facilities Administration and the Office of Metropolitan Planning and Development. We took planning money and earmarked housing subsidy programs: Sections 235 and 236 (interest subsidies), Public Housing, and Section 23 (lease housing). Despite the assisted-housing moratorium declared prior to switching to the Section 8 Housing Subsidy Program, we were able to salvage almost 50,000 units of prior subsidized housing programs because of the earmarking process with Model Cities.

How would you contrast OEO and the Model Cities Program?

As far as the old OEO, the staff of Community Action Programs (CAP) got on the train quickly. They realized that "Hey, we're serving rural counties; we've got to go to the state for block grant money and Washington can't help us." CAP agencies that didn't quickly coalesce at the urban/county/large-city level fell by the wayside. Some of the better ones got their administrative people working in Model Cities at the local level. But others just drifted off and tried to survive on leftovers—Labor, HEW, and Justice programs, etc., and OEO direct funding programs.

Was citizen participation in OEO different from citizen participation in the Model Cities Program?

The citizen participation process started strengthening in the last three or four years of Urban Renewal as planning for [its] Neighborhood Development Program (NDP) [was beginning]. A lot of pain [had been] generated at the local level with the turn-around into the Model Cities Program and the termination of competit[ion] for Renewal funds. The Renewal agencies—or their successor agencies—could not deliver on [many] of their promises to the large areas that had been folded-in under Neighborhood Development. A disappointed citizenry was out there [who] realized that the physical improvements [Renewal hoped] to package with social programs weren't going to be delivered. [However], the citizen participation operation [was] better in those communities where we were pressing for it during the terminal years of Renewal and the Neighborhood Development Program. We were able to get these neighborhood groups, along with groups that were delivering supportive services with Model Cities, Health and Human Services (HHS), and Labor funds, involved in neighborhood preservation and rehabilitation efforts.

What did you expect Model Cities to accomplish?

We hoped that it would increase the targeting to poor neighborhoods . . . and hopefully, finish off some of the grander plans of [Urban] Renewal for these neighborhoods. What happened, of course, was that a lot of the money earmarked for Model Cities under the Renewal and Housing Programs became destined for activities that were serving the broader economic development objectives of the city as opposed to dealing with areas most in need. Many of the large Urban Renewal authorities in our urban centers wanted to finish up the gilding of their downtown centerpiece activities designed to attract new development—some new housing, but certainly not housing for poor people.

Model Cities Program funds could be used as leverage to get more funds to finish [renewal] activities rather than taking 100 percent of those funds and plopping them into the Model Neighborhoods. Model Cities got short-changed and, I think, that hurt the program because of unfulfilled expectations.

People like Ralph Taylor, [HUD Assistant Secretary for the Model Cities Program during the Johnson administration and his successor], Floyd Hyde, [during the Nixon administration], pushed for citizen participation. They encountered a lot of very angry citizens as reflected by the visits that we used to get from inner-city citizen organizations and national organizations such as the Low-Income Housing Coalition (LIHC). However, despite many a report that came out criticizing us during the late 1970s and early 1980s, the program did more to pull minorities into the mainstream of community activism, training, management, and development than any other package of programs.

Talk about HUD during the era of Secretary George Romney and Secretary Floyd Hyde.

A lot of the key people that Romney brought in were influenced by the Ripon Society, a group of [Republican] progressive thinkers. Floyd Hyde, his deputy Bob Baeda, and Warren Butler, [deputy assistant secretary for the Model Cities Program]—all generally liberal and really savvy—had reason to salvage the program and set the stage for the program's transition to the Community Development Block Grant Program. [Their] agenda was designed to break down these—for better or worse—perceived fiefdoms of public housing authorities, Urban Renewal authorities, and park authorities and public works agencies. These local agencies with federally funded, categorical programs delivered in a so-called competitive manner, had free reign to do their own thing once the grants were received. The push to get [control] into the hands of the elected officials was a clear theme.

At the time, HUD Undersecretary [Richard] Van Dusen said, "The guys at Urban Renewal had their binge, now they're going to get their hangover." That quote reflected the tenor of the new Republican appointees' thrust to move control of federal programs to the mayors by playing hardball with agencies pushing for huge sums of money to complete their Urban Renewal plans. The dramatic shift was to downsize the influence of "grantsmanship" in federally funded categorical programs. Some groups that represented these independent, public and quasi-public agencies [dug in] their heels. They resisted the change to empower mayors despite the fact that they were the ones, back in the late 1960s and early 1970s, who were calling for some kind of block grant to give cities an entitlement based on needs assessment.

Some programs, such as those for economic development, didn't go well. What were the reasons?

One problem was a local, political problem and became a national problem as it emerged. The areas were too big! And there were too many—just the opposite of what we wanted when we started out. We wanted them not too big, not too small—just big enough to make an impact and small enough so that we could effectively deal with an array of problems and show that here was an approach that had some chance of success. Instead, we picked huge Model Neighborhoods with diverse populations without taking the steps to break them down into subneighborhoods where we could concentrate in certain areas that would make a difference.

Talk about the earmarking process and the delivery of funds and services.

[HUD] had earmarks nationally and earmarks locally and also at the regional office level—like the housing rehab programs and housing assistance program. My perception is that the 30 to 40 percent of Model Cities cash and later, Community Development Block Grant cash being spent on housing programs didn't make much difference in the neighborhoods. Basically, Model Cities never got the full impact of HUD Housing Assistance to target poorer neighborhoods. The criteria that HUD had for selecting areas for rehab programs just didn't mesh with the neighborhood selection process for Model Cities.

In many cases, the real rehab exercise was to bail out a lot of the Section 236 housing subsidy projects [done] under George Romney's Operation Rehab. [Those projects] kept coming back to us, five or 10 years later. The same result occurred with Section 312, the rehab loan program. The properties just came back in these poorer neighborhoods and we had to refinance them or redo the rehab.

We delivered the cash. The local government could use it, rather than us delivering reams of rules with a little cash on the side. That is a fact! Our message was, "Hey, we're getting out of your hair." Warren Butler moved every planner he could find on the payroll away from the program operations—every architect and engineer. We had to keep a few for their expertise because of federal environmental requirements. For Warren, it was anathema that we would have anybody from HUD second-guessing a local planner or a local Department of Public Works official about the size of a sewer pipe.

What was most rewarding about your work with the Model Cities Program and the Community Development Block Grant Program?

I felt good about the whole transition process from [Urban] Renewal to Model Cities, to Community Development Block Grants. It was a sea change in the federal program delivery system that was unsettling to local entrenched bureaucracies. One key area was the termination/transition process from separate categorical programs, to coordinated Model Cities' efforts, to block grants.

And I felt good about salvaging a lot of housing projects during the transition period that otherwise might have been frittered off into political deals . . . and salvaging the Loan Guarantee Program (LGP) in the mid-1980s. If [HUD had] put that program on budget in 1986, it would have been dead. OMB wanted to artificially establish arbitrary risk factors and calculate a whole set of projected losses, which would have made it a nonguarantee program. That the next several administrations kept the [Loan Guarantee] Program in the forefront was a major accomplishment. I would have liked to see the Community Development Program grow substantially by picking up programs from other agencies, but there was not the will to do that in the Clinton administration.

Looking back, the Model Cities Program was a time when the growth of state and local employment-payrolls was starting to take off—during the last two decades [the number of minorities hired] at state and local government levels has tripled. Many of the key hires in this period were from the ranks of those who cut their teeth on Model Cities and the Community Development Block Grant Program

There are damn few neighborhood-based organizations doing physical development or major social development work that, at some point, haven't received infusions of funds from the two programs that made a difference. The flexibility of [Model Cities and the Community Development Block Grant Program] enabled local government to respond to a wide range of needs. Relationships between local government and neighborhood groups are still being built. That . . . is another contribution of Model Cities.

Don Patch lives in Washington, D.C., and is retired.

Pat Henry
Federal Response Coordinator, Model Cities Program, HUD

As preamble, Pat Henry mentions that he was born in 1933 in Chicago, Illinois, before being hired to help manage the antipoverty program in New York City. His responsibility was for the OEO funded Manhattan Programs, which were, as described by Henry, "a pretty tight ship." Money was tracked, there was a process for citizen participation and proposals had to be prepared, however, weaknesses in the program were becoming apparent. The program was, he said, "nowhere near economic development and also nowhere near City Hall." OEO programs were really out in the neighborhoods. Management was with City Hall. OEO money that did get approved went directly to the recipient nonprofit organization, which ran a kind of paragovernment instead of a program. The big money, administered by the major city departments, was running parallel to [OEO programs] but not in sync.

Henry thought that "maximum feasible citizen participation" ought to be fine-tuned and that a relationship with city government needed to be developed. He was to see this idea become a reality in Model Cities in which local government was meant to take an innovative approach in the coordination of federal funds.

Henry began to work for the Model Cities Regional Office in New York City as a lead man for the cities of Pawtucket, and Providence, Rhode Island, and for Holyoke, Massachusetts. In 1970, he was offered a position at HUD in Washington, D.C., coordinating federal funds for the Model Cities Program.

"Lessons Learned"

A General Accounting Office (GAO) report [about] interagency coordination came out after a few years. GAO was very friendly to the concept of Model Cities and very friendly to the concept of mandated interdepartmental coordination of their funding for Model Cities. Their criticism was not of HUD but of other federal agencies that were not earmarking and committing sufficient funds in a way consistent with what they considered a federal mandate. I got the assignment of writing the HUD response to the GAO report. HUD was quite good at earmarking HUD funds for Model Cities [and] had earmarked $400 million a year for three years in a row. If you had asked, as we did at the time, what the total was from Transportation, Labor, and the Department of Health, Education and Welfare, it was pretty minimal. HEW had a gigantic overall budget . . . like a quadruple-sized aircraft carrier that could not be turned. It was just about impossible to get significant money from them. Labor was another story. Their model was to get in on the ground, get a process going, set priorities, and be serious about the value of success. And, they were interested in Model Cities because that's where the troubled demographics were.

What were local communities trying to accomplish through Model Cities?

In 1974, I went on loan from HUD to Cleveland, Ohio, to become that city's first Community Development Director and to start its Community Development Block Grant Program . . . that meant taking over the Cleveland Model Cities Program. Cleveland should have been in year five of the five-year Model Cities cycle, but the city was just beginning year one . . . and had lost the first four years of funding—$9.3 million per year—because of its nonconsistent program planning and priority setting process. There was a veto power being exercised in the Model Neighborhood, losing $37.2 million over the four-year period. I saved the first year CDBG budget in which I had a line item called "continuation of Model Cities"—$1.3 million. We continued Model Cities' health, dental, the recreation and mini-bus program, law and justice, manpower, elderly, and daycare. That kind of list jumps off the page. What were cities trying to do? They were trying to deliver services.

If you used the phrase "economic development services" there would be a big question mark on everybody's face. Economic development was not anywhere near the Model Cities Program in my experience . . . nor was Model Cities very close to the development of housing. Now and then Model Cities got into some housing rehab. The 312 Housing Rehabilitation Program, a categorical grant program, was by far the favorite HUD program in the neighborhoods and the favorite priority in the CDBG Program.

If you asked me what was the single most important issue in the OEO program, it was the recruitment of talented people who previously hadn't had a program within which to exercise that talent. This was especially true in Model Cities. People who became directors were very skilled.

Also very strong in Model Cities was that the program had a beginning, middle, and an end. People can focus on five-year periods . . . consensus-building loves momentum and it's really hard to retain momentum when the endgame is out of sight. You want to be able to say, "Alright, let's hit the ball, and let's evaluate ourselves." Evaluation, by the way, came into its own in Model Cities. At HUD we were determined to know what was being accomplished—the success stories that we could capture and explain—so we could give what we called the "lesson learned."

The critical component, it seemed to me, was in a city program's citizen participation model.

Cambridge, Massachusetts, decided to define the citizen participation process as having a veto power. Having City Hall say, "Alright, you got a veto power," was destructive to the process.

Mayors said, "Let them do what they want to do."

I think it was exactly that. Sometimes you hear money described as guilt money. Working in the neighborhoods was very hot . . . money was coming in and would keep things quiet—nonconfrontational. Money could do that. And in some places—Cleveland was one—the policy was to hire minorities only.

Wasn't the director of the Cleveland MCP shot?

That was the reason for my going to Cleveland. I put a team together to figure out what [the program] was doing. At the end of the three-day visit, the mayor and I explained to the citizens that the next phase of working in the neighborhoods was going to be with the Community Development Block Grant Program. And it would be run from City Hall and include many more neighborhoods than the ones in the Cleveland MCP.

The transition from Model Cities to CDBG . . . was masterful. Ask the question why did it make sense to shut HUD categorical programs down—some were very well conceived—in favor of CDBG. It's because lessons were learned. [First], the Model Cities Program's firm financial commitment of an exact dollar amount in the beginning of the year was revolutionary. It moved us away from a period of grantsmanship that was good for some places—very few—and began to create the good old level playing field. If you had a firm financial commitment you could do things. Second, the ability to use Model Cities money as local match money for other federal programs was masterful. With that policy, the concept of leveraging came into existence. The "Maintenance of Effort" policy, requiring that money generated from a new assessment may not be used to replace existing city services, was changed as well. I was disappointed that that policy was not imbedded in the CDBG—it was a losing argument. Since then state laws frequently use the phrase or something close to it, in other programs. Finally, the attempt to coordinate federal funds from the top down was a core part of the program . . . but disappointing.

If you could repeat the Model Cities Program, what would you do differently?

An economic development thrust in poverty programs, Model Cities, and also CDBG was glaringly absent. There was just no economic development strategy, agency, [or] economic development money. The closest to it was the Economic Development Administration (EDA) . . . which is very political and very difficult to penetrate; [and] Urban Development Action Grants (UDAG) really did fill a gap. The lack of emphasis on the need to have [an] acquisition strategy for improving physically dilapidated areas was a big lack in Model Cities. But it was understandable because the Model Cities dollar wasn't that much. Also, there never was, and still isn't, recognition for the need in urban centers for parking decks. No Model Cities money was ever spent for parking decks to make other investments possible. Whenever you try to figure out what the private sector needs to stay—employing people, generating sales tax, all the rest of it—there's always parking.

When looking back at Model Cities, what insight strikes you as significant?

One that jumped out at me was [during] my role as the Cleveland Development Director. Here I was, phasing out of Model Cities into the CDBG Program [and] trying to figure out what to do with this downtown that had a terrible negative self-image. Yet Cleveland was the third largest Fortune 500 location in the country after New York City and Chicago. Downtown, being a major job generator and a major revenue generator in property taxes, was off the charts. I did a downtown plan and began to set priorities. For instance, we needed hotels. Others like myself were saying, "We can't just keep talking about neighborhoods because people who live in the neighborhoods work in the center. We've got to reinforce this center." When UDAG came along in 1977, it was a good step in the right direction. In terms of CDBG, the pendulum never totally swung from the neighborhood to the downtown, but I think it began swinging closer . . . and it became politically acceptable to pay attention to, and invest in, downtown because that's where the jobs were.

Pat Henry lives in Princeton, New Jersey, and is currently the principal consultant for The Atlantic Group.

Chapter 2

Three Veterans of Housing and Urban Renewal

Warren Butler, George Gross, Dave Garrison, and interviewer John Sasso discuss the political considerations affecting the design of the MCP and its passage into legislation. During the mid- to late-1960s, Butler is HUD deputy assistant secretary for the MCP. Gross works in the HUD legislative office and will soon be House legislative counsel to the Subcommittee on Housing and Urban Development. Garrison, a lawyer and a lobbyist for the USCM, concentrates on legislation related to housing.

Butler recalls that collegiality and cooperation between Democrats and Republicans was greater in the 1960s than is true today. To Gross, the MCP is a logical response to domestic problems and negative reactions to the war in Vietnam. He describes the transformation of the Housing and Home Finance Agency (HHFA) to HUD as disorganized, and, because of negativity attached to Urban Renewal, he advises the MCP to keep its distance. Also, he notes the difficulty in obtaining support from other departments for an experimental program that resists definition. Suspicious of "urban renewal types," he wants a model of community involvement that is more organized and formal than OEO.

Butler, who is to brief Republican Rep. William Widnall of New Jersey, knows that if Rep. Widnall is comfortable with the republicanism of the program, 40 other U.S. Representatives will support it also. Another issue is the selection of cities for a program that is so small but consumes so much money. Butler relates an anecdote about Rep. Joe McDade of Pennsylvania that reveals how the number of cities in the MCP grew from 150 to 151.

Gross recalls that too much citizen involvement caused a negative perception of OEO, prompting Sasso to ask why Johnson would support so anti-
government a process as citizen participation. Gross replies that Johnson's involvement was probably limited to saying something like, "Look, we need a
goddamn program for the cities. You guys put it together."

The topic shifts to the Nixon administration. In 1969, Nixon requests a task
force to evaluate and make a recommendation on the MCP's future. The taskforce report concludes that politically, the program is too well established and
cannot be reversed. And, because the new administration is experiencing some
initial chaos, HUD is in an advantageous position to keep the MCP going. Also,
"Rockefeller" Republicans want the program to continue.

Garrison raises the question of interagency cooperation. Gross responds by
relating an anecdote regarding the New York Human Resources Administration
illustrating why agencies are unwilling to work together. However, interagency
cooperation—as a means to reduce future expenditures—is what appeals to the
Nixon administration.

Warren Butler, George Gross, and Dave Garrison: "An Idea of Community"

In Washington, D.C., Warren Butler's first assignment was to brief Republican Rep. William Widnall of New Jersey on the Housing Act of 1961. He had
no experience in housing but knew that the Senate would have a report on the
bill that he could utilize. As an intern asking questions, he learned that "in
Washington, you really didn't need to know a lot. You just needed the right
words" to induce someone else to "explain the entire thing."

By 1966, when the Model Cities Program was being formulated, Butler was
well established as a legislative assistant, having worked with the Republican
minority staff and the Democratic majority staff of the House Subcommittee on
Housing and Community Development. Following the election of President
Richard Nixon in 1968, Butler joined the Department of Housing and Urban
Development as deputy assistant secretary for the Model Cities Program.

After graduating from Boston University Law School, George Gross arrived
in Washington, D.C., to work at the Department of Labor. The following year,
1963, he joined the legislative office of the Housing and Home Finance Agency
(HHFA), soon to be reorganized as the Department of Housing and Urban Development. As the junior person in a small office, he "would get a little bit of
everything . . . Urban Renewal, public housing, water and sewer facilities," and
near the end of three years, preparation of the Model Cities Program.

In 1969, George Gross was assigned as counsel to the House Subcommittee on Housing and Community Development. The chairman, Democratic Rep. William Barrett of Pennsylvania was "an old-style politician from South Philadelphia," who got along particularly well with Rep. Widnall.

Dave Garrison grew up in the suburbs of Boston, attended Amherst College in western Massachusetts, and during the summer of 1964, prior to his senior year, traveled to Washington, D.C., to work as an intern for Rep. F. Bradford Morse of Massachusetts. In 1965, he returned to Washington. For the next three years, he worked full time as a legislative aide in Rep. Morse's office while attending George Washington University Law School at night.

Following law school, Garrison entered Volunteers in Service to America (VISTA) and was assigned to legal services in Washington, D.C. In 1970, the National League of Cities and U.S. Conference of Mayors hired him as a lobbyist for housing and community development.

Remembering the Model Cities Program

Butler: One thing, certainly different from today, was the collegiality that existed between Republicans and Democrats. It originated in the early 1950s with Rep. Bill Widnall, then the ranking Republican on the House Banking and Currency Committee, and Democratic Rep. Albert Rains of Alabama. Despite opposition by the Eisenhower administration, they worked together on legislation involving veterans' housing. Rep. Widnall really had been a maverick. The rapport that he built by his willingness to rise above partisan politics carried over to Democrats, Rep. Barrett of Pennsylvania, and Rep. Thomas Ludlow Ashley of Ohio.

In 1966, what were the political pressures propelling the concept of Model Cities forward?

Gross: The Model Cities Program was in large part, a response by the Johnson administration to a rising criticism within the Democratic Party: the war in Vietnam was swallowing up too many resources, and there was particular stress in the black/minority communities. In 1965, the Johnson administration, looking ahead to 1966 when the Model Cities Program would be sent to Congress as a major piece of legislation, set up a task force on cities. Robert Wood, undersecretary of HUD, headed that task force. This is when I came in. It was not a period when order and efficiency were hallmarks of any place in government, and certainly not at HUD, which had just become a [cabinet level] department.

I was given the job of writing a speech for Sen. Paul Douglas of Illinois introducing Model Cities legislation. There was a task force report, one of those huge blue books that I could use. I went to Bob Wood's office to get the report, and as the door was open, he heard me talking to his secretary. He came out and said, "I don't know how you're going to write a speech. We're trying to figure out just how the hell the program is going to run in here."

Did you feel the program had merits?

Gross: In the administration's view and in the task force's view, Model Cities had to move away from, but not kill, Urban Renewal. Model Cities was like putting an umbrella over everything you were doing before, plus adding many other programs, as many as people wanted. It looked like an administrative nightmare. How was the program going to work mechanically? How could you convince the secretary of the Interior, the [commissioner] of Education and others, that they should put their resources into our program?

Funding was the issue. A city's Model Cities plan might require a grant from a department such as Transportation. The city could use Model Cities dollars to fund its 20 percent local share. The remaining 80 percent had to be provided by the department.

Gross: An impossible expectation unless the president, who was extremely busy, pounded everyone on the head and forced every agency to work with HUD. [However], it was also true that in an age of riots and discord, something had to be done to help cities, despite the difficulties.

I don't want to sound as if we were opposed to the Model Cities Program. We were not. Tremendous time and effort went into drafting the bill that would be introduced in Congress. One part, the Declaration of Purposes, was extremely hard to figure out. What the hell was the purpose of this program? You couldn't define it. I liked the fact that Bob Wood billed the program as a "demonstration," [although] there wasn't enough money in the world to fund as many cities as were receiving Urban Renewal funding, so it seemed like a decent idea to fund 75 cities at the time.

Butler: I was still working with Rep. Widnall's staff. We hadn't seen the bill [introducing the Model Cities Program] . . . but let me back up. We had gotten very much involved with the Urban Renewal Program—often referred to by its critics as the "Negro clearance program." Nationally, we became a focal point for community groups, white and black, who wrote to us about problems they were having. [In many instances, Urban Renewal displaced people without relocating them to alternative housing.] The Housing Act of 1964, was the first time a tool was created for [housing] rehabilitation. My one claim to fame is that I wrote Section 312, the section on rehabilitation, from scratch. The legislative people were too busy doing the rest of the bill. And it became the law.

As cosponsors, we had Sen. Douglas and Sen. Jacob Javits of New York. Our orientation was toward the community, but we were suspicious of the old Urban Renewal types and Urban Renewal program activities. Although as a Republican, I had sat in on a series of seminars put on by the Institute for Policy Studies, which was about as left as you could get at that time. Wolf Von Eckhart, who had written *Back to the Drawing Board*, spoke; and Milton Kotler, who would write *Neighborhood Government* out of that series, spoke. I was tuned into the idea of community involvement in a more organized and formal fashion than had been characteristic of the Office of Economic Opportunity. When the Model Cities legislation came down, I was asked to brief Rep. Widnall who, in turn, would brief his Republican colleagues.

I said to Rep. Widnall, "On the whole, this is not something you will have any particular reason to oppose, particularly since it is a demonstration." Generally speaking, Rep. Widnall and maybe 40 other Republicans, who would follow him, were supportive of whatever came out of the Housing Subcommittee as long as they felt he was comfortable with it. And that is how a lot of things passed.

Talk about 1967 and 1968, the start-up years for the Model Cities Program. Each of you had to consider the program from a different political perspective.

Butler: I can relate a story I was told when I first moved to HUD in 1969. During the first year of Model Cities, there was an appropriations subcommittee headed by Rep. Joe Evins of Tennessee. Republican Rep. Joe McDade from Pennsylvania was a freshman on that subcommittee. When his turn to speak finally came around—he was last—he said, "Mr. Chairman, I'm very interested in this Model Cities Program. When I run down the list of all the cities, I note that there's a Model City in every [district represented by a member of] this subcommittee, except me. Is there an explanation for that?"

Joe Evins turned to him and said, "You weren't here."

And so the only city that was added to the original 150 cities was Scranton, Pennsylvania. And that made 151 . . . in order to deal with Joe McDade.

Gross: There is an important point to make here. The Model Cities Program was not a competition from which a group of cities was selected.

Butler: It was supposed to be.

Gross: But it wasn't. You couldn't even conceive of a program with 75 cities without Philadelphia, or New York. Or a city in Tennessee for Joe Evins, the House appropriations czar for HUD programs.

Butler: In theory, everybody could apply. In practice, everybody knew, with few exceptions, which cities were going to get in.

Cities were chosen according to congressional district.

Gross: That was one of the main reasons that people on the Hill later talked about ending Model Cities in favor of some broader, more comprehensive, program.

Butler: As a demonstration program, Model Cities couldn't exist at 75 cities and, as a program, it couldn't exist at 150. It wasn't big enough, and yet it took too much money out of the budget and away from other programs.

Before coming to HUD, I had been working with Republican Rep. Widnall on the Hill . . . and even at that point I wasn't paying attention to Model Cities until Floyd Hyde, the former mayor of Fresno, California, was selected as HUD assistant secretary for the Model Cities Program. In looking around, the Model Cities Program seemed as close to a Republican program as I saw.

Garrison: Why did you think the Model Cities Program was close to a Republican program?

Butler: It seemed to bring more resources to bear, not in isolation but in a coordinated fashion. What's the point, if you have a neighborhood facility but no money to put into it, or if you have parkland but no money to take care of it?

Garrison: That was a Republican philosophy.

Butler: It was the old, "New Federalism." If you had to have a program, it ought to go to local elected officials.

And it ought to have as few encumbrances as possible.

Gross: By the time Model Cities got underway, we had had some experience with the community action provisions from the Office of Economic Opportunity. One short-term experience was the impact legislative initiatives were having on the positions of local elected officials. The feeling was that there was too much citizen participation. Over time, authority would have to become more centralized in the hands of city government officials.

Butler: As a former mayor, Floyd Hyde's first position was that local government really should be in control. There was a citizen participation process, and up to that point, citizen participants, even in Model Cities, were former OEO people. The feeling of the Republican administration was that this was still community control. If you look at the citizen participation policies' for the OEO Program and compare them to those in existence a year later, you would see a tremendous change. Where once communities had given veto power to their citizen organizations concerning the dispersal of money, now authority and responsibility for the program shifted toward local government.

Garrison: Model Cities differed from OEO in one important respect: [in Model Cities], money literally went from HUD to the city. But from a mayor's point of view it was not sufficient. The mayors still felt they were captive in an OEO-like process. And that helped determine much of the conversation around the Community Development Block Grant Program.

Butler: From my standpoint, the Urban Renewal did not function very well because money did not go through local government. Urban Renewal agencies were creatures of the state. After a board was appointed, [the agency] ran itself. Urban Renewal agencies received money directly, and I never felt they were very responsible to the local community by which I mean elected officials, community people, or neighborhood people.

So, I [was] sympathetic to the Model Cities process. But on the other hand, I had seen OEO and felt that despite the value of citizen participation, it tended to be extreme. And I was to see the same [extreme] in Model Cities.

Gross: One of the issues in the 1969 Housing bill involved rewriting the citizen participation provision. Republicans were in office and favored strengthening local government control. Many Democrats agreed.

I credit President Johnson for establishing OEO, which led to the Model Cities Program. However, in my opinion, citizen participation, as formulated under OEO, challenged local government, the very government that Johnson represented.

Gross: Johnson's connection was no more than a broad thrust. As the president, entering his first full year in office, he knew that he must deliver something. He was not an expert in these areas but he had to act politically. He would have moved toward OEO and the Model Cities Program even if there hadn't been any riots in the streets. This was an age of experts like Bob Wood whose task force put together Model Cities, and Fred Hayes who had worked on the Poverty Program. These were programs President Johnson agreed to because they were the work of experts. What Lyndon Johnson probably said is . . . "Look, we need a goddamn program for the cities. You guys put it together." I don't think he gave it much thought. But, if the war hadn't been going on and there hadn't been riots in the cities, he would have paid much more attention to what was going on.

When President Nixon took office in 1968, the Model Cities Program had been in existence for two years. How did the Nixon administration regard the program?

Butler: The first thing done was to put together a task force to evaluate and look at Model Cities in progress. This was March of 1969. The task force visited about a half dozen Model Cities. Portland, Maine, was one, also Dayton, Ohio, and Seattle, Washington. The task force concluded that we should continue and go forward with the second 75 cities already selected. I think the political realization was that the process was so far along, it couldn't be reversed. Maybe the amount of money allocated in the appropriations bill could be changed, but not the number of Model Cities.

The situation was chaotic. You had a completely new administration. No Republican had been in office since 1960, and no one was completely in control. So if you could convince HUD to move forward, you would be able to take advantage of the moment. Floyd Hyde wanted Model Cities to continue, and others in Nixon's administration had much the same feeling. Those doing the evaluation were considered Rockefeller Republicans. They saw the program as a counterbalance to OEO. The question was funding.

Garrison: Interagency cooperation was one part of the program, which, in retrospect, seemed to be the least effective. Why was it a part of the mix?

Butler: Interagency cooperation was part of the whole idea to focus on a neighborhood. Urban Renewal changed as a result, away from a concentrated effort in a downtown area, to a neighborhood approach . . . because if it didn't, it wouldn't be around much longer.

Gross: The concept belonged to Bob Wood. HUD could not change a city or even a part of a city by itself. It could clear land and build facilities, but if education was to be upgraded, the program had to deal with education, and if daycare or job training or the other things aimed at inner-city problems had to be upgraded, the program somehow had to get all the pieces together.

When I was in New York in the Human Resources Administration (HRA), we dreamed up the latest version of a comprehensive approach: every family would have a coordinator who, once the family's needs were identified, would go to other agencies and get the aid needed. Coordination at the family level!

Even though HRA might be 10 times as big as other agencies, the client could be a mother with children whose biggest need was an apartment—not a check, but an apartment. HRA had its own police force, but it didn't have apartments. We might need five different services to really serve a family. We finally had a meeting in City Hall to outline a program. The attitude from the Housing Department was, "Forget it. We need *our* housing units for *our* needs.

If we use them for your needs, you might as well make our whole department a subunit." And you know what? Nobody else had anything to say. The meeting was over.

Butler: One of the most difficult coordination problems was within HUD. Remember that HUD came together from the Housing and Home Finance Agency, which was a series of agencies—the Federal Housing Administration, Fannie Mae, Urban Renewal, and so on. We used to have a joke that HUD was the Department of Housing *or* Urban Renewal because of the lack of cooperation in the assignment of resources.

Early on, there was the recognition that interagency cooperation wasn't going to happen. It couldn't happen at the local level. There were different delivery systems [for funding] and different places where decisions were made. There were different cycles for when the funds went out. There were agencies that were not part of city government . . . or county government. To make anything happen, there had to be a willingness to cooperate at the federal departmental level, at the highest levels. What appealed to President Nixon's new administration was the idea that maybe, by being more efficient, the amount of money needed for the future would not be as much, and maybe, by being more efficient, things could happen.

Warren Butler lives in Washington, D.C. He is a partner in the Community Capital Group. George Gross died in 2004. He had been an attorney in Washington, D.C. Dave Garrison is vice president of the National Academy of Public Administration.

Part Two

People, Conditions, and Programs

"When I was mayor of Fresno, there weren't two blacks in city government. I chose a black, Jim Aldridge, as Model Cities Director. Not many years later, he was the City Manager at $100,000 a year."

Floyd Hyde

The Model Cities Program lifted the "constraints of racism" on the neighborhood pool of resident talent, notes Ron Gatton (chapter 3). Job opportunities opened through citizen participation and the practice of hiring neighborhood residents—a program requirement. Local leadership also encouraged resident hiring. Mayors understood that involving residents at all levels of activity increased the program's legitimacy and lessened the city's burden.

Part Two concentrates on Model Cities Program directors, who found themselves confronted by political unrest, economic strife, turf wars among rival community factions, bureaucracy, corruption, bigotry, and citizen disagreement over identifying and prioritizing problems. Many agonized over the ideological choice of confronting the established system or working from within as a strategy for change. Others, by shear determination or astute planning, succeeded in overcoming indifference extending to deliberate resistance. Their stories—of strategies, mistakes, opportunities, and ambitious plans—are grouped according to similarities of experience.

Chapter 3

Citizen Catalysts

Prior to becoming director of the Mission District MCP in San Francisco, California, Larry Delcarlo is active in the Mission Coalition Organization (MCO), a neighborhood power base that employs Saul Alinsky-style, activist strategies in its effort to get jobs for neighborhood youth with businesses located in the community. One example involves the neighborhood branch of the Bank of America, where residents overwhelm the bank by cashing checks written on green tortillas—the bank had previously advertised that it would honor a check written on anything. Another targets the CEO of Pacific Telephone and Telegraph by distributing flyers to the CEO's neighbors in their upper class community—the flyers ask them to call the CEO and ask why he refuses to talk to the MCO. In the Mission District MCP plan, neighborhood activists have ensured that the program is accountable to the MCO. The MCO identifies neighborhood needs, which then become components in the plan—an annual community convention provides the opportunity for input from every neighborhood organization. San Francisco has another MCP, Bay View Hunters Point, where citizen participation is in the form of a commission with members appointed by the mayor. DelCarlo contrasts the effectiveness of the mayor-controlled commission, which never establishes a community agenda, with the community-controlled coalition, which consumes too much time and energy in program management. Ongoing in the Mission District, is the debate between proponents of community control, who want parallel but separate agencies, and proponents

39

of institutional change, who want neighborhood agencies integrated into city government.

Iowan Ron Gatton travels to the West Side Christian Parish in Chicago, Illinois, to work in the Civil Rights Movement. Then, thanks to a HUD scholarship, he attends the Maxwell School for Citizenship and Public Affairs at Syracuse, New York, where he is recruited for the HUD Intern Program. He is assigned to the MCP, then drafted for a HUD experimental program—termed "annual arrangement"—in Gary, Indiana, and eventually recruited to become director of the citywide MCP—named "Planned Variations"—in racially divided Dayton, Ohio. The city, reeling from the loss of manufacturing jobs, is facing a devastating budgetary shortfall. However, Gatton—along with the city manager, police chief, and superintendent of schools—works within the newly devised Priority Board System to maximize use of the city's meager funds and reverse the process of decline. The MCP program, in Gatton's opinion, suffers the negative effects of operating at a time when the culture of poverty is misunderstood.

Young Dave Thompson's parents make him "pay attention" to events marking the Civil Rights Movement. He becomes a community organizer for OEO until the advent of the MCP, when he begins teaching Model Neighborhood residents how to participate in, and petition, local government. He contrasts the extremes of citizen participation under OEO with citizen participation under the MCP in which the environment is more open to debate. Thompson observes that hostility between citizens and city council is the result of incompetence on both sides. In his opinion, city councils that placate citizens do not serve the minority community or the city, whereas constructive participation produces more sophisticated citizens with regard to city planning and allocations.

In high school, Jimmy Threat scores well on standardized tests; however, white guidance counselors steer him toward the study of agriculture and away from law or medicine. After several educational detours, he studies economics at the University of Pennsylvania's Wharton School of Business in Philadelphia. In the late 1960s, Threat accepts an offer to become director of the MCP in Kansas City, Missouri. His first challenge is to restructure citizen participation—away from exercising absolute power and toward building consensus and partnerships—otherwise the program has no chance to succeed. Also, he must reconcile the objections of seven different neighborhood groups, each wanting complete control of its share of funds, and still submit a cohesive plan to HUD on time or lose money. In the process, Threat learns that listening is more important than talking.

In rural Iowa, Richard Wright is athletic coach, teacher, and counselor until he is offered a job directing a federally funded, antipoverty program in Des

Moines. Although Des Moines is a small city, strained relations between police and community and explosions—a police station, a Drake University building, and a Black Panther House—create turmoil. The departing MCP director, who is viewed as an outsider, leaves the plan submission process in shambles. As the new director, Wright faces a citizen group that wants complete control of the program and complete control of him. Citizens bring weapons to neighborhood meetings. In Wright's opinion, their hostility toward the program is, in part, a reaction to Urban Renewal's earlier disregard for people. Wright reflects that one weakness in the program is its emphasis on social services rather than economic development. Ironically, the emerging cable TV industry presents neighborhood citizens with a real economic opportunity; however, the city wants the citizens to stay out.

Peter Richardson serves an internship in San Francisco, California, in order to complete his master's in city planning. Six months later, San Francisco city officials ask him to return to help them figure out an acceptable comprehensive plan to save the city's MCP from being dropped by HUD. However, one application must cover two distinctly different neighborhoods: Hunters Point—a black community with a lot of "noise . . . and enthusiasm," and the Mission District—a Latino community under the control of the well-organized, very political Mission Coalition Organization. Widespread distrust requires Richardson to collaborate secretly with the MCP regional administrator while publicly enduring hostility. When MCP money finally arrives, the staff grows from five- to 80 people. In Richardson's opinion, the San Francisco MCP lacks focus but provides a little something for everyone. For Richardson, the program's appeal is its invigorating call for creativity.

Larry DelCarlo
Model Cities Program Deputy Director
Mission District, San Francisco, California

During the late 1950s and early 1960s, the Mission District, a working-class community in San Francisco, California, was in transition. For resident Larry DelCarlo, it was a training ground in activism. Immigrants, many from Central Latin America, were moving in. Working-class residents were moving out, and with them went the neighborhood's resources.

Because the new Spanish-speaking residents didn't understand English, and the dispatcher in the Laborers Hiring Hall spoke only English, new residents

Photo 2: John A. Sasso, Joseph Alioto, and Moon Landrieu

didn't go out to work. Joseph DelCarlo, a neighborhood activist and also Larry DelCarlo's father, joined with others in the Laborers Union to organize a caucus of Spanish-speaking laborers. As a result, the union hired a Spanish speaking dispatcher and also addressed the need for new members to learn the language of their trade. The caucus became a powerful political base within the Mission District and established a tradition of activism that would later define many of DelCarlo's strategies when dealing with corporate resistance to jobs creation for the Mission Youth Program and, later, for the Mission District Model Cities Program (Mission District MCP).

Green Tortillas and a Community Convention

We had tried desperately to find jobs for young people, hitting the bricks and going round to corporations—in San Francisco, we have many. So we thought, This is a great opportunity. We asked Chevron, and Pacific Gas and Electric, and thought, They will give us jobs. But it wasn't that easy. We decided to hook up with the Mission Coalition Organization (MCO), an organization using tactics styled after community activist, Saul Alinsky.

My parents, who were both involved, suggested we start an employment committee. We began using community activist tactics against corporations that wouldn't meet with us. We staged an action at a branch of the Bank of America in the inner Mission District. We had heard that that bank accepted checks written on anything, so we got 200 people to stand in line, each person carrying a check written on a tortilla dyed with green food coloring—the bank's operation was totally disrupted; [then] we promised to return periodically during their busiest times. Before the end of the day, the bank officials took a few of us in the back and said, "What do we have to do here?" From then on, the Bank of America began to provide summer jobs for the youth of the Mission District.

On another occasion, we were trying to get Pacific Telephone and Telegraph to provide jobs. We were getting nowhere and weren't allowed to meet with anyone powerful enough to make a decision. But we knew the CEO lived in Hillsborough, so we organized a caravan of about 30 cars to travel the 25 miles south to his neighborhood—a lot of CEOs lived in Hillsborough; it was one of the wealthiest communities in the Bay Area. We brought printed fliers, and we were going to visit his neighbors. We got there, parked our cars, and fanned out, knocking on doors and leaving our fliers . . . being early Saturday morning, people were home.

We told everyone that people in the Mission District needed jobs. We said, "Please call your neighbor, Jerome Hull, CEO of Pacific Telephone and Telegraph, because he doesn't want to talk to us." We told them we looked forward to getting to know the people of Hillsborough a whole lot better because we'd be back every Saturday until the company met with us. Finally the police escorted us out. On Monday morning the public relations department for Pacific Telephone and Telegraph called our office to say that the CEO would like to talk to us about jobs.

What was your strategy for the Mission District MCP?

The Mission Coalition Organization was very powerful . . . we wanted to create a program that would be accountable to this larger organization and thus to a lot more people than just the funding agency. That was the strategy.

During the planning year, before I became deputy director of the program, Mayor Alioto and the MCO had engaged in a long battle for the controlling vote on the Mission Model Neighborhood Corporation (MMNC)—the citizen participation group. The mayor wanted to appoint two-thirds of its members, but just the reverse happened. The MCO appointed two-thirds, and the mayor appointed the remaining third.

The MCO wanted the citizens to be accountable to them. Before being appointed deputy director of the Mission District MCP, I became chairperson of the MMNC to make sure that happened. We set up a number of committees—housing, employment, childcare, legal services so that any organization wanting to fund something, build something or [even] change a bus route, would need the sign-off of the Mission Model Neighborhood Corporation. And the only way an organization could do that would be to negotiate with us and make compromises in support of what we wanted for our neighborhood. We became very powerful that way.

Was the Mission District under pressure from developers?

That's how the Mission Coalition Organization got started. The Urban Renewal Program, with the Redevelopment Agency, had just completed its Western Edition Project. Areas were just bulldozed to make room for housing and business offices. A lot of people were displaced. The Mission District was next. We formed the MCO to keep the Redevelopment Agency out of our neighborhood. We won that fight. And having experienced that power, we said, 'Let's keep this organization together; we need to do lots of other things.'

What were the priority programs?

Programs arose from needs identified by the MCO. We needed legal services because it related to jobs . . . and housing because the landlords took advantage of so many immigrants or because immigrants didn't have the right documents. So jobs, housing, legal services, and childcare were the four primary areas. No program was developed in isolation. Each program area developed an agency and all the agencies were housed in one office, a storefront really. They met together regularly, so each knew that what one was doing was connected to what the others were doing. If someone were being placed in a job, that person would probably need childcare. If two and three families were living together in substandard housing, then obviously those families needed housing. It was that simple.

Tenants' rights emerged. We negotiated with landlords and asked them how we could help improve their property if they themselves couldn't afford to. From that [dialogue] came the Community Housing Rehabilitation Program. It was one of the actions developed from the MCO agenda and supported by funds from Model Cities.

The community went along with this agenda? It sounds too good to be true. Was there strife or disagreement?

Oh, there was always debate and struggle within the organization. To make it work, we had an annual community convention. We had representatives from every local organization you can imagine: the elementary schools, the Merchants' Association, the Homeowners' Association, and even the radical groups protesting the war in Vietnam. Every group in the Mission District was represented at our annual convention. Also, this was when the officers for the Mission Coalition Organization were elected. If a group didn't participate, it didn't have a whole lot to say once the decisions were made.

The conventions were tough. We fought with each other, sometimes in physical fights, but when it was over and the agenda was set, nobody dared to shoot it down. We were one of the few representative organizations in the country at the time.

Did you have any involvement with Bay View Hunters Point, the other neighborhood in the San Francisco Model Cities Program?

Only while receiving planning funds. A council of representatives, five from the Mission District and five from Bay View Hunters Point, came together regularly to collaborate and to make recommendations to the mayor. The process was tough because the citizen participation structure for Hunters Point was a city commission, whose members were appointed by the mayor, as opposed to a nonprofit corporation for the Mission District. The Hunter Point commission became a city department. The Mission District remained independent from the city.

At times during the planning year, we'd say, "We don't want this Model Cities money. It's destroying our organization." I remember Mayor Alioto calling us in to give us hell for our tactics right after the MCO had taken an action against Pepsi Cola. Pepsi had a huge factory in the Mission District and refused to talk to us. In fact, the company tried to get us arrested by calling out the tax squad on us. A week later we learned that the CEO for that factory was also a huge contributor to Mayor Alioto's campaign.

Mayor Alioto gave us an ultimatum: 'Make a decision! You can continue this militancy or run the Model Cities Program. I'm not going to allow you to do both."

We stood up in unison and said, "OK, the choice is to continue our militancy. You can keep your Model Cities money." And that was the end of the meeting.

That night, while we were discussing what to do next, Mayor Alioto sent one of his people to say that the mayor wanted to open the dialogue again— maybe something could be worked out. And so, we were able to do both: receive the money and continue our militancy . . . I should say advocacy because we weren't violent, which made a big difference. The people in the Mission District were in a different ballgame than the people in Bay View Hunters Point. The Point set up a commission to do projects that the mayor wanted done. A community agenda was never really in place.

Were you able to accomplish what you wanted?

The things we wanted to do, we were able to do. We had control on most of the major developments, but lots of little things went on that we couldn't control. As we focused more on running the program, complying with all the regulations, and having good audits, we focused less on community advocacy. At about that point, the MCO had to confront the problem of putting energy and leadership in the organization or running the Mission District Model Cities Program. We really couldn't do both.

You became the establishment. Suddenly you had responsibility.

That's right. Our leaders became directors of programs. We had a critical debate within the MCO: whether to have community control, which meant running our own agencies, or force institutional change by telling the city what services we wanted and how we wanted those services provided. Many of us were on the institutional change side. We reasoned that to compel institutional change was the more powerful position. But we lost.

The community control side argued that city departments didn't know how to provide services for our neighborhood. The control side said, "Who knows better than us what our needs are? We should run our own agencies." So we set up parallel institutions, a "paragovernment," rather than deal with mainline institutions. We made our own rules, which, of course, we couldn't enforce because of the regulations attached to funding. We had to play by the established rules. However, the programs we did start worked pretty well.

In retrospect, should you have used that opportunity to initiate institutional change?

Yes. When I became director of Community Development in San Francisco, my job was to monitor or be responsible for monitoring about 150 agencies, all receiving funds through the city. The money, rather than being used to make institutions accountable and to build strong organizations, just kept the programs running.

Now that I've been on the inside of city government for 27 years, I can see clearly the mistake we made—people used funds to run their own programs. Institutions that have changed over the years, changed because people from the community got in and made changes from the inside.

Larry Del Carlo lives in San Francisco. He has been instrumental in developing programs as diverse as conflict resolution training for gang members to creating a refugee center in Central America. Currently, he is director of Business and Community Development for San Francisco Unified Schools.

Ron Gatton
Model Cities Program Director: Dayton, Ohio

For Ron Gatton, "the church was an avenue to the outside world," away from the isolation of Iowa. In 1965, after earning a bachelor's degree at Grinnell College, he traveled to Chicago, to the West Side Christian Parish. The parish was the Chicago center of the Civil Rights Movement and the community-organizing vehicle for Dr. Martin Luther King and the Southern Christian Leadership Council (SCLC). As Gatton's involvement increased, he became convinced that "government had an essential role to play in achieving the movement's goals."

The critical moment in his career came after HUD awarded him a Fellowship to the Maxwell School for Citizenship and Public Affairs at Syracuse University. "I didn't necessarily intend to work for HUD, but since they'd been kind enough to pay my way through graduate school, I figured the least I could do was see the recruiter when he came to the campus." The recruiter's efforts worked. In 1968, Gatton joined the HUD Intern Program. When he was assigned to Model Cities, Gatton said, "I didn't understand it very well, but I knew it was where I wanted to be."

Dunking in the Line of Fire

My first year as a HUD intern was spent in a series of rotational assignments including public housing, Urban Renewal, and financing. I was assigned to Steve Hahn, the lead man for the cities of Dayton, and Columbus, Ohio. Before the end of the year, Steve was promoted—HUD was short on people, so at age 23, I replaced Steve as lead man. [Next], I went to Detroit, Michigan, as lead man for Syl Angel, [the previous] director of the Columbus MCP . . . [until] I was drafted as lead man for Gary, Indiana.

HUD chose Gary to experiment—the idea was to bring together all HUD programs and other federal programs to bear on the city's problems. The program in Gary was a "demonstration" and the intellectual predecessor to the Community Development Block Grant Program. We'd say to the city, "We'll give you what you want for the coming year [termed an 'annual arrangement'], but we expect you to build your capacity," to expand functions of city government to meet people's needs.

The program I was recruited for in Dayton was a "citywide" Model Cities Program (Dayton MCP) under Planned Variations. Dayton was terribly divided racially. The program probably saved the city from further riots and violence, but it was also divisive because the white population, expressing a classic fear at the time, thought that blacks were going to take over everything. The city was about 35 percent black. The white population included many Appalachians who had come to work for General Motors. Most of these jobs had disappeared by the early 1970s, which created direct competition between racial and ethnic groups for the remaining jobs.

At the time, Dayton was unusual in that the city had a progressive liberal city manager, James Kunde, and three liberal people in key positions. The superintendent of schools was an outspoken advocate of forced busing. The police chief was probably the most progressive in the country. He initiated the Daisy Cops—when trouble broke out, he would send in cops with bouquets of daisies in their holsters. And, as director of the Dayton MCP, I was the third.

During my first year, the Eastside—where the negative-on-liberal-issues white population lived—invited the superintendent of schools and me to sit on a dunking machine at their Octoberfest. We agreed and were considered such sports that the event was editorialized in the local newspaper. When we showed up, festivities were delayed while the police chief had the dunking stand moved so it wouldn't be in the line of sniper fire. Today, it's difficult to remember how real the threats of violence were then.

One of your goals was to bridge the racial gap?

Yes, but let me provide some perspective. The black community was integrated in the sense of economic and social standing. Frankly, you had a lot of black people with a college education working in low-level jobs. The leadership potential within the community was tremendous. Opening city government to the black community by establishing a priority board in every section of the city was very important.

I remember having the priority boards review a draft of the city budget at the same time the City Council was reviewing it. The City Council was very annoyed; in public, Jim Kunde pretended to be annoyed, but he had actually given the okay. Citizens from all parts of the community were reviewing expenditures such as the purchase of police cars, things that had previously been the prerogative of the business community and City Council. I was excoriated for this process, but, to this day, the city budget in Dayton is developed at the neighborhood level.

The Dayton Model Cities Program had three legs. One, the city wanted to make sure that the riots didn't happen again. There was an element of buying people off—a lot of dangerous people were on the city payroll, people who were likely to cause trouble. Two, people who had been previously under-employed came into city government—into areas such as the school system—and had opportunities they had never had before. In one instance, a lawyer, who had ranked second in his class at law school and had been pressed by racism to conduct his practice in a storefront, emerged as a leader in his neighborhood and in the city. Three, we wanted to change how other agencies did business and improve economic development and social services. We had some far-out projects such as unionizing domestic workers and reducing recidivism among ex-cons.

Frankly, the most important leg of the program was opening up opportunities within the system. Nothing ever came of the Domestic Workers Project except causing consternation in the suburbs. That project crashed and burned when two strong people fought over the directorship. The Ex-con Program and a program for Vietnam vets continued on and became institutionalized through other agencies.

What effect did political considerations have on the program?

The best way to answer is that ultimately we—Jim Kunde, the police chief, the superintendent of schools, and I—had to leave. We had pushed the community farther than it was willing to go. However, because of a courageous mayor, city manager, and City Council, all that we wanted to do, we did.

Jim Kunde had seen the handwriting on the wall for the city's economy. Dayton's population had decreased from 270,000 to 240,000, a precipitous drop at the time. We had $10.5 million in Planned Variations money and Kunde wanted to use some of that money as a catalyst to improve the city's economic future. We put about $1.5 million into the Citywide Development Corporation and about $.5 million—administered by the Citywide Development Corporation—into each of the six neighborhood priority boards for their own development projects. The citywide projects were successful early on. It took several years for the neighborhoods to do economic development activities. The pot of money was sitting there but couldn't be accessed unless the neighborhood was involved in the project. It pushed the issue of creating job-producing activities down to the neighborhood level.

Later, when Pat Harris, secretary of HUD under President Jimmy Carter, testified on the Hill as to what she wanted to accomplish, she used the Dayton Citywide Development Corporation as a model for financing techniques. The creativity in the program was the use of a combination of public/private funds to leverage what was a modest amount of money into major reinvestments.

What do you believe is the legacy of the Model Cities Program?

Local government is totally different today. The Model Cities Program, with some preparatory help from [OEO], was the catalyst for change.

In Dayton, we had great success opening things up for middle class blacks, but we had little impact on the very poor, regardless of race. At that time, we did not fully understand the culture of poverty, or appreciate the extent to which dependence is debilitating, or that government can only do so much. The white backlash that characterized national politics in the 1970s through the 1980s was motivated by fear. It's interesting to ask what might have happened if we had

had an effective leader to see the Model Cities Program through? Could the backlash have been avoided?

Ron Gatton served as HUD regional administrator in Chicago during the Carter administration. Currently, he lives in Chicago and owns and directs his own consulting and development business.

David Thompson
Executive Director, Western Regional Citizen Participation Council

From childhood on, David Thompson was audience to his parents' discussions on social issues. Places—a third floor apartment in Harlem belonging to friend of the family, Mary McLeod Bethune—became fixed in memory because they marked an important event.

"I was probably more interested in going out to play, but my parents sat me down and said, 'Now, you have to understand. . . . '" His parents made him pay attention—*Brown v. The Board of Education*, Martin Luther King in Montgomery, Alabama, the bus boycott.

After a year of undergraduate school at Fisk University in Nashville, Tennessee, Thompson began to participate in sit-ins with the Student Nonviolent Coordinating Committee (SNCC). During that time, he met John Lewis—a believer in nonviolent protest—and, after moving back to New York, joined the Congress of Racial Equality (CORE) on Long Island.

On Long Island and under contract to OEO, Thompson progressed from community organizer to consultant for citizen organizations. After organizing the Western Regional Citizen Participation Council (WRCPC), located in San Francisco and funded by HUD and OEO, he began teaching citizen groups from various Model Cities Programs how to participate in, and petition, local government. According to Thompson, during the early days of citizen participation, "No one knew exactly what was going on." Accomplishing a goal was more idea than plan. "The cities didn't know what we were doing; the citizens didn't know what we were doing; we just knew that our focus was on the citizens."

Citizen Organizer

We began with these questions: how would citizens participate; what powers and authorities could these boards have; who would be on the boards? Those neighborhood residents who came forward and were active often came out of voluntary service—something nonprofit or with a political connection. The biggest problem came from people who were pure opportunists, but without support, they usually went away. Church affiliations were not a major influence, although that is probably less true in the South. Quite frankly, the church didn't want people's interest diverted to something other than the church.

Other questions we asked were about delivery systems for services. What kinds of models were in the community? How did community development corporations deliver services—housing, that kind of thing?

Not clear, was the how of interfacing with Model Cities. The program was operated by the cities [and was] not a freestanding agency. With OEO, because citizen participation groups wanted a community control model, relationships ranged from simple avoidance to hostility. In a meeting with HUD and OEO, I remember feeling like a contractor, thinking, "You guys have no idea how difficult you're making my life. I'm not here to play out your philosophical differences."

When we set up the Western Regional Citizen Participation Council, we had funding from both HUD and OEO. With OEO, because it was a grant, we got a check up front, a lump sum. With HUD, because it was a contract, we didn't get the money until delivery of the service. The problem was that we had no cash flow. I wanted an agreement with OEO that we could use grant money as cash flow so we could carry out our contract with HUD. We would have a "memorandum of understanding" as to how that could happen. I realized that HUD and OEO would never agree. So I went to my office and wrote a letter to each of them telling them that I would be using grant money to accomplish contract goals. I made sure that the accountants set up a system that would adequately account for each agency's funds. Then I went ahead.

As time passed, OEO became a less important player, while our relationship with the regional office staff at HUD improved. Our relationship with Model Cities Program directors improved substantially. The environment, as a result of the efforts of the National Model Cities Directors Association (NMCDA) had become more open to debate and discussion because of that organization's efforts to bridge the gap between citizens and MCP leadership. The importance of a working relationship between citizens' groups and public interest groups was the ability to present a united front when dealing with HUD.

Early on, citizen participation meetings often had the feeling of "us and them?"

There were hostile meetings between the city and the citizens, but generally where those occurred, you had incompetence . . . on both sides. Because programs were interdisciplinary and interdepartmental, we felt able to talk to anybody we needed to, and we had a better relationship with a [city] council than most department heads . . . they treated the council as something to be avoided. Information was hidden, not shared.

From your perspective, what was the impact of citizen participation in the communities?

Cities like Richmond, California, and Tucson, Arizona—cities in which I organized—didn't necessarily have a direct role in human service areas, but they had a stake in them. They were beginning to fund some related components, to get involved, and to partner with people at the human services level. The citizens who were involved became much more sophisticated about planning and the allocation process. They were looking for innovative projects they could do at the neighborhood level and making change at the delivery level. These changes have stood the test of time, despite subsequent belt tightening and programmatic alterations at the federal level. And despite the program changes, local institutions that are well grounded in the community and add value, survive.

Is it because of Model Cities that now there is a mechanism for how people petition their government?

Yes. For example, Richmond had some earlier neighborhood council activities prior to its Model Cities Program. These councils were strengthened by the addition of Richmond MCP staff people, and by the development of a coordinating committee. We became useful to the City Council, the mayor, and the city managers in managing the politics of the community, since we could help them with the demands being made by the minority segments—not by keeping people quiet but by being constructive. We had the ability to put local interns in place, to do things the city couldn't do but were necessary to building capacity. For instance, the mayors were delighted to pass an issue on such as housing to someone who could handle it for them.

Twenty-nine neighborhood councils now exist in the city of Richmond. There is an unwritten law: if you want a zoning variance or whatever, you talk to your neighborhood council before going to the Planning Commission. Because, if there were a controversy, the commission would expect that you had at least talked it over with the neighborhood council. That planning process has remained in place . . . and we've gotten better at the work. Now, the neighborhood councils are the "fifth estate" in the community.

Dave Thompson lives in Richmond, California, where he is director of Community Development.

Jimmy Threat
Model Cities Program Director: Kansas City, Missouri

Before World War II, Richmond, Virginia, where Jimmy Threat grew up, was a segregated city. As a student, Threat had scored well on standardized tests and caught the notice of his white guidance counselors. According to Threat, they advised him that "too many blacks were pursuing law and medicine [and that he] ought to look at agriculture because that was an area with lots of jobs" ... and furthermore, "the federal government was always an employee of last resort" and "an employee of first resort'

Threat was directed toward Tuskegee Institute in Alabama. When he told admissions that he wanted to study etymology, he was referred to the School of Agriculture, where someone corrected him, saying, "You mean entomology."

"No," said Threat. "I don't want to study insects. I want to study words."

Threat decided that if Tuskegee didn't offer etymology, he would go to a school that did. Cornell University in Ithaca, New York, admitted him in 1941with the expectation that he would begin classes in 1942; however, Threat was drafted into the army. After his discharge in 1945, he enrolled at Morgan State University in Baltimore, Maryland, but then met a girl, a student at Virginia Union in Richmond, Virginia, and, shortly thereafter, Threat became a student at Virginia Union.

In 1952, Threat, no longer interested in etymology, began to study economics at the Wharton School of Business in Philadelphia. In 1953, he married and then worked briefly in Philadelphia for the Industrialization Center, and for the Human Rights Commission until the city of Newark, New Jersey, recruited Threat as director of Human Relations and Human Rights. However, the riots and instability that characterized Newark in the late-1960s, persuaded Threat that the better choice was to accept the offer to become director of the Model Cities Program in Kansas City, Missouri (Kansas City MCP).

Reconstruction

Kansas City had already retained a consultant from East St. Louis, Illinois. He developed a concept that involved a series of committees and [a citizen participation] board that was much like the [one in] St. Louis. The board [exercised] absolute legal power [rather than building] consensus or a partnership. My first challenge was to reconstruct [the board] in a manner that would give me some opportunity to succeed.

How did you work with the board?

You have two ears and one mouth. You listen twice as much as you talk. I became an excellent listener.

The [board] had appropriated money for a plan . . . and [had] hired consultants from all over the country. [Because] the city wasn't one contiguous area, I set up what would be seven different neighborhood groups and appropriated about $5,000 for each group for planning. There was a good chance [that] I was going to get seven different plans. I worked with these citizen groups and their consultants . . . that [effort] wasn't very productive; they all wanted complete control over the money.

If [the plan] got to Washington, D.C., before June 1, 1969, we [would] receive $3 or $4 million more. I didn't want to pass that up, [but] we had a protracted schedule that would have had us complete the plan in September; if [that happened], we would have less money. We told the citizens, got enthusiasm up, so that they [began to] work with me. We divided the plan into three parts.

Part one was problem analysis. [The groups] did all right with that part.

Part two was a five-year plan, just some schedules.

Part three was the implementation period, the big plan. I was trying to meet a deadline . . . and at the last minute [the citizens] came picketing my office, bringing their blue books—their citizen plans—and demanding that we incorporate [all of them]. I refused.

After talking with my staff, [we] came up with an idea. As part of the [overall] plan, we would recommend that each of these neighborhood groups receive some money to carry out three functions: continued planning, [technical] assistance, and neighborhood improvement. [One] of the seven groups was very small, so money was given on a per capita basis, but each [neighborhood] had enough money to hire at least two staff people.

And that's how we got through the first midnight hours . . . and began the implementation of our plan. In the wee-small hours of the morning, we overcame all objections.

What was your strategy?

You harness the power of government with the skills and mandate of the people. [But] not like OEO [in which] people thought they had maximum feasible citizen participation.

We [began] to set up corporations: a youth action coalition corporation, a special-education corporation, and a daycare corporation. We used Title 4A to set up the day care program and got the city participating as a full partner. We set up a Model Cities Health Corporation and, with the support of private money, just recently completed a $6 million facility that serves the neighborhood. [Today], the daycare and healthcare facilities stand next to one another and [are] a beautiful sight.

We set up each corporation [with] 50 percent consumers—Model [Neigh-borhood] people were the consumers—and 50 percent local business people. The attractive thing was that Model Cities [could give] money to each [corpora-tion] to operate. [Although] we put a lot of effort into economic development, we were never really able to pull it off. [But], we did a lot more in various hous-ing assistance programs than most cities tried. We had an extensive second mortgage program and a housing allowance program—the forerunner of Section 8—that was a demonstration and funded by HUD. These were the golden nug-gets that survived from the Model Cities Program in Kansas City.

How would you characterize the relationship between citizens and city in the Kansas City MCP?

As a real partnership!
When I [became] director of Community Development in Kansas City, I had the same conditions [encountered during the Kansas City MCP]. We had independence from the city but integration with the city when that was the best way to deliver services. [Under Community Development], the only thing I had to do was phase out funded citizen participation. We still had citizen participa-tion as required—a large committee that evaluated programs and programmatic approaches. But [the Kansas City Community Development Program] never abdicated power to the citizens.

Jimmy Threat is retired. He lives in Kansas City, Missouri.

Richard Wright
Model Cities Program Director: Des Moines, Iowa

On March 13, 1955, the roads in rural northeast Iowa were frozen making it possible for the doctor to reach the farmhouse where Richard Wright was born. His parents ran a country store that provided food, clothing, and a home for them. On Saturday nights, when there was enough gasoline, the family took trips to a nearby small town where they "people watched." Eventually, Wright's fam-ily gave up their country store and moved to Garnavillo, Iowa, a town of 600 people. The building where Wright attended high school was the same building where his mother taught school and his father was a custodian.

After receiving a bachelor's degree in education in 1957, Wright taught, coached, and earned master's degrees in Guidance and Counseling before be-coming director of admissions at Loras College in Dubuque, Iowa. However, the academic life came to a close when a colleague asked Wright to oversee a fed-eral antipoverty program the Iowa Civil Rights Commission was taking on.

Funding for the program, aimed at low-achieving students, came from the Office of Economic Opportunity. The commission, budgeted at $130,000, was having difficulty managing the federal program, budgeted at $1 million. When, after one year, the director left, Wright—the only employee "who knew where the front door was,"—took over until the program ended in 1968. The following year, Wright became Educational Planner for the Des Moines Model Cities Program (Des Moines MCP) and shortly thereafter, the program's director.

Trust

We had one year, 1968, in which planning took place. By the time we got to the end of [the year], the director had gone back to Iowa State University and others had gone on to other jobs. I was left to assemble the plan—a 480-page document. We tried to get funding but had to wait six months for the political scene in Washington to get straightened out.

What were the demographics of Des Moines?

The perception around the country is that Des Moines is smaller . . . rural. But the same dynamic, found in big cities, is also found in Des Moines. There were pockets of poverty, minorities lived pretty much in one spot, housing was not good, police/community relations were strained, and the Black Panthers were viewed with great suspicion. A series of explosions [had] occurred—the city police station, a building at Drake University, and a Black Panther house [were blown] sky-high. Even though cities such as Cleveland, Los Angeles, and Chicago got the publicity, there was unrest in communities like Des Moines as well. The breakouts were a little different, but the dynamics were the same. Because of their experience in Urban Renewal, minorities and many low-income whites living in other sections of the city didn't want any connection with federal programs.

Describe the Model Neighborhood.

Three or four were considered; [however], the one selected had a high concentration of minorities—about 40 percent—and was the most vocal as well. There were some Hispanics and Southeast Asians, [but] the predominant minority group was black. The [Des Moines MCP] staff was viewed with distrust even though the director was black and black persons had been hired from the neighborhood. Staff members were "outsiders" who wouldn't know what the neighborhood was all about. Developing the Model Cities plan was anything but smooth. The citizen board tried to establish complete control. [Trust], building a good working relationship takes years, but the relationship can be broken in 20 minutes . . . it was important for the citizens to see fair play and know that I meant what I said.

What characterized the citizen participation meetings?

They were chaotic, humorous, and terribly intense. We expected people who were not even on the board to come to meetings. Some community participants carried guns; some had shady backgrounds, but most of the residents were solid, hard-working people who wanted good things to happen in their community. In one [incident], an argumentative minister on the citizen board showed a gun to a woman who became hysterical. She called her sister, a neighborhood resident, who called the cops, who sent police cars out to where the meeting was being held. The police couldn't figure out where to go. Around midnight, when [the police] got to the door, a large black man met them saying, "What are you people doing here? There's nothing going on." So the police turned around and left.

Another incident involved the second director of the program. The board members verbally abused him regularly. One night, during a board meeting, he got up, walked into his office, slammed the door, and didn't come out. The citizens didn't know what to do. They sat [with no one] to yell at for about 20 minutes because the director wouldn't come out of his office.

On another occasion, the director was gone and his door locked; however, the water fountain was located [inside] his office. Someone wanted a drink of water, so the citizens just removed the door.

Understand. The neighborhood residents had been pushed around through the years by programs such as Urban Renewal. Residents wanted to deal with conditions in their own neighborhood. They were led to believe that they were running the program . . . until the City Council and city manager found out that HUD was going to require the city to stand behind an audit. That helped straighten out how, and on what, money was going to be spent.

What long-term effect did the Des Moines MCP have on citizen participation?

Before Model Cities, few people went to a City Council meeting. Since Model Cities, and now in Community Development, people, especially low-income representatives—white, black, Southeast Asian, Hispanic—show up at council meetings. They have learned how the system works. Today there are 46 neighborhood groups. [Although] the participation mechanism has been watered down somewhat and is no longer the "grassroots" participation it used to be, what is there, came primarily as a result of Model Cities.

What were the program's goals?

The citizen-based strategy was more toward social services. The weakness was that we never quite knew how to do economic development—the kind that brings about jobs that last and pay enough to buy needed things—primarily because the citizens had a lot to say about where the money went. They were heavy on education, on human services such as childcare and elderly programs. However, the citizens believed that economic development really meant the money was going downtown where the big money already was. And big money, if given the choice, would try to move the little people out of the neighborhoods close to downtown in order to pursue private interests. Model Cities had good education and training programs, but never a good marriage with the people who had money and could hire from the neighborhood.

Did the Des Moines MCP establish daycare and health centers?

Model Cities brought in the money that could help subsidize low-income childcare. Before Model Cities, funding was difficult to come by. Model Cities had the matching funds to start childcare programs that exist to this day. The citizen's role was to recommend the programs; the city's role was to use the funds in a matching manner to expand services.

In this part of the country, the county is the principal body dealing with human service programs. The city uses its community development money to supplement the county effort—elderly services, daycare, senior citizen centers, transportation, and Meals on Wheels. Many of those services were started during the Des Moines Model Cities Program. The citizens would have liked business programs, but hell, they were more long-range, and the citizens were after something they could do right now. Now, HUD is putting a bigger emphasis on economic development.

Did political considerations prevent any programs from being run?

Des Moines was getting into the cable television business and it was Time Warner, I believe, that wanted to see about grassroots citizen involvement in cable television. The citizens were on top of it; this would have been a major economic development opportunity, but it was a political hot potato. The City Council had ideas on who should run cable television, and frankly, [it was] one of the few times the council told the citizens to stay out. The council eventually hired a local group who made millions of dollars.

Did the program have an impact on individuals?

Many people who were on citizen boards became elected council members, state legislators, and county supervisors. The present mayor of Des Moines, who is black, worked for the Des Moines MCP. He came around to a citizen board meeting a few years ago when he was running for City Council.

One of the board members said, "What do you know about the Community Development Block Grant Program?"

The candidate turned, looked at me and said, "Well, Dick Wright fired me." And he's the mayor now, and I'm no longer with the city.

The Model Cities experience was a very positive thing although little research and evaluation has ever been done on it. You know we were always trying to stay alive. After that first year of planning, there wasn't time to sit down and plan. You didn't always know who your friends were, so you didn't have much chance to step back and let things happen. Once you started down that road, you couldn't go back.

What would you have done differently?

In economic development, if you're going to subsidize, make sure you develop the kinds of community businesses and the kinds of jobs that can really help. Also, I don't think the City Council was of one voice in regard to the program. The council was in some disarray—at times pitting one side of the city against the other. We could have done more to anticipate and deal with these potential conflicts

Looking back, I would have tried to make sure that the council and city manager stated more clearly what they wanted from Model Cities, including citizens and staff. One city manager, who had been with the city for about 10 years, tried to keep all seven councilpersons happy. He apparently had arrangements with each. In that scenario, it is only a matter of time before the fireworks begin. [In Des Moines], the Model Cities approach brought inner-city residents into local government decision making, [but] the process could have been more successful if the council and manager had developed a strategic plan to work with them.

Richard Wright lives in Des Moines, Iowa. He continues to work as a community development consultant.

Peter Richardson
Model Cities Program Director, San Francisco, California

In the early 1960s, Peter Richardson was an undergraduate at Williams College in the ordered small town of Williamstown, Massachusetts. In 1970, he earned a master's degree in city planning from the University of Pennsylvania in Philadelphia. Part of that experience had included a summer internship with the

City Planning Department in San Francisco, California. Following graduation, Richardson went, with two other University of Pennsylvania graduates, to Springfield, Massachusetts, where, in Richardson's words, "The three of us, with a lot more energy than experience, took on the Springfield Model Cities Program." Six months later, city planners in San Francisco asked him to return. The San Francisco Model Cities Program (San Francisco MCP) was about to be "unfunded." The city, facing elimination from Model Cities, wanted Richardson to prepare a comprehensive plan that would save the program.

"Missionary Spirit"

The Hunters Point neighborhood, which was the black community in San Francisco, initially formed its own Model Cities organization. The mayor subsequently brought in the Mission District, which confused matters. Part of my initial task was to figure out how a single application could be created, blending these two very different neighborhoods—the Mission District being a Latino community. Hunter's Point had a lot of noise and bluster, and enthusiasm, [but] not much organization. The Mission District had a tightly controlled community organization that worked pretty effectively with the city on a political level.

Various plans had been submitted, but the city never got one plan together that HUD could fund. HUD finally said, "You've got three months or that's it." Peter Clute, the Model Cities administrator in the San Francisco regional office, really wanted to get the [program] funded, so he and I collaborated in secret. I would write, and he would say, "I can approve that."

What was the primary focus of the program?

Among the many great attributes of Model Cities, was that the program provided a little bit for everybody . . . and it had no particular focus. Everybody had a piece of the action. I don't want to be too cynical . . . there was a $7.5 million program, split between these two neighborhoods—you know, sliced and diced according to eight program dimensions. There was a housing component in each; there was education and criminal justice . . . all those things.

There was a lot of resentment in Hunters Point; [the program] was being, quote, taken away; Mayor Alioto was stepping in, and HUD was collaborating with the mayor.

[Members of] the Mission Coalition Organization (MCO) recognized the pitfalls . . . and didn't want to take responsibility. They wanted to hold the mayor accountable for seeing this thing work . . . which made for some schizophrenia. The MCO was also interested in the employment features of the program. Agreements were negotiated to assure Mission residents, members of the MCO, [and] people who came through the labor unions—there was a strong labor influence at the MCO—had first shot at jobs. And there was accountability ... if you weren't going to give a job to somebody with those credentials, be prepared to explain why.

Were there pressures, political or otherwise, that affected your ability to develop your program?

I was a young white kid trying to function in a Hispanic neighborhood and a black neighborhood, which was ironic. I was 27 years old at the time. For a brief ... six months, after succeeding the guy who had hired me as deputy director, I was the director. When the money finally came in, the San Francisco MCP went from an organization with four or five people, to an 80-person staff. It was nuts!

What did the program mean to you personally?

I don't know that I've ever done anything harder. A lot of us in Model Cities felt a missionary spirit. We believed in comprehensive development—there was a lot of money, at least it seemed like a lot of money to me. We believed that you could dispense maximum feasible [citizen] participation ... some of us still believe that [Model Cities] was a great concept.

Because the Mission District was strong politically, it always had an entrée to City Hall. What happened to Hunters Point?

The Mission District could, and did, flex its political muscle and cause the mayor to pay attention to them. They did fine. It was my belief that to deal more effectively with Hunters Point, the director needed to be a minority person, preferably black. In fact, my successor was black. Unfortunately, he was beaten up two months after he took over.

I [was also] threatened in the office ... by a person who didn't get a job. He was lit up on drugs, came in with a gun, busted up a meeting, and put [the gun] under my jaw. A Filipino, a huge guy, decided he would station himself outside my door for the balance of the time I was there.

Where was Mayor Alioto in all of this?

His message to me was, "I don't understand this stuff. I believe in it, but see what you can do about keeping these people out of my office."

I had become personal friends with Ben Martinez, [head of the Mission Coalition Organization], and, to some extent, with Larry DelCarlo, [director of the Mission District MCP]. We had an understanding: in public they needed to yell at me ... you didn't want to appear too cozy, and we didn't.

Overall, the creative juices [needed to deal] with a whole range of things were just invigorating. If you looked around a room [full] of Model Cities directors, not too many were over 35. [This] was a young, committed group.

Peter Richardson lives in Burlington, Vermont. Currently, he is a consultant on housing issues.

Chapter 4

Confrontation or Assimilation

Terry Duvernay grows up in segregated New Orleans, Louisiana, feeling great affection for his neighborhood and its people. Because of his potential, he is encouraged by teachers to continue pursuit of a Ph.D. but, instead, decides to work in an antipoverty program. Soon, he becomes director of the New Orleans MCP for which the targeted area is his own childhood neighborhood. Because Civil Service status is denied to those working in the MCP, access to, and integration with, city government is difficult. Cautiously, the MCP builds allegiances with city department personnel willing to cooperate. Support comes from the administration of Mayor Moon Landrieu. In addition to the goal of improving his neighborhood, Duvernay is determined to bring blacks into the Civil Service. His leadership of the New Orleans MCP is so successful that he is appointed the city's first black CAO.

Carlyle Cox's childhood is steeped in the wholesome values of Oklahoma. In 1951, he travels to Emory University in Atlanta, Georgia, to study religion. Almost to the point of completing his dissertation, he is assigned new advisors, who demand new requirements. He quits but continues as minister in a church in downtown Atlanta until a prescient awareness of his grandfather's death prompts him to leave the church. He becomes a community organizer for an antipoverty program and is soon recruited by the mayor of Gainesville, Georgia, to join the Gainesville MCP. Nearly half of Gainesville—population 15,000—lives in extreme poverty. Cox adopts a spend-quickly-and-invest-in-the-community policy for the MCP and develops an "us and them" style of citizen participation—for example, the ex-con and the judge who put him away serve as cochairmen on the Criminal Justice Committee. Because of the resulting upheaval, the city council plans to let the MCP application pass into oblivion. Cox musters supporters and citizens to a meeting with council members at a Holiday Inn in which council members are out-maneuvered. Cox's strategy of investing in the community lays the foundation for continuing economic success long after the MCP ends.

In New Jersey, journalist Donald Malafronte reports on antipoverty programs and art and architecture for the *Newark Star Ledger*. When the mayor asks him to become his chief-of-staff, a position that includes directing the Newark MCP, Malafronte is delighted, since to him, city planning and architecture are solutions related to the same problem. Because the city has applied for, and intends to run, the Newark MCP, Malafronte determines that an election of citizen participants is necessary to neutralize an attempt, orchestrated by activist Imamu Baraka, to seize control of the program. Since HUD fears the potential for violence, the election must hold to the highest standards of honesty. Further, the core of the Newark MCP—generate jobs and upgrade the community by bringing a medical school into the Model Neighborhood—is opposed by activist Tom Hayden, who opposes the project and misinforms the press as to the medical school's prospective impact on the neighborhood. On a humorous note, Malafronte relates an anecdote about a prolonged project with the Public Works Department that results in the MCP mantra: "Will that be sufficient?" In retrospect, he believes that too much power was inappropriately passed to community groups and that insufficient knowledge of economic development contributed to the failure of many MCP job programs.

Terrence Duvernay
Model Cities Program Director: New Orleans, Louisiana

Terrence Duvernay was born in New Orleans, Louisiana, in 1943. He grew up living with his parents, grandparents, a sister, and cousins in one side of a "shotgun double" in a neighborhood near the train station and the music of Rampart Street. As described by Duvernay, it was a few blocks in a pattern of segregation, "like a checkerboard" across the city so that domestics could live near their employers.

When the time came to think about college, Duvernay, despite his academic promise, was in no hurry. His sister, impatient with her brother's nonchalance, secured his signature and submitted an application to Dillard University in New Orleans for him. Once there, he wrote papers about "growing up . . .about peo-

Photo 3: Terrence Duvernay

ple and institutions," and "about the interactions of families and why people had jobs, or why they didn't." Following graduation from Dillard, he began to work for Project Cause, an antipoverty program in New Orleans. About his life's goal, he said:

> My idea, when I left college, was to work at City Hall, but City Hall was segregated. You couldn't go to the offices above the first floor . . . and you couldn't go to the cafeteria below the first floor. You could only pay your taxes on the first floor. I was going to stay in New Orleans and work in City Hall. I had no idea how I was going to do that, but that was my goal.

When Duvernay passed the exam and completed the training for the Louisiana Department of Employment Securities (LDES), he was told to go back to the LDES and let them know that he was ready to go to work. The man in charge said, "I'm really happy to see that you folks from New Orleans made it. There's only one problem: we're not ready to hire any black folk yet."

Blocked from civil service, Duvernay decided to apply to graduate school at recently desegregated Tulane University in New Orleans. Because he had graduated *cum laude* from Dillard, he was awarded a full scholarship and a stipend of $300 per month . . . nearly equal to what he would have earned had he gone to work for the Louisiana Department of Employment Securities.

At the Walls of Civil Service

My sociology professor at Dillard told me about Total Community Action, a poverty program that he and the head of the labor unions in New Orleans had put together. One targeted area was the neighborhood I grew up in. So now, I was working part-time in the summer to get jobs for kids, age 16 to 21, and doing follow-up counseling to make sure all was going well.

One night, while I was on break, I got a call: it was the man from LDES. He said, "I was very impressed with you . . . and by the way we've been ordered by the Department of Labor to start hiring black people, and we'd like you to be the first black hired with the department." That was six months after I had been turned down.

I said, "Thank you very much, but I'm a full time student . . . so go find somebody else to be your first black."

I wanted to work full-time for Total Community Action, so I told my major professor at Tulane that I wanted to put a pin in my dissertation. Soon after, Sherman Copeland, a Dillard classmate, told me about the New Orleans Model Cities Program (New Orleans MCP). Jim King, the program director, offered me the job of Education and Social Services Planner . . . I didn't want to leave Total Community Action; [however], one of the three [Model Cities] target-areas was the neighborhood where I grew up.

I started in 1969. Mayor Victor Schiro didn't know we were there, but Ben Levy, his chief administrative officer, did. He was the brain behind the program and responsible for us coming aboard.

What did you want the program to accomplish?

I wanted my life's dream . . . to turn my neighborhood around. Our program was divided into three components: housing and physical development, manpower and economic development, and education and social services. Each component had a planner and associate planner. The idea was to create jobs and businesses and bring money into the community—rebuild houses, improve infrastructure, pave roads, cover canals; and in my area, improve education. We created multipurpose community centers, community schools, and alternative education programs that taught parents how to teach kids.

Was the program inside, or outside city government?

We saw Project Cause, the poverty program we had come from, as outside. We felt Model Cities ought to be inside, an integral part of city government. We were hired without civil service status—in New Orleans, civil service was the epitome of public service and white folk . . . weren't going to let that go. The compromise, which allowed us to be hired, was that we could move up and down in the New Orleans MCP, but we couldn't move anywhere else in city government.

We utilized [those] departments of city government willing to work with us. Now that was a struggle, because most of them didn't want to talk to us. Once we gained allegiances—the Department of Health, the Planning Department and the Social Services Department, were helpful—directors said to their staff, "Work with these people . . . help them, or you won't be here." So we did our planning in conjunction with people who were already in city government. Ben Levy was behind a lot of that because he believed in us.

Mayor Moon Landrieu's support for the New Orleans MCP was significant. Tell me about his election.

Moon Landrieu was a Louisiana state legislator during the heyday of the Jim Crow era. School desegregation was going on. The state legislative body was treading on rights, left and right; all the Jim Crow laws passed 50 to 1. Very enlightened people . . . were voting with the crowd, except this one guy, Moon Landrieu.

When he ran for mayor, nine other people were running. A man named Jimmy Fitzmorris was supposed to win in the first primary. The real fight was for number two. Sherman, [now] the deputy director of the New Orleans MCP, and groups of black folk . . . had formed political organizations—Soul, Bold, and Coup—that went into the neighborhoods and worked politically. This was the first time they made a difference.

As it turned out, Jimmy Fitzmorris came within a whisper, but he didn't win. Moon went into a run-off with Fitzmorris. On the eve of the election at the end of a debate, Fitzmorris—pulling out an old lie—said, "Moon isn't it true that you have Mafia connections?" A bombshell! In the backlash, the electorate told Fitzmorris to go to hell. Moon was the new mayor, carrying 99.9 percent of the black vote.

The departure of Jim King and Sherman Copeland from the New Orleans MCP, and also the departure of the city's CAO, Ben Levy, and assistant CAO for fed-

eral programs created an administrative vacuum. Moon appointed you director of Model Cities and assistant CAO for the city of New Orleans. What were you able to accomplish?

We built three multipurpose community centers that are still centers of program delivery . . . and three housing corporations that are still providing housing. We paved the streets. If we had an impediment, it was that we ran out of money.

We changed mindset; people felt empowered. Programs and services could be delivered from the neighborhood, and, because of our leadership, city government changed. We implemented a Comprehensive Employment and Training Act Program (CETA) and created all the federal programs that followed. We had an impact on civil service. When I left, every department had a black director or a black deputy . . . 35 percent of the employees were black. Some became City Council members or state legislators. It all started with Model Cities.

New Orleans was a stone's throw past segregation when Moon Landrieu appointed you CAO for the city.

I told Moon he should choose his executive assistant, Tony Gagliano. Moon said, "Tony is one of my choices, but from a competency standpoint, there's not a dime's difference between the two of you. I could always say, 'Gee, the black guy finished second' . . . not that I'd have to explain to anyone. But when I look at what we need right now, you're the best person for the job. I don't know what's going to happen when I step out with this decision, but I know it's right."

Moon built up the suspense at the press conference the next morning. We were in City Council chambers. When he announced that Terrence Duvernay would be the city's new CAO, people jumped to their feet in a standing ovation that I can still hear. In 1969, I was the eighth black employee in city government. In 1976, I was the chief administrative officer for the city of New Orleans. That was change.

During the Carter administration, Terry Duvernay worked for the Office of Management and Budget under Harrison Wofford. Later, he became chief of staff for secretary of HUD, Moon Landrieu, and, during the Clinton administration, he was appointed deputy secretary of HUD under Henry Cisneros. Terry Duvernay is deceased.

Carlyle Cox
Model Cities Program Director: Gainesville, Georgia

Carlyle Cox grew up in Muskogee, Oklahoma, during the 1930s and 1940s, when "work in school or church were about the only things anybody did." His parents ran a mom and pop store; his grandfather, who was an elder in the church, owned a farm where Cox milked cows.

In 1951, Cox rode the train into Atlanta, Georgia, to attend Atlanta Christian College. He progressed quickly, entering Columbia Theological Seminary, and next, Emory University to work on a doctorate. Almost to the point of completion, two professors on his dissertation team decided to leave for other schools; their replacements informed him that he would have to start over. "I didn't have another two years to spend on research . . . I threw in the whole can of beans."

While at Emory, he had begun serving as minister in a church in downtown Atlanta and had continued in that capacity after ceasing work on his doctorate. Awaking late one night sensing that something was wrong, he waited, anticipating news from home. At 3:30 a.m., his mother called to tell him his grandfather had died. Following the funeral, Cox returned to Atlanta, faced his congregation on a Sunday morning and said, "This is the last time I will be with you . . . chapter closed."

Having recently experienced the integration of his own inner city congregation, he began to work as a community organizer for the Atlanta Poverty Program. He was assigned to Perry Homes, a 1,000-unit public housing project for low-income blacks. The white businessmen who ran the city held the paternalistic attitude: "We're gonna help these poor folks."

Later, as head of the regional Vista Program in Atlanta, he met the progressive mayor of Gainesville, Georgia, who persuaded Cox to come help run the Gainesville Model Cities Program (Gainesville MCP). A year and a half later, Carlyle Cox became the program's director.

Showdown at the Holiday Inn

We didn't know what we could do at first. The population of Gainesville was about 15,000. The program focused on 45 percent of the city, the southeast and southwest quadrants . . . an extremely poverty-stricken area of about 7,000 people. The black community lived in the southeast quadrant. There weren't even streets, just alleys. Many of the shacks had no running water—two or three spigots were just stuck down the alleyway. Sometimes as many as 40 shacks shared two or three outhouses. The southwest quadrant was home to a low-income white community. It was in total dilapidation; the infrastructure and

housing stock, was almost as bad. The nicest housing in the area was two housing projects just completed by the Public Housing Agency. We literally had to
"re-house" our community. [This] was probably 70 percent of our program.

The remaining 30 percent went to individual and social needs. People, who
weren't even a half-mile from the hospital and the Health Department, didn't
know how to access services. So we started a community service center. We had
a new building, a closed-down black high school at the edge of the city. It had
been built in a last ditch effort to avoid integration—black students were going
to have better than ever. Well, the whole thing dissolved with integration . . .
there was a lot of anger. The white community refused to go to a black school,
so the newest school was closed. [Inside the building], we had to shovel out
trash and broken glass, three feet deep in some places.

How did you organize citizen participation?

We brought "us and them" together in 10 committees . . . by having joint
chairmen. For instance, a fellow just out of prison and a superior court judge
chaired the Criminal Justice and Juvenile Delinquency Committee . . . the judge
had actually sent the guy away. The chairman of the School Board and a dropout
jointly chaired the Education Committee. A welfare recipient and the Welfare
and Family Services director jointly chaired the Income Maintenance Committee.

How did you get the "bureaucratic" professional to participate?

We didn't try to deal with just half a city. We tried to have participation
from all aspects of the community—first-time recipients and the people who
dispensed the revenue. Most people were low- and moderate income, but we
wanted people, citywide, making the decisions. The city was too small for a
program that was independent and separate.

What was the effect?

The real effect was tremendous upheaval. The dynamics in the committees
were stirring the whole community. We had spent close to two years just planning. Late in 1969, the city manager told me, "The City Council"—five white
men—"has decided not to accept the grant for implementation. We're not even
going to submit the application to the Department of Housing and Urban Development. We're just going to let the planning grant run out and in about 90 days,
wind it up."

Now that's where it was. On a Friday afternoon! I spent a lot of time and
talk that weekend [with] citizens that had been much involved. HUD had just
told us that we were going to get more money than we had originally thought.

We had adjusted our plan for those dollars. So we decided if we were going out, we were going out with a bang.

I pulled in all the chairmen, the key players, the judge, the head of the hospital, the chief of staff in the city, and the residents—both extremes on the power spectrum. I said, "We're going to have a citizens participation meeting at the Holiday Inn." It seats about 250 people. "We're going to give a full report to the City Council.'

I went to see the city attorney, Bill Gunner—who later became President Carter's right hand man—and said, "Now Bill, the mayor heads the full meeting any time the council is assembled?"

He said, "The City Council can assemble wherever it wants to. When the council meets, the mayor is the chairman of the council. If there's a quorum, it's an official meeting."

The mayor was with us. I said, "Mayor, the staff is not going to be around. Everybody's equal." Two hundred people—50 of them very rich key people—heard these reports. One by one the [committees] reported—we want a family planning program, a fetal monitoring system, an outreach program—all 10 parts of our program.

Then the citizen participation chairman said, "Mayor, in front of this auspicious body, I would like the City Council of Gainesville to go into session and vote on submitting this plan to the Department of Housing and Urban Development for funding."

The mayor said, "I call this meeting to order." Another guy sort of said, "Ah, yeah."

"I have a second. All in favor . . . don't just raise your hand, stand up."

We had the clerk recording it all . . . and we submitted the damn thing to HUD. That is what citizen participation can do. Publicly, the City Council members supported it. They couldn't say they didn't.

Tell me about the financial strategy, the principle that you adopted.

We understood that the way to achieve the most success was to do some sensible projects quickly. We adopted a principle: spend money quickly . . . but make investments in the community, investments that continue long after the dollars are spent. For example, the Housing Committee said we needed places for new subdivisions. We bought about 290 acres of land for peanuts . . . and put two subdivisions on part of it. One tract was too far out to build on. That was in 1970. Now, people say it's time to build that far out. A black woman on our staff, Frances Williams, just completed a 100-unit, subdivision. It's located on 40 acres of the land we bought in 1970. So in 1999, we're still recycling.

In 1970, there wasn't anything close in that could be done quickly. We had to tear down, and that's not quick. We set up a public nonprofit housing group and funneled all our housing programs through this group. It's still in effect today. We put in maybe $1 million from Gainesville MCP funds in the first three or four years. Today, we have cash assets of about $4.5 million that we're still using from that original money.

We spent, but at the same time we bought housing, totally "rehabbed" it, and sold those units as people could afford them . . . and recycled that money. In 1984, we were approaching $9 million in program income and assets that, after negotiating our Program Income Statement with HUD, we committed to the city to be used over and over for community development purposes.

We started The Gainesville Small Businesses Group to make loans for business and industry. It's still going and has $2 million in a revolving fund. We built our first industrial park with funding received from Model Cities, Community Development Block Grants, and the Economic Development Agency (EDA). Now we have six,, and they are full—thousands of jobs. We're working on our seventh.

We have a community service center in the heart of our city. Today, it's a full city/county department—funded by city and county, state and federal monies—and doing inner-city transportation, day care, and elderly programs. We have changed the focus of our center and the types of services it offers, probably 10 times.

Carlyle Cox is city manager of Gainesville, Georgia.

Donald Malafronte
Community Development Administration:
Newark, New Jersey

As a journalist for the Newark Star Ledger, Donald Malafronte reported on Newark, New Jersey's antipoverty programs, the Civil Rights Movement, and wrote a column on art and architecture. In 1964, Mayor Hugh Addonizio asked him to become his chief-of-staff—an appointment that included responsibility for the city's various antipoverty programs. When emphasis shifted to the Newark Model Cities Program (Newark MCP), it was an opportunity for Malafronte to focus all his varied interests in one direction. For him, "city planning and art and architecture were all part of the same thing. In the 1960s, the notion of creating something wonderful with architecture was of great interest to those who were young and that included me." Malafronte, who was now head of the Community Development Administration, director of Model Cities, and assistant to the mayor, was in a unique position.

"Will This Be Sufficient?"

An [earlier] Community Action Program, named the United Community Corporation (UCC), was a pure form of community action and run entirely by the community with the blessing of the city. A mistake! Model Cities was the antidote; in the application, written from the mayor's office in 1966, we described a large central area that was the worst area of the city. The core of our program was bringing a new state medical school at a university hospital into the Model Neighborhood. If we could divert the school from its original suburban destination of Madison, New Jersey, we could rebuild the neighborhood using the school and its campus. Surrounding the concept in our proposal were the usual employment, human resource, and law enforcement programs. These were tied into programs in Urban Renewal. The proposal wove together physical renewal and human renewal—a package.

Because the community ran the United Community Corporation, there was the notion that the community would also run Model Cities. In fact, Leroy Jones, a social activist better known as Imamu Baraka, organized a vote in a small church on a corner in a small neighborhood and [then] declared those people selected the Model Cities Community Board. This board would run the Newark MCP, he announced. Washington dutifully took note. The board of about 30 persons had elected themselves to run a program that the city had written the application for and intended to run itself. So we had a debate with HUD and the state's new Department of Community Affairs.

Our position was simple: the board was illegitimate. We said, "That's not the way to do it." Instead, we divided the community into districts, each district to elect four representatives. We ran a big summer campaign with something like 500 candidates. People were nervous about upsetting the community election and bringing a city-sponsored election into play, particularly after the riot of the previous year. Calls from Washington came in daily, but we said, "Don't worry. We'll take care of it." We had state and federal observers, and the American Arbitration Association to judge whether the election was fair. The turnout of 5,000 persons was one of the highest for an antipoverty election anywhere in the country. The election of the Model Neighborhood Council was a bona fide community election, and when it was done, there was not a single shred of doubt left as to the community's voice.

Prior to the election, the local newspapers took every self-proclaimed community leader seriously. After the election there was a great silence. The first meeting was entertaining, a 1967 style confrontation with several council members on the [political] far right, [and] several members on the far left. The rest were in the middle and didn't want any part of the confrontation. After the third meeting, the extremists didn't bother to show up and things settled down.

The city entered into an agreement with the council to have a joint veto provision—no program could be approved without the positive vote of both council and city. We had just had the riots. The joint veto diffused the possibility of further difficulty through either side.

What caused the riots?

Bringing the medical school to Newark was the centerpiece of the program. In 1966, we launched a campaign to [ward] off the school's proposed move to Madison. The campaign included a considerable amount of posturing and negotiations back and forth with the state and the feds—who would pay for it, and how much land would be provided. During the furious round of negotiations, the community became more or less forgotten. We were so deeply involved in forcing that medical school into the center of Newark that we lost sight of the community; the quality of communication we had previously built up was lost. Tom Hayden, a radical activist at the time, was a leading opponent of the medical school relocation. He had amazing access to the media and was drumming up all kinds of business by saying that thousands of people would have to be moved. At one point the New York Times ran a piece that said, 'Medical School Plan Involves Relocation of 50,000 Minority Persons.'

I said to the reporter, 'The neighborhood has 1,500 people, not 50,000.'

The reporter said, 'But that's what Tom Hayden said.'

I said, 'For Christ sake. Can't you put in the story that the census indicated 2,500 persons lived in the neighborhood in 1960 and that number is down to about 1700 to 1800 now?'

'I only reported what Hayden said,' he told me. The man and the paper had no sense of responsibility.

Baraka was often perceived as a radical. He wrote in a violent style but I don't think he was a violent person. He wanted improvement, even though he ran and lost in the Model Cities election. Tom Hayden, on the other hand, intended to create a riot. He saw himself as a revolutionary. The idea of rioting to keep a medical school out of Newark was so stupid I can hardly believe it happened, but it did. Once the riot ended, we all came back to our senses. Everyone sat down to several weeks of community negotiations—percentages of minorities to be hired, how people would be relocated, community oversight, and so on. The negotiations, referred to as the Medical School Agreement, cleared the way for construction. Today, the school and hospital employs almost 10,000 people and is one of the biggest employers in the city.

You have a story about an interaction with the Public Works Department having to do with the cleanup effort after the riots.

Actually, the initiative was part of the Newark MCP. I spoke to the director of the Public Works Department. I said, "Listen, we've got to clean up all these empty lots." He described some huge pieces of equipment . . . bulldozers and that sort of thing that he would need, and said it would take a couple of months. Okay. We ordered the equipment and, several months later, it arrived.

Then he said, "However, you understand that we need something to carry them. You can't just drive a bulldozer down the street. We need carriers."

"If I get carriers, will that be sufficient?" Okay. We ordered the carriers. Two- or three- months later the carriers arrived. We loaded the equipment, and I asked, "Now, can we clean the lots?"

"Well, uh, of course. Now, I just need [operators] to run the equipment."

I said, "Why didn't you tell me this the first day . . . the bulldozer, the carrier, the operators. We could have budgeted all of it. Will this be sufficient?"

"Yes, this will be sufficient."

And "Will this be sufficient?" became our Model Cities mantra. The man from the Public Works Department didn't think he could get the money if all the costs were out on the table. On the other hand, if Mayor Addonizio wanted a thing done, all he had to do was say, "Clean up these lots," and it was done by afternoon . . . for me, equipment was needed. So I learned that to get things done in Newark, you needed to be the mayor's person, and that's what I became. The mayor was agreeable. However, when he was indicted and convicted while running for a third term, his power ended.

The new mayor, Ken Gibson, was a solid guy and his own person, and I stayed on with him for a while. He had been the cochairperson of a jobs and employment community organization run by black community leaders before there was an antipoverty program. Indeed, a negative of the antipoverty program was its "professionalization" of social services. The programs replaced social service agencies run by volunteers and local groups. The extensive social service structure that was previously in place disappeared.

Did the Newark MCP have a lasting impact?

The medical school and the hospital transformed the neighborhood. In many ways the Model Neighborhood, 30 years later, has become a model neighborhood. The idea of tying the physical renewal of the city with human resource programs under a single coordinating agency in the mayor's office was a change that worked for many years. Quietly, those efforts have once again drifted in the direction of a decentralized approach, or more accurately, been sorted out among individual departments. Public Works does more than it did before. The Health Department does more than it did before. After 30 years, the mayor's Policy Committee still continues to set the tone for the city's efforts to improve itself. So, all in all, I think it still works.

Did citizen participation survive in any fashion?

I think it has not. When the perception was a black community oppressed by a white administration, citizen participation was an issue. That all changed with the election of Mayor Gibson in 1970. Ken Gibson was not a believer in extending the community participation aspects of the Community Action Program and the Newark Model Cities Program. It became irrelevant in Newark. What community are we talking about? My own belief is that the most valid community leadership, is the leadership that gets elected, not self-appointed. Voting is the best form of community participation. An important part of Model Cities in Newark was moderating community action and putting power back into the hands of the city government after too much power had been inappropriately passed to community groups.

If you could do it over again, what would you do differently?

I don't think a lot of us who ran Model Cities programs understood economic development. You don't create jobs from federal grants. If you get federal dollars, use them to create businesses and opportunities for businesses. Create real jobs that people can have for the rest of their lives. I felt crushed every time a federal program was phased out, and people who had worked for seven or eight years had to look for work again. Maybe I'm beating myself over the head needlessly, because Model Cities happened at a time when broader participation in society was more important than economic development. One thing that the antipoverty program, the Model Cities Program, and Community Development Program did do, was to bring an amazing number of minority people into leadership positions, people who would never have had the opportunity otherwise. Discrimination wasted so much talent. But it wasn't about giving. I used to tell minority groups, "I'm not going to give you anything. We got elected. We're going to make decisions. Then you're going to get elected . . . and you'll make the decisions."

I remember how quickly good will was developed when people felt that there was some equality. We were much criticized in our program for establishing the joint veto provision. Every lawyer said it was the worst possible thing: you never have 50/50 boards. But within the context of having just gone through some very violent times, we wanted to establish trust and peace. The fairness of the Model Cities election allowed the community to trust that the district representatives on the board were really their representatives. Each side backed away from the dumber, more radical ideas that could have been imposed on the other side. After a few months, everybody just settled down. Board members began to notice that the person sitting across the table was okay—a kind of friend. An extraordinary rapport developed among blacks, whites, and Hispanics in the Newark MCP. The board was about 65 percent black but also included Italian-Americans from the North Ward and Hispanics as well. The greatest part was in understanding that everyone was trying to do the same thing—make life a little better for everybody.

Donald Malafronte lives in New York City. He is president of the Urban Health Institute in Roseland, New Jersey.

Chapter 5

Leveraging the System

Franklin Raines, age 23, interrupts his studies in Oxford, England, to return home to Seattle, Washington, to work for the Seattle MCP as director of Budgets, Contracts, and Evaluations. He designs a financial tracking system that requires close monthly monitoring of contracts and results in more budget power for the mayor. To Raines, developing the capacity to apply for, and accept, supplemental grants should be a condition of all MCP programs. His system is "get the grant money, account for it, have a plan, tie it all together, contract out, and monitor the contract." With the mayor, Raines establishes a citywide Office of Management and Budget, which, he observes, works well in Seattle owing to the absence of institutionalized services. From his experience in the Seattle MCP, he learns two important lessons: that monolithic informational systems don't work and that doing exactly as a group demands may not serve the group's best interests.

David Dennison grows up in an Urban Renewal area of Philadelphia, Pennsylvania. He begins to work for the city as a clerical worker. Meanwhile he takes courses and soon becomes a HUD intern. The city of Newark, New Jersey, recruits him for its Community Development Administration, which is responsible for the Newark MCP. On his first day, a paper pile—a "foot-and-a-half of binders, programs and projects"—confronts him. Also, because Newark has just elected its first black mayor, "the black community is euphoric." However, Dennison realizes that the community has no experience in the exercise of power and no clear goal. A power struggle ensues in which black activists, who helped campaign, believe that they are entitled to program control; meanwhile, whites retain control of the city council. Activists disrupt community meetings as a form of persuasion. However, by holding simultaneous meetings in different locations, the MCP stretches activist manpower and neutralizes the situation. Dennison observes that the private sector's role in community development is critical. Also, he plans quarterly meetings for all participants in programs or projects receiving federal funds through the Newark MCP to prove that funds are well utilized and to caution residents that funding does not last. Because the city learns to coordinate "grantsmanship," opportunities for leveraging resources increase.

Nathaniel Winston Hill, a teacher in Little Rock, Arkansas, is witness to the use of federal troops to force the integration of schools. When the Little Rock MCP needs a director, Hill, who is well respected, is appointed. He observes that city government tolerates black people heading programs serving black people but not black people heading programs that are citywide. Also, because the city wants no part of "funny money"—MCP money—Hill insists on an honest accounting of funds so that no taint can be attached to the program. Determined to change city government's perception of black people, Hill seeks parity with city officials. Through such MCP projects as the Career Opportunities Program—a kind of college prep for neighborhood youth—he encourages black people "to get experience and move on to something better."

Franklin Raines
Model Cities Program, Assistant Director for Budgets, Contracts, and Evaluations: Seattle, Washington

In 1972, 23-year-old Frank Raines took a break from his studies at Oxford University in England to travel to Seattle, Washington. Seattle was home. His father, a custodian in the city Parks Department, and his mother, a custodian for the Boeing Company, had raised a family of seven in the Central Area section of the city.

Raines spent the summer working in the Seattle Model Cities Program (Seattle MCP). At summer's end, Walter Hundley, the program's director, asked Raines to work full time. Raines accepted and, following a brief return to Oxford, resumed working for the program through October of 1973.

Follow the Money

I shared Walter's view that the program was there to leverage limited dollars. We were going to get the people with more dollars to do things for the neighborhood, things we didn't have money to do, and they otherwise wouldn't have done. "If you do childcare, we'll fix up the building. If you plant trees, we'll subsidize the costs." We had money that was not allocated, and within a plan, we could be opportunistic. We could subsidize whatever the other entity did in its normal life and say, "If you invest in our neighborhood, you'll be able to do more than if you invest somewhere else."

Just before I joined the Seattle MCP staff, the program had become more closely affiliated with the city. Under Planned Variations, two neighborhoods had been added to the program and in a reversal of usual expectations, Mayor Wes Uhlman began using the Model Cities staff—many of whom were minorities—as a kind of brain trust. One thing he wanted was more power over the city budget. As assistant director for Budgets, Contracts and Evaluations, it was my group that monitored contracts—how they were working, did we need a change in management? In our program, budget and contract management was in one place. Using that example, we worked with the mayor to create a citywide Office of Management and Budget. Despite the small size of his staff, the mayor was getting more budget power. It was the only large-scale operation that wasn't a bureaucracy.

Information processing was critical. We had a fabulous system for tying dollars to performance by having a logical breakdown from the overall program structure, to a particular program, down to a particular project, down to the activities and who was doing the activities. This is still unheard of in most government agencies, but we could do it in Seattle. Therefore, we were able to control the dollars . . . because we monitored every month we were able to intervene. If a lot of money was being spent on miscellanies, we'd want to know where that money was going immediately, not a year or two later when data came in from the accountants.

Model Cities planning requirements had a logical structure. We took those requirements and made them our plan and that's how we ran our agency. You could literally walk from our plan, through our budget to accounting, and trace every dollar. Although the Seattle MCP shut down long before its long-term impacts could be evaluated, we knew where the money went; we pushed the discipline down to the agencies. People didn't get paid until they reported what had been done for the month according to contract and invoiced in our way.

Did tension exist between city agencies and the Seattle MCP?

Yes, but it wasn't racial tension; it was tension between the old-line—the civil-service people who got to their positions by lasting longer than anyone else

Photo 4: A Model City Project

lasted—and the new-line. This was before the mandate that made Model Cities an integral part of the city. In the beginning, Walter brought in people who had never been in government; they didn't have to take a civil service exam or bother with the city's rules. Certainly there was tension with the City Council about the control of program money. The council saw only big lump sums— hard to trace. We knew every detail, but if we had shown the council, it would have been subject to appropriations control.

What impediments existed to achieving the program's goals?

This was an early point in real community development. It wasn't the level-and-start-anew approach of Urban Renewal. There were no organizations like nonprofit housing in existence. We had to create—a daycare program, an economic development program—nobody knew if these programs were going to work or last. We made parks; we bought synagogues and turned them into community centers; we put utility lines underground. These were things that helped to keep the neighborhood viable through a difficult recession—Boeing [had] dropped from 15,000, to 30,000 or 40,000 employees. At one point I went to a meeting of the Investment Committee and voted against a project that I knew wouldn't work. Walter said, "We can't do that. People will be angry. Some things we have to do because it's a symbol to the community."

The infusion of people into the social service organizations and city government was a huge outcome of the program. Several people worked their way up in Seattle City Light—a bastion of white male engineers. One person, Norm Rice, who had been a grantee of ours, became mayor of Seattle. Model Cities was a big recruiting tool for a new breed of mayors, who brought in people they wanted without requiring them to start from scratch in the civil service. What we didn't have were know-it-alls from college who were out to save the ghetto. Walter was a very practical guy who didn't attract people like that.

In your opinion, did Model Cities change the way that cities deal with issues?

In the past, cities, other than New York, didn't have the capacity to apply for or even accept federal grants. They didn't know what to do and had no vehicle to apply for grants because they had never done it. Model Cities created that capacity—applying for supplemental grants was a condition of [the] program. Cities knew how to build highways, but they had never dealt with the U.S. Department of Health and Human Services. Seattle developed a Human Services Department that was 90 percent grant funded. It was just like running a section of Model Cities—you get the grant money, account for it, have a plan, tie it all together, contract out, and monitor the contract.

I think one of the reasons Model Cities didn't do well in New York City was that human services were institutionalized; there was a huge bureaucracy . . . and a lot of competitors. These entrenched competitors would say, "Just give me the money. Why do I have to go through you?" In Seattle, we weren't treading on anyone else's toes. There was no human-services bureaucracy, no housing bureaucracy. And although Seattle City Light was a bureaucracy with a huge budget—a budget we always wanted to leverage—we could say, 'That under-grounding thing you do, do it in our neighborhood." We were paying for it. City Light had the crews. There was no debate. They didn't have to care about the neighborhood to do business with us.

It was our ambition to get the city to redirect its spending. Over time, after the neighborhood got the park, yes, the city would support it. But in the beginning, we just wanted the city in the process, and it was Model Cities Program money that brought the city in. Within the program, the battle was how not to commit more and more money. The danger, in committing all the money to sustaining the same organizations every year, was that the program would become a bureaucracy. With Planned Variations we could continue to expand services because we could shift the overhead costs.

You stayed with the Seattle MCP for a little more than a year. How did that experience help your career?

I learned not to build big monolithic information systems. The Seattle MCP tried to build a new information system with Boeing . . . it never got finished. Seattle tried to build an information system for us . . . it was horrible. Instead, break the system into chunks. Tell the designers what you need and have them bring back something that fits what they think you said. You say, "No, no," [then] send them away and have them come back again. You don't build anything until you've agreed. I carried this lesson to the U.S. Office of Management and Budget, and put out an order, "No more big systems." In fact, it was known as one of "Raines' Rules."

I have a healthy skepticism about what can and can't be done at the local level. I have learned to listen, to identify with but not literally do what a group says it wants . . . because the group doesn't necessarily know what form it takes to get what it wants. In meetings, you have to be patient and not pursue your own agenda. Don't go to the bathroom or have a smoke, and don't get up when someone is talking. You are helping to empower people; but at the same time, you have to interpret what is going on. You don't do something stupid because of a vote . . . you go back to the next meeting and say, "Let's talk about it."

We hired people out of citizen participation. At every meeting, if they complained that we weren't doing x, y, and z, we said, "Come work with us on that issue." Over time, the quality of citizen participation went down because the smartest people were now working with us, which gave us a talent pool. When Planned Variations money stopped, we had to lay people off; we had to begin the process of shutting down the program. The trauma was trying to decide what the city would or wouldn't pick-up. And although much of what had been the core of the Seattle MCP made the transition to the Community Development Block Grant Program, it was without the "entrepreneurship." In government or business, it's tough to keep an innovative program from being absorbed by the bureaucracy.

During the Model City era, we had money and subsidies from HUD programs. But we didn't have the market, the financial resources from private entities, and the community groups like community development corporations. Today we have the market and the community groups, but we don't have the subsidies. If we ever have all three at one time—because if you've got the subsidies, you've got the market available to you; and if you have the groups, you can implement—then you can really rock and roll.

Frank Raines lives in Washington, D.C. During the Clinton administration, he was director of the Office of Management and Budget and, until recently, was chairman and CEO of Fannie Mae.

David S. Dennison
Deputy Director, Community Development Administration: Newark, New Jersey

To David Dennison, the neighborhood in Philadelphia, Pennsylvania, where he grew up, "was like any other ghetto neighborhood, an Urban Renewal area similar to those that others have grown up in."

We didn't realize that's what it was, because it was home. I went to public schools like everyone else . . . and after graduating from high school, I got a clerical job with the city of Philadelphia. I was making $1975 a year and thought I was rich.

When his enthusiasm for clerical work waned, Dennison, after completing the requisite courses at Temple University, became a fingerprinting expert for the Philadelphia Police Department. Within several years, he acquired a good background in research, analysis, and legal skills but was soon taking courses in education and social welfare, having decided that he "really didn't want to be in the Police Department."

In 1966, Dennison, by now a HUD intern, was assigned as an Urban Renewal representative to the HUD regional office in Philadelphia, an office that also oversaw areas in nearby New Jersey. By the time Dennison had spent three years at HUD and earned a master's degree in public administration, New Jersey recruited him to work as deputy director of its Community Development Office. He was to set up a funding program with guidelines to assist those cities in New Jersey that wanted to apply to the Model Cities Program.

By 1970, Newark, New Jersey, had elected its first black mayor, Kenneth Gibson. Soon after, Newark asked Dennison to become deputy director of its Community Development Administration (CDA). The entreaty came by phone from CDA director, Junius Williams, who said to Dennison, "Look, we need somebody right now."

"You guys are crazy," Dennison said. "Nobody's coming to Newark to work within one week."

Williams said, "Listen brother, I need some help. You've got to come."

Dennison went, "drove to Newark like a crazy man," walked into Williams's office at Branford Place, a storefront . . . with the window blinds drawn so people couldn't see in. Williams was sitting behind a desk "completely covered with a foot and a half of binders, programs, and projects. He got up, talked for two seconds, and said, "Sit down, this is your desk. Good-bye."

"Now, the thing about Newark," as Dennison learned, "was that there were two CDAs." In the mayor's office, there was the Community Development Administration or Big CDA, funded by the city's operations budget, and under Big CDA's jurisdiction were the Planning Department and Community Development Agency or Little CDA—actually, the Newark Model Cities Program (Newark MCP) funded by HUD. "That confused a lot of people," especially

'HUD officials who were trying to distinguish between funding requirements related to the Newark MCP and funding requirements related to HUD programs administered by the city.

The Coup in Newark

The black community was euphoric. They had won the election . . . and they were proud. They didn't know exactly what they wanted, but they wanted something. In the midst of this, Mayor Gibson was trying to organize his government and establish priorities—whom to talk to, how to determine inclusion and exclusion. This was new behavior among different ethnic groups. How do we talk to each other; how should we be with each other; how do we make this transition? It was a different vibration than I had ever experienced before.

The perception was that an extraordinary amount of power had changed. People asked, how do we deal with the "spoils of power?" Expectations were unrealistically high, and the white community—the Italian community primarily—didn't believe it had happened. They took a let's-wait-and-see attitude. They had lost a mayor, but nothing really had changed. Meanwhile, Mayor Gibson was trying to make appointments and balance different ethnic groups.

One day while I was sitting in City Hall, Steve Adubato from the North Ward, came in and said, "I'm here to see the white people's mayor. I'm Italian, and there is no precedent in my history where an Italian has followed a black man."

I said, "Mayor Gibson is not available at this time. If you would like to leave a message, I'm prepared to take it."

He said, "I'll wait for the white people's mayor," but nobody came out to talk to him and eventually he left.

Interestingly, as time passed, Adubato became the mayor's staunch supporter. In Newark, we had elections for the Model Cities Participation Board. We encouraged him to run. Once he got on the board, he fought a lot of things, but the interaction turned him around. In years to come, he became a positive force for the program.

The dynamic that smacked the blacks was realizing that the City Council, the legislative part of city government, had a majority of white councilmen—the mayor appoints people to critical boards such as the Board of Education and the Housing Authority, but the City Council has to confirm those appointments. In my first four years in Newark, the public complained that the mayor wasn't [improving] education or housing. Mayor Gibson kept telling them, "I just don't have the votes."

It wasn't until the Community Development Block Grant Program came along that the City Council gave the mayor more clout. Still, the redevelopment entity was under the jurisdiction of the Housing Authority, an independent authority needing resolutions from the council, not the mayor. Mayor Gibson had to negotiate a lot of compromises to get anything done.

Describe the climate from 1970 to 1974.

The Black Power movement was still very strong. LeRoi Jones, the Black Nationalist social activist known to the local folks as Imamu Amiri Baraka, was a skilled organizer and had been heavily involved in the pre-election. He wanted to make sure to the victor go the spoils . . . he figured he was a victor. A lot of activists in the movement had helped hang signs and performed other tasks to get people elected. They wanted the benefit of that effort. The mayor wanted to support requests for jobs, but skills in some instances were required . . . something not known by a lot of people.

At the meetings at Branford Place, Baraka's support staff would be lined up all around the conference room. You never knew what was in people's laps to help the negotiations along. Reasonable workable agreements always resulted. We were a happy family taking growing steps together.

It was self-defense.

We'd be discussing projects, the processes required by the government; we had to come up with a legal and equitable process that afforded access and participation that everybody agreed to. Often, I would interview two or three individuals from the Black Nationalist movement at a time. Those who lacked required skills and were not referred for employment didn't appreciate our position. It was not uncommon to receive a request for an "encouragement" meeting from supporters of the rejected party.

In community planning meetings, to persuade residents to their point of view, activists would send one or two people to a meeting with a deliberate intent to disrupt by reciting some scripted speech. Because of the black community's experience with police brutality, when "freedom of speech" rights came up it became critical for [community] residents to police their meetings. Frequently, we conducted several meetings simultaneously in different sections of the city, which neutralized the manpower resources of any group intent on disruption. Things were always on edge—people jockeying for power, influence, and a money stake. People, black and white, were intimidated. I don't want to exaggerate, but it was an unending hot seat for four straight years.

These were the preconditions. What did you want the Newark MCP to accomplish?

Well, the critical thing was that certain areas had physical deterioration from the rebellion.

Why don't you use the word "riots?"

It was a rebellion against injustices, not just rioting.

Are you saying that a riot is an action without a purpose . . . and that a rebellion has a purpose?

Absolutely! Many in the community were incensed that the white establishment press—the newspapers—were defining and writing that blacks were rioting. Who blessed it as a riot? Blacks stood in front of the National Guard tanks to stop the killing. They were willing to give their lives to improve their living conditions. It was not a riot; it was a rebellion.

Our Model Cities executive team had the desire and the leadership to stabilize certain communities and show what a comprehensive program of physical, social, and economic development could do. We had the capacity to build anchors, anchors that could be catalytic. We created a Housing Development Rehabilitation Corporation that demonstrated effective housing stabilization projects and used all the tools that we had to leverage program funds. We developed comprehensive support projects dealing with health and human-services issues. The transportation system was also a concern—many areas weren't adequately served—and the infrastructure was in bad shape because it had been bled for so long.

The Model Cities leadership saw that Newark was strategically located. The Port Authority was there, an international airport, and access to major highways from the north, south, and west. A proposed linking highway threatened to cut right through the heart of the black community. One of the biggest challenges, prior to, and after, Mayor Gibson's election, was to get approved an alternative revitalization plan for the land that had been cleared and proposed for the highway. The leadership fought and fought, and eventually won the right to redevelop the parcels for something other than a highway.

So that was the hope for Newark.

Looking back, what do you personally feel good about?

I was struck by the critical requirement for the role played by the private sector in community development. I was hungry to learn more, to come up with a collaborative public/private partnership model that could impact difficult places like Newark. Newark was a natural laboratory. I decided to enter a Ph.D. program at the Union Graduate School with a concentration in organizational behavior. This led me to develop a collaborative municipal/corporate model. Within two years, utilizing this model, the city had formed a public/private team and taken a different approach in preparing a funding application to the Economic Development Administration. I feel good that I personally improved my capacity to assist others in mastering their environment, especially using collaborative public/private partnership methodologies. Growth and development in Newark included asking, 'How do you do urban development; how do you pull in and deal with political realities; how do you deal with politicians, the press, and the different legal authorities, especially when all you have is influential power."

What lasting change took place in Newark?

In Newark, the words of Jessie Jackson, 'I am somebody," were never truer. I noticed this attitudinal posture in the first two and a half years. It was a mindset that self-determination was alive and well in Newark. That can-do attitude enhanced the receptivity for other change. The staff looked to think outside the "supposed" restrictions of the box . . . and that was more reason for wanting to learn about the dynamics of organizational behavior.

For example, the Newark MCP tackled integrating Newark's predominantly white police and fire departments. Jobs in those departments required taking a statewide civil service exam. We designed a special police and fireman cadet program. Candidates had to live in, and work in, the Model Cities areas. They would receive the same training as conventional recruits. We negotiated with the state civil service office, which agreed to upgrade all cadets—without the civil service exam requirement—to full policeman or fireman status after successfully performing for one full year. The police and firemen unions fought this back door access but lost and, as a result, several young black men gained entrance to these departments.

Also, we began to hold quarterly meetings for everybody in programs or projects that received funds from the Newark MCP—including employees in city departments and agencies. My goal was twofold; [one], for all providers to hear and appreciate the comprehensiveness and integration of their contribution, and [two], to sensitize the recipient [to the fact] that a federally assisted program easily becomes temporary when people take the assistance for granted.

To gain access to jobs, we structured job classifications and job requirements within the program that were duplicates of jobs in traditional city operations and departments. People were assigned to work closely with their duplicate department whenever the opportunity presented itself. The business administrator told the newspaper that the program was operating a "shadow government." No matter, the end result was that some of the best candidates for key openings in traditional city departments came out of the Newark MCP.

The mayor's Policy and Development Office coordinated a review of all federal funds impacting the city and requiring the mayor's sign-off. Under Planned Variations, the Newark MCP created a Chief Executive Review and Comment Office. This gave us the opportunity to improve our leveraging of resources with entities interfacing with areas we served. We had no legal authority, but we could influence . . . and we could coordinate "grantsmanship" efforts more comprehensively. As a result of this coordinating role, our agency soon became the primary source for managing federal and state grants, an amount roughly equal to the city's traditional operating budget.

The Newark MCP was digging up all kinds of money . . . to meet the needs of the police department and for demonstration programs run by the board of education. At the same time, the [program was] structuring access to city government and authority, and grooming people for the future.

David S. Dennison lives in Washington, D.C., where he directs his own consulting firm.

Nathaniel Winston Hill
Model Cities Program Director: Little Rock, Arkansas

While growing up, Nathaniel Winston Hill lived on Ninth Street in Little Rock, Arkansas, in the midst of a concentration of black businesses and nightclubs. "Just about every Saturday night," he recalls, "there was a shooting or a killing." A block from Hill's home stood a vintage World War II building brought from nearby Camp Robinson to house a YMCA. The YMCA, Hill's employer throughout his youth, was a gathering place "where black professionals in the neighborhood came to play dominoes."

When Hill was still a child, his father had become ill and was unable to work. His mother supported the family with earnings from work as a domestic and supplemented the family's diet with leftovers from dinners cooked for others. Despite the hardships, all three brothers graduated from college; his sister became a nurse; and Hill, after earning a master's degree in physical education from the University of Arkansas, began teaching in a segregated school in the depressed, eastern edge of town. Hill said of his work:

Teaching was a joy. Parents looked up to teachers—like a preacher or a lawyer. If I didn't discipline a child for something he did in school, the parents wanted to know why.

In 1968, when Little Rock needed a director for its Model Cities Program, Charles Bussy, the only black member on the Little Rock City Board, had the "pick." Hill, free of political entanglements and well respected as a teacher and as the director of an educational incentive program for young people, was the ideal choice. Also, Hill brought with him a determination, born of personal experience, to change negative attitudes affecting race relations.

Without Blemish

I was married in 1956. My wife taught school in Crossett, Arkansas and I taught in Little Rock. Each weekend I drove [over 100 miles south] to Crossett to be with her. One Monday morning, while driving back through Pine Bluff, I was pulled over for speeding. [Since] I didn't have any money with me, I said to the officer writing the ticket, "I know where police headquarters is. I'll just stop by and pay the ticket."

The officer went to his car, made a call to the station, then came back and said, "Well Nathaniel, headquarters is going to send an escort out here for you."

At headquarters, I called my pastor, who lived in Pine Bluff, to ask if he could help me, but he wasn't home. I called the principal of my school who told me to call Lawrence Davis, the president of the University of Arkansas in Pine Bluff, but he wasn't home.

[Just then], a little fat fellow, who was sitting in the corner of the [police station], said, "Lock that n___r up. He wasn't supposed to get but one phone call. He's had five."

I called the president's office at the university again and said, "Please, somebody, come get me. They're talking about locking me up." About five minutes later, someone from the university called to say that he would be at the police station in five minutes and would pay my fine.

The desk sergeant said, "Nathaniel, do you know a Mr. Collins?"

I said, "No."

The sergeant said, "Well, you be sure and pay him back."

This time, the jailer spoke up, "You mean to say you're gonna let this n___r go? You let him go, we'll have to have every policeman in the state of Arkansas trying to track him down."

[When] the sergeant motioned me out, I eased on out the door. If it was a set-up meant to scare me, it did. I found Mr. Collins who [was] a black policeman on the university campus, thanked him, and [put] his check in the mail the next day. That was life in the South.

In 1957—the memory is as vivid as if it were yesterday—U.S. Troops were brought in to enforce a court order to [integrate]. Everyday I rushed home from Carver [Elementary] School in East Little Rock, bypassing Central High, to see what was happening on television. And there they were...vehicles [with U.S. Troops] coming across the Broad Street Bridge. It was like D-Day. We just jumped up and shouted "Yeah!"

By 1968, how politically expedient was it to put blacks in positions of authority?

I think [political expediency] was the main reason the board told Charles Bussy that he could select the director of the Little Rock Model Cities Program (Little Rock MCP). When, after two years of National Model Cities Directors

Association (MNCDA) meetings, I looked around, 95 percent of the Model Cities directors were black. Black people could head programs serving black people, but they couldn't head programs that were citywide. Model Cities wasn't going to be around long, [so early on], I started to think about bridging the gap between Model Cities and local government.

How did you go about hiring your staff?

I didn't want an all white staff—the same [that] people had [always] seen—and I didn't want an all black staff. I wanted an integrated staff so the program would reflect what we stood for. I wanted to make life better and to show city hall that black professional people [could] do a good job.

What were your goals for the Little Rock MCP?

I had total responsibility for the program. The city's Finance Department didn't want anything to do with "funny money." I had to have my own accountant, sign checks, and operate the program. I wanted no financial blemish; other programs had been cited for mishandling of funds. I didn't want to be one of them.

The Model Cities area [was Little Rock's East End]. People had lost hope. The few paved streets carried people through the depressed area to the airport . . . most of the streets were without curbs and gutters and had open drainage ditches. Houses were falling apart, schools were not [maintained], and the [only] park was under the airport's landing path. Because of flooding—the area was near the river—one or two children drowned in culverts every year. When the river rose, the city closed the floodgates, which caused water to back up into the neighborhoods.

[Model Cities] was right on the heels of desegregation. I wanted the city to provide services to depressed areas. I wanted to change how people in city government felt about black [people]. White people looked at the area as blighted—a rough area. Blacks looked at it the same way. No one wanted anything to do with people in the East End.

Concurrently with the physical aspects of the program, we began a Career Opportunities Program. Because several people in the Model Neighborhood wanted to be physical therapists, we used Little Rock MCP funds to start a program in physical therapy at the University of Central Arkansas. We also began a program with the local colleges that helped youngsters develop [into] teachers. Many [participants] did become teachers and are now employed by the Little Rock School District.

Unbelievably, there was [just] one doctor in the entire area and no recreational [facility], so we turned our attention to health care and activities for children. The committees—[made up of area residents]—developed a plan for a one-stop facility for people with problems . . . any kind, such as employment, legal, physical, or dental. The facility, the East Little Rock Community Complex, housed a gymnasium, swimming pool, library, and daycare program, [which was actually] a preschool program contracted out to, and run by, the Little Rock School District. But the [school] district wouldn't put money into the program, so we pulled away. We thought that since the city was [partially] funding the preschool program, the city might as well get credit. That was an important decision because, for the first time, the city of Little Rock was actually operating social programs.

The community complex was 26,000 square feet. Building that facility was of great importance because it proved to the residents that the city was investing in their future. It wasn't Urban Renewal, and it wasn't just dealing with the infrastructure because we knew that physical programs had to go hand in hand with social programs.

The high point of [Model Cities] was that you could try things. If other programs had failures, they were immediately shut down. But [with] Model Cities, if something didn't work, we could say, "Well, this way won't get the job done." We weren't penalized for a failure as long as we learned from it and moved on to something else.

Is there a legacy deriving from the original program and philosophy?

[From the beginning], I encouraged black people working in the program to use it as a stepping stone, a way to get experience and move on to something better. We thought Model Cities was going to terminate after five years. I began looking [for citywide responsibility as a way] to keep [the goals of the program] going. As the Little Rock Model Cities director, I went to department heads, hat in hand. The only way they would be happy to see me would be if I had something to offer them. And how could I do that?

The opportunity came when the city manager [put me in charge] of bringing about a merger between the city's Health Department—[a service that existed prior to the Little Rock MCP]—and the county's health department. being successful put me on an equal footing with the chief of police, the fire department and parks department and enabled me to do more for the Model Cities area.

[For me], the whole legacy of the program is neighborhood participation. We now have Alert Centers all over the city where neighborhood committees can rally round—where residents, working with city officials, can solve problems in their neighborhood. Before Model Cities, black people didn't go to city hall with problems. Now, they [do].

Tell me the significance of the "suit of clothes."

It's what most black churches do for a preacher as an expression of love. When I retired, the staff gave me a dinner . . . at the East Little Rock Community Complex, the complex that the program built in 1970. When I walked in, the place was jammed-packed with people. I was given a suit of clothes. Then, near the end of the dinner, the mayor read a resolution: "Upon" my "separation from the city, the complex" would be "renamed the Nathaniel Hill Community Complex." To have a building named after me made me feel . . . I really had done a decent job for the city.

Nathaniel Winston Hill lives in Little Rock, Arkansas. He is retired.

Chapter 6

Personal Experience

In high school in Tucson, Ariz., and, later, in the Marines at Camp LeJeune, North Carolina, during WWII, Cressworth Caleb Lander participates in several effective efforts to counter racial discrimination. Following the war, he returns to Tucson, Arizona, where he is politically active and works in antipoverty programs. Appointed to the Tucson Housing Authority, Lander challenges its practice of holding closed meetings and intimidating public housing tenants by conducting midnight inspections. When Lander becomes director of the Tucson MCP, he develops the strategy of "co-optation"—of drawing city government into the program, thereby gaining access to city government. Projects initiated with the city's cooperation include transportation for handicapped workers, strip-paving dirt roads, a Head Start Program, and a Small Business Development Center. Particularly interesting is a major sanitation project that provides 350 homes—many lacking indoor plumbing—with a specially designed bathroom/water heater module that can be attached to a house or stand separately. In addition, many residents get their first sewer, electrical, or water line. Lander reflects that if the Tucson MCP had adopted a hostile attitude toward city government, the institutional change brought about in city departments could not have been accomplished.

Walter R. Hundley grows up in West Philadelphia, Pennsylvania, during the Depression. When he enters college to prepare for the ministry, he finds himself moving politically to the left. He moves to Seattle, Washington, to become minister in the nondenominational, multiracial, Church of the People. When a rift in the congregation dissolves the church, Hundley pursues social work and devises solutions to juvenile delinquency. A critical thinker and active in the Civil Rights Movement, he attracts the notice of Seattle's mayor who appoints him director of the Seattle MCP. Hundley rejects any plan that builds "a segregated city within a city." Rather, he wants the white community to understand that the program also serves their interests. One successful project, utilizing the resources of the Seattle MCP and the Historic Preservation Act, turns the older, run-down center of Seattle into a thriving business area and tourist attraction. Another project named Community Police—neighborhood residents intervene in domestic disputes within the Neighborhood—is so effective that it breaks down Police Department resistance to hiring minorities. However, a Minority Contractors Association is not so successful. To illustrate the pressures on the program, Hundley relates an anecdote about men brandishing guns at a neighborhood meeting and demanding a share of Seattle MCP money.

In the 1960s, East Boston, Massachusetts, is the future site of Logan Airport and the hometown of young Tom McColgan. When residents organize to protest the city's seizure of land by right of eminent domain for construction of the airport, McColgan develops empathy for the victim's point of view. Pursuit of a master's in public administration takes him to Holyoke, Massachusetts, a city that McColgan describes as "a classic sociological exercise," because the least economically able live on the "flats" next to the river. In 1973, he begins to work in the mayor's office and soon becomes director of the Holyoke MCP whose primary focus is on physical renewal and social programs. However, by not "partnering with neighboring industries," McColgan recognizes and regrets an opportunity lost. In preparation for the CDBG, McColgan must organize the administrative framework that will operate all the city's categorical programs, grants, and ongoing MCP projects from one location.

Cressworth Caleb Lander
Model Cities Program Director: Tucson, Arizona

In 1925, the year Cressworth Caleb Lander was born, his grandfather, certain his grandson was destined to be rich, gave him the name "Cressworth," a combination of Kress and Woolworth, the two major stores in Tucson, Arizona. At the time, Tucson was a small town. Everyone knew everyone or knew the person's family. In the black community, family members held fast together in mutual support against the "sting of segregation." This was particularly true within the Lander family whose belief in self-determination was the family virtue.

Photo 5: John A. Sasso and Cressworth C. Lander

Although Lander attended segregated schools throughout elementary and junior high school, he considered his education superior because his teachers "were the kind that taught seven days a week." He learned to pay attention to events around him. For example, in the late 1930s, Tucson High School was integrated, but activities within the athletic department, with the exception of track, were not. Four black athletes who had almost single-handedly won the state high school track championship—a matter of great pride to the school—used their accomplishment to challenge school officials. Their position: "If other sports weren't opened to black athletes, they would not compete." As a result, in 1939, Tucson High School overturned its racist policy and allowed black athletes to participate in all sports, even contact sports.

After graduation from high school, Lander volunteered for the U. S. Marine Corps. He was sent to Camp LeJeune, North Carolina, where he experienced his "first real taste of segregation in the South." While waiting at a train station for a bus back to camp, Lander, along with other black servicemen, witnessed a scene that left them in disbelief:

We looked across the way. In the waiting room for whites there were German prisoners being served donuts and coffee by the good citizens of Wilson, N.C. That was an irony . . . and more than an individual could take; to be a member of the U.S. Marines, fighting for your country, and have to wait in an unheated 25-degree, segregated waiting room while German prisoners of war were treated to donuts and coffee.

In another incident in Wilmington, North Carolina:

We were attempting to get back to base. We were all lined up according to how you came to the line—first come, first serve. Someone from the bus company came up and said that the blacks had to be in the back and the whites had to be in the front. The buses weren't going to leave until we fixed up the line in a segregated system. Well, the blacks didn't like it, but neither did the whites. We decided, blacks and whites both, to take over the bus, put the driver off, and drive the bus back to Camp LeJeune. The next day the bus company had to send someone to the base commander to get the bus.

With boot camp completed, Lander, owing to his office skills, was assigned to personnel management at Camp LeJeune, was soon promoted, and eventually became head of the Personnel Office. By 1964, after "decocooning" airplanes for use in the Korean War, earning a bachelor's degree in business administration from Los Angeles State College in 1959, and returning to Tucson to work as a real estate broker, he became proprietor of Lander Mirasol Liquor Market on South Park Avenue. A white businessman, Mr. Frank O'Reilly, whom Lander had worked for as a young boy, was the friend who backed him when the banks would not. Lander was so determined to make the store succeed and to repay Mr. O'Reilly that he defended his store against would-be burglars with a .38 caliber pistol late one Sunday evening. No shots were fired, but guns were drawn, chase given, police called, and an arrest made. The defense lawyer tried to characterize Lander as a "gun nut" . . . he had made these boys "come into the store." No one was buying. The judge praised Cress Lander, saying he was a "courageous man and the fastest gun in the West."

Co-optation

After World War II, I worked in the Young People's Progressive Political Party. We went into rural areas to sign up underserved and underprivileged blacks. We registered approximately 5,000 to 6,000 new voters who could back local candidates. We then asked for job opportunities and were able to place the first black in the treasurer's office, and in other county and city jobs throughout Pima County.

In 1969, after organizing and working in OEO sponsored, and local, anti-poverty programs, you became the first black appointed to the Tucson Housing Authority.

Some things were wrong with the Tucson Housing Authority. The board met monthly in a private room in the back of the Pioneer Hotel. People from the community were not invited to what was, in effect, "a public party." With help, I was able to get the location changed to the Santa Rosa Center. For the first time, the Housing Authority started to have open meetings; people from the community could express their desires, their problems, and seek relief before the Board of Directors.

The board, mostly Tucson businessmen, was not happy with me. I had admonished the director for the way public tenants were treated—there were midnight inspections, without notice, to find out if males were living in the house and there were inspections for use of improper materials. People didn't have the sense that the [house] was their home. The effect was to make public housing residents feel subhuman.

I called for an investigation of public housing. The board wanted me removed, but Jim Corbett, the mayor of Tucson, backed me. Within 24 hours, there was a mass resignation and I was named chairman of the Tucson Housing Authority.

Why was the Model Cities Program so important to the city of Tucson?

I was aware of what could happen if we organized the community, if we had funds to provide basic services. The potential Tucson Model Cities Program (Tucson MCP) budget for Tucson was approximately $3 million, about six percent of the city's budget. I saw an opportunity to really do things for the city. In our antipoverty program, we didn't have the type of money that was necessary to deal with the infrastructure—streets, transportation, and parks. The legislation indicated that 75 cities would be selected in the first round and another 75 in the second. I said, "Well, we're going to have to make Tucson one of those cities."

We wanted to put an application together. I started to work with people in the community. We called the HUD regional director in San Francisco and expressed our need for a program. We talked him into making a trip to Tucson, and then walked him around the South Park area and the downtown area. Sure enough, the city of Tucson was selected in the second round.

Although the largest minority in Tucson was Mexican-American, you were selected as the director of the Tucson MCP. What happened next?

To make things right I selected Fred Acosta, a Hispanic, as deputy director. I knew he was a good activist. First, we attempted to buy into some of the established systems in Tucson so that Model Cities wouldn't be an outsider. I went to the city attorney and said, "We need to hire an attorney for the Tucson Model Cities Program; I want that attorney to be part of your staff." Then we went to the superintendent of the Tucson Unified School District and asked for a representative so that education could be a real priority—he assigned two people, one whose salary we paid. We went to the Arizona Department of Economic Security—they were responsible for welfare and all the benefit programs in Pima County—and said we would pay for one of their people to be on our staff. In the health field, we brought in Bernice Epstein, who had done work for the University of Arizona.

The "Co-optation Model" is what we called the Tucson MCP. We tried to co-opt City Hall, to bring them into our system, and thereby, have them bring us into their system. We were buying credibility for our program because we wanted to be looked upon as a legitimate agency.

We bought into the major part of the community in terms of staffing. And, because we wanted to implement a good fiscal system, we brought in two recent graduates with master's degrees from the University of Arizona. We hired people who lived in the seven neighborhoods of the Tucson MCP. Once we assembled our staff, we started to work with community activists to establish neighborhood associations. We looked at the problems and, with the assistance of our staff and some outside consultants provided by [HUD], the neighborhood associations started to put together a plan.

What major needs were identified?

People, who were handicapped, needed rides to medical facilities, to recreational facilities, and to job facilities. We had basic services—trash pick-up, police and fire services—and some measure of community service with the parks and recreation department, but not the scope of services that city government and state government is involved in today.

People on the eastside of Tucson had always used citizen participation to get redress for their grievances. Minorities on the south and west sides had not, so the Tucson MCP started to teach them that they too had a right to appear before the mayor and council.

Streets needed paving so people didn't have to walk through the mud. We came up with an idea to strip-pave 35 miles of road in and around downtown Tucson. The Transportation Department said these were nonstandard roads, but we convinced the mayor and City Council that it was better to have 35 miles of strip paving than to have no miles of standard paved roads. Citizen participation was a major factor; we packed the chambers and overrode the position of the City Council.

We had a health problem. Within two miles of City Hall, there were 350 outdoor privies . . . without attachment to any kind of sewer system. With the help of Bernice Epstein, we devised a module that was a bathroom with a water heater. The module could be attached to an existing house or freestanding. We used to tell people on the eastside that the mosquitoes and flies from those privies were spreading disease and germs, and for some reason, those flies refused to recognize the boundary lines of the Model Neighborhoods. During the period of Model Cities we replaced 350 outdoor privies and, in many cases, put in the first sewer line, the first electrical line, and the first water line to a property.

We developed a "rehab" program for residents in owner-occupied units, in effect, turning the neighborhoods around. For the first time property values started to increase . . . communities were reborn because of the Tucson MCP.

We took an economic development package to the mayor and council . . . to set people up in business. A number of council members objected to competition with existing businesses in the area, so we had to take a different tack. We set up a Small Business Development Center and made small loans to people in the community. Now, you see many franchised restaurants and other businesses in the south and west sides.

What impact did co-optation have on legitimizing those services?

The city of Tucson picked up a program we devised for transporting people to various destinations, which is now the Van Tran Program. Also, we had a Head Start Program but no kindergarten. We made a proposition to the superintendent: we would place a kindergarten program in each of 13 elementary schools in the Model Neighborhood . . . and fund the cost. The superintendent thought it was a magnificent idea. He said, "Once you get the program in the inner city, I will be forced, by pressure in the community, to provide kindergarten services to the entire city of Tucson." He was right.

What lessons did you learn from the Tucson MCP?

If you give people an opportunity and the resources to put their ideas into practice, people on the lower end of the economic spectrum can make real changes in their community. In order for change to take place . . . sometimes the changes can't be radical. We were able to buy into existing programs . . . if we had been standing on the outside, throwing rocks, we could never have brought about the institutional change in Tucson that took place during the period of Model Cities.

The program was terrific, but we didn't have enough time and resources. If I could do it over again, I would go a little deeper . . . to provide the assistance that families need to move to first class citizenship.

During the Carter administration, Cress Lander was appointed managing director of the Civil Aeronautics Board in Washington, D.C. In 1980, he returned to Tucson, where he served as that city's director of Housing and Community Development and then, director of Community Services until his retirement in 1991.

Walter R. Hundley
Model Cities Program Director: Seattle Washington

At age 71, Walter R. Hundley continues to remain at ease in the middle of a fracas, a skill he learned as a child while living in West Philadelphia, Pennsylvania. "I wondered if I'd ever grow up to lead a full life because of the mayhem that went on." There was also the economic disruption of the 1930s. Hundley didn't have enough money for college, but he did have a good public school education, further enriched by high school teachers holding doctorates who, because of the Depression, were grateful for the opportunity to teach Philadelphia's youth.

After graduation from high school, Hundley decided to join the army. Before enlisting, he first had to fulfill an obligation as delegate to a statewide Baptist Church Sunday-School Convention in Pittsburgh. When he returned to Philadelphia, he found a letter waiting for him, an invitation and scholarship to Lincoln University, an all black, all male, small liberal arts college in Pennsylvania. He was 16 years old.

"I grew up at Lincoln," said Hundley. The president of the college was Horace Mann Bond, a real intellect and the father of Julian Bond, the former director of the National Association for the Advancement of Colored People (NAACP). "The student body considered him a 'hat-in-hand, shuffling-for-the-white-man,' kind of person. We knew he was brilliant . . . and resented his groveling to get money for the college. In any case that was part of my growing up."

At Lincoln, Hundley's political perspective moved to the left; nonetheless, his ultimate goal remained focused on teaching religion. A white professor and graduate of Yale Divinity School in New Haven, Connecticut, had taken an interest in Hundley's career. With the professor's support, Hundley gained admission to Yale. While at Yale, an older student, a former assistant U.S. Attorney in Seattle, Washington, told him about The Church of the People, an unusual, somewhat left-wing, nondenominational church that was located there. The congregation of whites and a few minority blacks and Asians was looking for a minister, preferably black, to integrate their church.

Hundley, just married, put himself and his wife on a plane and went to Seattle. "That was 1954. I had to brave the establishment of Seattle because many people considered the church Communist, although they didn't know the difference between Stalinism and communism, not to mention socialism—these differences rankled." Most members of the congregation were elderly and still living a radical version of the 1930s. When more young people started attending the church, a rift occurred and the church dissolved.

Hundley turned to social work, beginning at Monroe Reformatory, a state prison for young offenders. Soon after earning a bachelor's degree in social work from the University of Washington in Seattle, he became director of a demonstration project, the Metropolitan Youth Development Council, funded by the Ford Foundation. The project's objective, according to Hundley, was to "devise solutions to juvenile delinquency by concentrating the money on a target group . . . to meet all the needs for the group—social, educational, and welfare." The concept was a "harbinger of the Model Cities Program. Our studies didn't conclusively prove that this intense approach significantly changed the delinquency pattern among our group, but the program was exciting." When top sociologists from the East and West Coasts came to look, "they gave the program high marks; so it was considered a success, even if the kids in the program didn't fare as well."

In 1965, Mayor Norm Brayman asked Hundley to help write an application for Seattle to the Office of Economic Opportunity. The Central Area— eventually a Model Neighborhood in the Seattle Model Cities Program (Seattle MCP)—was a predominantly black neighborhood and a component in the OEO application. It was one of the first areas to be funded. During the initial organizational process for the Central Area Motivation Program (CAMP), the first director appointed proved ineffective, and, although, the residents perceived Hundley as someone "working for the white guys," after several months of going nowhere, they asked him to become director of CAMP. He accepted.

"Not Just a Black Program"

The Civil Rights Movement was getting some steam in Seattle. I became chairman of the local Congress of Racial Equality (CORE). CORE believed in direct action so we picketed, staged sit-ins, and something we called "buy-ins." We'd go into a grocery store, fill our carts with food, then go to the counter and say, "Oh gee! I changed my mind." We never took direct action against major employers unless we had been frustrated by weeks of negotiations.

We were also moving toward integration in the school district. We had one of the most successful school boycotts in the nation. We set up "Freedom Schools" for kids on the days we boycotted. Parents and other volunteers, including teachers, were at alternate sites to conduct classes.

Then Model Cities came along. We had a lot boiling in addition to the OEO Program. Mayor Brayman was a real right-wing Republican. Earlier, we had picketed against him because he ran against the open-housing measure. He had once said to me that he didn't want federal money coming into the city because "that was the nose of the federal camel,"—in fact, he brought more federal money into the city than any previous mayor. The mayor's assistant was Ed Devine, very liberal and a good friend. At his urging, Mayor Brayman decided to apply to Model Cities.

As director of the Seattle MCP, what political considerations did you have to face?

If a white guy had been appointed, I'm almost positive that the program would never have gotten underway. Mayor Brayman understood that. From a different perspective, once the program started there was a tendency, for the police department particularly, to end-run the program. The mayor didn't break any bones about it. He just told them right out, "You cooperate."

We had one political battle before we could begin the program. We couldn't distribute Model Cities Program money because we needed a legal sign-off to send to the fed from the city's attorney, a rock-ribbed Republican. According to the state constitution, public money could not be given to individuals except for the poor and needy. By his interpretation, our program plan did not meet that standard. We worked with the mayor to convince him, but he would not move. It looked like we would not get the program. Finally, the mayor turned to the Republican governor who told his attorney general, Slade Gorton, to write the legal sign-off.

As soon as we started, we began to let people know that this was not just a black program. We extended the Model Cities area to include the International District—primarily Japanese and Chinese—and Pioneer Square, which adjoins the International District. Pioneer Square was an old business district falling into disuse. The city had applied for an Urban Renewal grant: thinking tear down and build in because the district was right next to downtown. Cooler heads prevailed. With the resources of Model Cities and the Historic Preservation Act, we realized that we could preserve and renovate these old buildings, some of which were built right after the Seattle fire in 1889. The area became the Historic District. Now, it is a thriving business center and tourist attraction.

It was my responsibility to help the black communities understand that they had to share in the program. I remember being invited to several other cities to talk about what we did in Seattle. One of the cities was Chicago. When I read Chicago's program I said, "Oh no, I'm not going there." The Chicago program wanted a segregated city within a city, apartheid—black against white. They were going to have their own health department, their own education system, and their own police department. I knew that nowhere in America would that work. It would be setting the people up for a big fall. In Seattle, I argued that we had to build into the system. Model Cities wasn't going to last.

What were your expectations for Seattle?

I didn't think we would revolutionize the city or make a drastic dent in the crime problem, but we could establish some institutions and modify others. We could give the residents of the Model Neighborhood more opportunities for the future.

For example, we'd been after the police department for years: they ought to have more minorities. The department sternly resisted. We made a proposal: let civilians in the Model Neighborhood—without the leather uniform and without the holsters—intervene in domestic disputes or with kids acting up. That was the wedge. When the police realized how effective the community police could be, they began to use that group as a base for the selection of regular cops. Today, the police department is completely integrated.

Another example was a proposal for an Income Maintenance Program. It was really a "workfare" system. We used Seattle MCP money to subsidize welfare clients that we were trying to put into the labor market. The program provided money to the state to run the experiment in Seattle. I don't think the state used the money effectively. It wasn't enough money to be a real subsidy and, to me, that's a huge fault. After Model Cities, the Maintenance Program was discontinued.

Didn't you need daycare, health benefits, and transportation to succeed?

We asked the state to provide those components. The Income Maintenance Program was the only SMCP program for which the money and control went directly to the state welfare system. We didn't have day-to-day knowledge of what was going on. Our requests to "come on board" were refused. With other projects done with other agencies, we were part of a team.

How did other programs fare?

In the health area, we were ahead of the trend. The citywide neighborhood health clinics that we have now just didn't exist before. Some we started through the city and county health department and others through the private sector. With Model Cities money, the Children's Orthopedic Hospital, a private hospital, started the Odessa Brown Health Clinic in the Central Area. The Group Health Cooperative, a liberal HMO, built two community clinics in housing projects for the poor. The Black Panthers looked at what we were doing and started a clinic. All continue today.

Some groups, black primarily, would try to thwart a program if they didn't have control. For example, we set up the Minority Contractors Association—all construction in the Model Neighborhood that used Seattle MCP money, would be done by minority contractors. Here was an opportunity for companies to grow. But, with few exceptions, infighting prevented them from working together. At one point we had to hire a white contractor to build a swimming pool because there were no minority contractors who could handle that job. We started a monitoring program to make sure that the majority of employees were minorities. Later, the city continued that function for all city contracts by establishing a Human Rights Office whose staff checked to make sure that the employees hired met the contract standards. I hoped for a strong permanent minority association with clout, but it didn't quite happen.

You have stories that illustrate the mood of the time?

Before our program was endorsed, we had an areawide meeting with the regional officer for Model Cities. More than 1,500 people, making a whole lot of hubbub, were in a Baptist church. People were jumping up and expressing their views. In the middle [of the meeting], a wild community activist came walking down the isle. Everybody knew her and said, "What the hell's she up to?" A couple of guys began to edge their way toward her . . . she was capable of anything.

She came right to the stage, opened her coat and let a couple of doves lose to fly around over peoples' heads. Someone called the cops and said there was a bomb . . . and yet, everyone stayed to continue the discussion. The regional fed observing the meeting wasn't sure if he ought to certify the program; people were volatile. We said, "God bless us, buddy. If people had acted like sheep, we'd have worried. People knew they had the freedom to speak, and holler and react. All that turmoil led to a conclusion . . . that's what the program was all about."

Another story is funny now, but it wasn't then. A black group wanted to share in the Model Cities money by way of a rip-off. Someone I trusted had invited me to one of this group's meetings for a talk. I went alone. About 20 guys waved their guns at me, trying to make me split the loot with them. You know how skinny I am. I wasn't sure I'd get out of that room alive, but if I was going down, some of them were going down with me. For some reason that stopped them. They began to laugh and from then on we really talked. By standing up to them, the program gained respect. I never had a problem with them again.

Does any of the original philosophy from the Seattle MCP remain today?

Yes, particularly in the citizen participation process, [which] had begun with OEO, but in Model Cities, we organized the community to a much greater extent. Mayor Wes Uhlman, who followed Mayor Brayman, set up an Office of Neighborhoods to work with neighborhood groups. Now, it's a part of city organization. Projects aren't done without first holding hearings in the neighborhood.

Also, we gave a lot of confidence to neighborhood people, to get into politics, to apply for jobs they had never had before, jobs outside the neighborhood. People didn't admit it, but they used to be scared. Now, they're everywhere because they know they have a place in the system. We opened up the system.

Following the Seattle Model Cities Program, Walter Hundley became the second person to direct the city's first Office of Management and Budget. He was next appointed commissioner for the state parks and recreation department and continued in that position until his retirement in 1988.

Tom McColgan
Model Cities Director, Holyoke, Massachusetts

East Boston, where Tom McColgan spent his childhood, is situated on an island. Although, connected to Boston in 1933 by the Sumner Tunnel, the community was somewhat isolated. In the late 1800s, East Boston had attracted Jewish immigrants who, in turn, were followed by the Irish and the Italians.

In the 1960s, when McColgan was about 12 years old, construction for Logan Airport began. Residents rallied in protest against the taking of their land by eminent domain, making East Boston one of the first communities to engage in civil disobedience. In fact, the Maverick Street Mothers, a group of mothers with children in baby carriages, rolled their carriages in front of "tub-dump" trucks—18-wheelers used to dump fill into the harbor to increase the length of the airport runways. Already lost to the community was Wood Island, a 150-acre open space of beaches, picnic areas, and ball fields. McColgan's first exposure to public development was from the perspective of a potential victim.

McColgan's education, a Massachusetts affair, progressed westward across the state from Boston College High School with the Jesuits, to the College of the Holy Cross in Worcester, to the University of Massachusetts in Amherst. Finally, after arriving in Holyoke, he began an internship that would satisfy the requirements for a master's degree in public administration. Being in Holyoke— a depressed community, known as the "paper city," because it was heavily supported by numerous grants—was, according to McColgan, the "classic case of being in the right place at the right time." In 1973, his internship complete and his westward progress halted, McColgan began work in Mayor Bill Taupier's office as part of the Management Assistance Program, a city agency financed by HUD.

A Classic Sociological Exercise

In 1973, Holyoke was a second round Model City that was one year away from conclusion and still had a full array of ongoing programs. The director, Jerry Hayes, needed someone to think and work through an organizational model for combining all the categorical program grants that would be consolidated by the Housing and Community Development Act of 1974. At the same time, I took over as director of the Holyoke Model Cities Program (Holyoke MCP).

Mayor Taupier had a reputation for being an interesting character.

Bill Taupier was a fiscal conservative who truly believed in Urban Renewal and in a radical approach to the city's problems. Taupier's approach was to go after everything. For a city of 50,000 people, Holyoke had six active Urban Renewal areas, two Neighborhood Development Programs, and a number of water and sewer grants, and park grants. Taupier was comfortable with the fact that in Massachusetts, cities operated at the will of the state. Long before David Halberstam wrote The Best and the Brightest, Taupier was looking for the best analytical thinkers for key management positions. He ignored ethnicity, he ignored race, and he ignored gender.

My job was to take the framework provided to all cities, [under the Community Development Block Grant Program], and develop the organizational— the administrative and executive framework—for all the categorical programs to operate out of one central location. And one of the consolidated programs was the Holyoke MCP.

What was the focus of the program?

Early on, the toughest political decision in Holyoke was to decide which neighborhood would actually be the Model Cities neighborhood. The city had two neighborhoods that were in serious disarray, South Holyoke and The Flats. Because The Flats was in tougher shape, it got the nod. It was a truly diverse neighborhood where the early Hispanic population had gravitated, primarily because of the availability of a large number of dirt-cheap housing units. It was a dense neighborhood, primarily multifamily, with cold-water flats built between 1890 and 1920.

Holyoke is a classic sociological exercise. The Flats are on a plain at grade with the Connecticut River. As you go up the hill—and Holyoke goes up the side of a mountain—the higher you go, the higher the income, the better the housing, [and] the better the neighborhood. Yankees, seeing the opportunity to harness waterpower so they could run mills, created the town in 1853. In 1862, it became a city that billed itself as the first, planned industrial city in the United States. But The Flats, whether black, brown, or white, was closest to the mills and the poorest section of the town. It was ringed by the first-, second-, and third level canals, [which] originally powered all of the mills. The canals cut-off the neighborhood from the rest of the city and were the reason for building tenement buildings. The plan of attack was to try to focus, not only on the [physical] development, but also on the quality of life, which meant social services. Heretofore, [social service programs] had not been part of HUD programs.

Prior to Model Cities, did Holyoke provide any social service programs?

Welfare programs were being administered by the state . . . and there were a number of programs for the elderly. That was it. So the two cornerstones of the

Holyoke MCP were addressing the housing issues and the health, economic, and language issues. To nobody's surprise, the lion's share of Model Cities dollars went toward the softer human service programs.

Later, the Holyoke MCP Community Development Corporation, which eventually became the Old Holyoke Development Corporation—it is still in existence—created the Riverside Development Corporation, a subsidiary to undertake industrial development. The plan was "dedensification,"—move away from multifamily construction on the Urban Renewal sites. Think subdivisions; think suburban within an urban setting; however, the only sustained commitment that ever materialized was a 100-unit conventional, elderly public housing [project] that looks like new construction to this day.

Was there a strain between the social service end and the physical development end?

Actually, there wasn't. There was almost unanimity to have things like "Operation Mobility." Model Cities bought two mini-buses to go all around the neighborhood; the concept was to take residents [out of The Flats] to job training, to doctors, etc. The problem was that nobody ever rode the buses. We used to talk about getting a few local funeral homes to put a couple of stiffs in the buses for the HUD people to see when they were coming out for their monitoring visits.

How effective was citizen participation?

Citizen participation changed radically from beginning to end during the Model Cities years. Originally, the Holyoke Model Cities Policy Board had members from the French, Irish, Puerto Rican, and black communities. Interestingly, in the 1970s, a number of folks who lived in the Flats were bilingual in French and English. This diverse group had grand plans and took [their] authority seriously. Holyoke was one of those communities that vested all of the final decision making in its Model Cities Policy Board.

In what way did the policy board change?

The policy board consisted of 15 people—12 residents and three at-large from other sections of town. Early on, there were elections, but they eroded and the board became polarized. The Hispanic representatives left. When we had our final meeting of the Model Cities Policy Board six year after it started, there was not one Spanish face on that board.

Holyoke was a small city. The Flats was a poor neighborhood [with] drug/crime problems, and problems that were racially based. The fires of expectation were fueled far too high; people weren't able to achieve economic and social equality so quickly.

What did the program accomplish, and what couldn't it do?

I think we overestimated how quickly we could dedensify. The city could not keep up with boarding and securing the number of units that were abandoned. Owners just walked away. We quickly realized that we were feeding the problem because we had no intervention strategy. So we boarded and secured knowing that the buildings would be vandalized and burned. We had overestimated how quickly we could move to the physical side of development. [Today] the neighborhood is less dense; there are a number of well-kept subdivision-type developments that were done by the Old Holyoke Development Corporation. These developments have been replicated in other poor neighborhoods in the city. That piece seems to work, but it came 20 years later.

One successful physical development activity was the Model Cities Service Center, constructed smack-dab in the middle of The Flats. The center housed employment and training programs. It contained a health center, a daycare center, and an elderly drop-in center. Today, all those functions still exist in that building.

Did the way the city conducted its business change as a result of the Holyoke MCP?

I think that public involvement—citizen participation around its community development program—is much more intense than in other communities. After Model Cities, the government was so delighted with the fact that final authority was back in its hands that it bent over backwards to make sure that folks were included in [the] process.

But the process was not well attended. People realized that they were now in exclusively advisory roles. [They] said, "Why should [we] bother? All we're doing is giving advice. The city doesn't have to follow it." It was a shock to former members of the policy board who had survived and been asked to be part of the transition. Still, Model Cities did affect the way the city looked at comprehensiveness in public development . . . the influence of focusing all your resources on a limited area.

In retrospect, what would you have done differently?

In hindsight, I think we should have done more planning around the marketability of the neighborhood. What did we need to do? We had some big solutions for some small problems. We had a program [named] "Operation Mainstream." People actually monitored how somebody went through job training—

back through school and through employment counseling. A lot of people in the public services got so caught up in the numbers, in showing that they were cost effective, that they lost sight of the goal. I also think we needed to put more money into better thought-out social services and open some of the development options to the private development community. Even though The Flats was ringed by industrial plants, we never attempted to partner with neighboring industries.

In the early 1970s, the idea of "public/private partnerships" didn't exist. What, for you, captured the spirit of the program?

Most emblematic, in an idealized way, of what we were trying to do were the daycare graduations. All the faces . . . mothers, young enough to be my daughters, were there because all of them were either working or were in a training program. That program seemed to truly succeed . . . exactly the way we wanted it to be.

Tom McColgan lives in Springfield, Massachusetts, and is commissioner of economic development for the city.

Chapter 7

Programs in a Crossfire

James Kunde, age 25, is acting city manager of Dayton, Ohio; however, the mayor tells him he is too young for the position. Kunde matures in Jackson County, Missouri, where he is county manager in a climate of political reform following the "Pendergast era." In 1970, Kunde returns to Dayton to become city manager. The Dayton MCP has already started against a backdrop of riots, a greatly diminished tax base, and competition between racial and ethnic groups for remaining jobs. A city staff member suggests that neighborhood groups decide how the city's last dollars should be spent—possible because Dayton is one of the first cities to have a program-based budget. The result is the "Priority Board System," which calls for a citizen-activated organization in each neighborhood. Also, Kunde wants to apply a key lesson from the MCP: that the system must build commitment to the neighborhood or else the most able people move away leaving the neighborhood worse than before. Because the Dayton MCP is citywide under the designation "Planned Variations," the federal government makes an additional $10.5 million available to the program. To ensure quality participation, safeguards are designed into the system.

Jan Shapin is raised on a family diet of socially progressive ideas. During summers, she works in Washington, D.C., for various senators and congressmen, and, following college, she organizes for Community Action Agencies in Oregon. Returning to Washington, she works for the Redevelopment Land Agency (RLA), which is responsible for developing the District of Columbia

MCP. HUD approves funding but rejects the District MCP plan. The RLA assigns Shapin and another RLA staff member to coordinate development of a second plan, but from the outset, the district's halting movement toward self-governance effects the process. The planning committee—mayoral appointees from a list of volunteers plus loaned staff from city departments—is unwieldy, and the plan it develops is "ragged." Meanwhile, the district holds its first campaign to elect a mayor; simultaneously, the district MCP initiates a campaign to elect an official citizen committee. Ironically, the same citizens appointed to the previous ad hoc committee are elected to the new committee; however, the now official committee does not endorse the district MCP plan on the grounds that it is the work of the ad hoc committee. Instead, the plan is given to a consulting firm, which delivers a "big, smooth" version bearing little resemblance to the original plan but showing a similarity to plans developed by the firm for other cities. To illustrate the frustration of the situation, Shapin relates an anecdote about bureaucracy and the pace of progress in the district.

In 1968, New Englander Jeff Swain is a city planner in Rochester, New York. Rochester is in decline, in part, because corporations such as Kodak, Xerox, and Bauch and Lomb no longer provide a stable economic base for the city. An incident between teenagers and police at a Friday night dance sparks riots that spread throughout the city and become the forum for previously suppressed issues—people without jobs and disenfranchised minorities. Activist Saul Alinsky organizes the highly contentious FIGHT—Freedom, Independence, God, Honor and Truth—whose strategy is to pressure Eastman Kodak for jobs. Meanwhile, after considerable delay, the city decides that the membership of the citizen participation board will be half elected residents and half city appointed members. A remark by the city manager telling citizens that the Rochester Program belongs to them guarantees further conflict. Neighborhood representatives want new institutions, not institutional change. The city council sits back with a "Let-them-have-their-program" attitude. Because of internal strife within the Rochester MCP, Swain, who has not offended anyone, is appointed director. Candid in his assessment, Swain notes that the economic component, which he describes as reactive, does not work. Swain relates an anecdote about a contentious citizen meeting in which a member of FIGHT informs Swain that a man standing nearby has a gun and is there to protect him.

Cal Wilson has a football scholarship to the University of Indiana in Bloomington and is one of the reasons the university goes to the Rose Bowl in 1968. After college he marries, is drafted but opts to join the Marines and, following his discharge, moves to Tuskegee, Alabama, to wait for his wife to finish her master's degree. A series of odd jobs lead to the position of Manpower Specialist with the Tuskegee MCP. The program is in its third year and on its sixth director. Wilson becomes its seventh. The program is considered "high risk" because there is no industry and no economic base. Wilson, who wants the program to provide the infrastructure to attract big business, finds that because the city is predominantly black, businesses are reluctant to move there. The Tuskegee MCP constructs an Industrial Park that is not promoted effectively; however, the Incubator Program, a program for small businesses and affiliated with Tuskegee University, is successful. In retrospect, Wilson believes that had the Tuskegee MCP worked with the private sector, the program would have had a better understanding of economic needs and would have been more successful.

James Kunde
City Manager: Dayton, Ohio

James Kunde, born on New Year's Eve 1937, had by age 25 and again at age 28 served as acting city manager of Dayton, Ohio. However, the mayor told him that he was too young . . . to "stay in touch" and come back when he was older. In the interim, Kunde worked in Kansas City, Missouri, where he became the first county administrator for Jackson County.

In Kansas City, a group of reformers had just taken over the county government and, in the process, had cleared away all remnants of the old "Pendergast" era—so named because of Tom Pendergast, the corrupt political boss of the area's Democratic machine. Perry Cookingham, the city manager during the reform movement of several years earlier, stepped forward to bring together an informal group of experienced advisors. This action helped Kunde determine who could be trusted and who the competent professionals were. "It made survival much easier," said Kunde . . . "in any case, it was an adventurous time." In this Dickensian-like atmosphere, Kunde became the Development Director of Kansas City. He remained in that position until 1970 when the city of Dayton, Ohio, asked him to return as its city manager.

The Priority Board System

When the Dayton Model Cities Program (Dayton MCP) started, the city was already experiencing some of the worst riots in the country. One reason for the development of the riots had to do with Wright Patterson Air Force Base, one of the earliest equal opportunity employers. Although the base was located on the east side of the city, most of the African American population lived on the west side. A long, difficult commute separated black people from good jobs with few other equal opportunity employers in between.

Riots weren't the only problem. General Motors was out on a long-term strike [with] 30,000 workers out at the same time, and National Cash Register, employing 24,000 people, was going through a conversion [that] would eventually reduce its workforce to 4,800. Because the city's chief revenue source was income tax, the city was facing an extreme budget situation. We had to cut 300 positions and virtually every program.

Based on a suggestion from one of our staff, we decided to give each neighborhood the opportunity to decide how its share of our last dollars would be used. Fortunately, we had one of the nation's first program budgets . . . because what we had in mind couldn't be done with the old line-item budgets. Neighborhood discussions and decisions would center on the city's programs. We wanted to apply the lessons we had been learning from our Model Cities Program without repeating its mistakes. The key lesson being if you only give opportunity to people, the most able will capture the advantage and quickly move away, leaving the neighborhood worse than before for those left behind.

We wanted to give neighborhoods the power to spend money, but we also wanted to avoid the staffing wars that had complicated the initial program. Therefore, the city would provide staff people, but the neighborhood would have veto power over any staff assignments. [Also], because the staff was on the city's payroll—the same pay and benefits as other personnel—they could be supervised under the regular city system.

We made sure that staff assigned to the program learned to completely respect a neighborhood's decisions. We named the process the "priority board system." We used natural boundaries to redraw neighborhood lines, respectful of traditional lines but promoting integration of race and income. To make it work, we called together every citizen-activated organization in each neighborhood. We said, "If you can organize a process that is ongoing, effective, and represents the choice of the neighborhood, we'll give you staff support and a pro-rata share of the city budget to prioritize and allocate." Every area of the city agreed.

The priority board idea intrigued the federal government and the new director of the citywide Dayton MCP, Ron Gatton. Dayton became a Model Cities experiment under the designation Planned Variations with the result that additional MCP money jumped the city budget to $10.5 million. Gatton ensured that the original Model Neighborhoods were not lost in the citywide program. Also, knowing that technical assistance would be critical, he initiated a Citywide Development Corporation staffed with competent people to back-up neighborhood organizations in structuring their improvement efforts.

As the program got bigger, the staffing of these neighborhood priority boards became more of an issue. We decided to stick with regular city staff and put them on sabbatical in order to provide continuity. This assignment became very popular for young aggressive staff. Eventually, federal dollars disappeared, but the priority boards grew stronger and became the basic budget decision-making system for the city. An unwritten rule emerged: if you wanted to move up, you had to show outstanding service in the priority board system. At the department director level, we developed a three-dimensional matrix to evaluate performance. It included effective service to neighborhoods; performance in departmental responsibilities such as planning, street maintenance, or purchasing; and effective participation on a task force such as race relations, housing, or economic development.

Did the City Council feel that its power was usurped by the neighborhood priority board system?

This is an important question and the main reason why the priority board system—the most long-term, successful part of the Dayton Model City Program—wasn't swept up by other places. The budget crisis was one of two reasons we could do it in Dayton. The cuts had to be severe, but, if the neighborhoods had the ability to make their own decisions, they could also shift priorities—add things they needed and delete things they could do through their own volunteering. The cuts stopped being only a City Hall problem.

The priority board system allowed the City Council to avoid difficult decisions?

Exactly! The second reason has to do with the end of an era. During the 1950s and 1960s, the most successful cities had a home-based business group that recruited public officeholders—in Dayton it was the All-Dayton Committee. The committee had begun to reach out to minorities. The right wingers in the city formed a counter organization against bussing and other similar issues. At the same time, Dayton, like other cities, was experiencing a change in industry. For example, National Cash Register, even though it kept its corporate headquarters in Dayton, became internationally focused. General Motors also became an international corporation—their five Dayton divisions became branch plants.

These pressures virtually killed the All-Dayton Committee. That's both good and bad. More opportunities for minorities opened up; however, special interest groups replaced the core of business leaders who originally ran the city. I dealt with the older, corporate-style City Council, which didn't exercise a lot of power but responded to directives handed down by the city manager and his staff. Since then, I've talked to other cities about the priority board concept; they all say that city council members would have a problem giving up power. Why would a person want to be in that office if the major decisions affecting budgets were made by the neighborhoods?

How extensive is the legacy of the priority board system?

The priority board system couldn't be precisely copied in other cities . . . it has lasted in Dayton. Other cities, seeking stronger citizen involvement, have moved toward the model through things like special grant programs for neighborhood-based organizations. In Dayton, the system began to have problems of institutionalization—the current city manager initiated a comprehensive planning approach that has revitalized participation in each priority board area . . . it seems to be working well. The Citywide Development Corporation, another strong legacy of the Dayton MCP, has served as a model for many other cities; one example is Cleveland, Ohio.

In retrospect, were the program's activities appropriate for the situation?

We stumbled into a set of really good answers—being young and not knowing what to do can be an advantage. If we had not faced crisis after crisis, we probably would not have instituted what amounted to an informal "learning organization model." We used local and outside universities to facilitate discussions with city department heads—on issues such as task force management, or how to think through changes and crises. Initially, the Dayton MCP only provided opportunities to individuals. When those same individuals left the neighborhoods, the program lost leadership. Building neighborhood commitment was the focus of the priority board initiative and the citywide Model Cities effort that grew from it. And, although we didn't have the metaphor at the time, "social capital" was created within each neighborhood because neighborhood residents could make meaningful decisions together. That's something we didn't anticipate.

We were just beginning to learn a key lesson: that we needed to provide opportunities, not just to people, but to the neighborhoods in which people lived. We needed to provide opportunities such as building communications centers, revitalizing workplaces, putting neighborhood schools into the business life of the community, and providing good jobs where disadvantaged people can get to them.

James Kunde lives in Arlington, Texas. He recently retired as director of the Coalition to Improve Management in State and Local Government. He currently teaches in the School of Urban and Public Affairs at the University of Texas at Arlington.

Jan Shapin
Model Cities Program: District of Columbia

In 1961, Jan Shapin's father, who had been working for Walter Reuther of the United Auto Workers in Detroit, Michigan, moved to Washington, D.C. There he joined the Kennedy administration as deputy director of the Housing and Home Finance Agency (HHFA), thus giving Shapin, who was attending Reed College in Portland, Oregon, the opportunity to spend her summers in Washington working for various congressmen and senators. After receiving her bachelor's degree, Shapin remained in Oregon to organize Community Action Agencies in the state's rural counties. In 1965, she returned to Washington to work for the Appalachian Regional Commission, a quasi-federal agency that made investment decisions promoting economic development in rural areas. After a year of graduate school and the realization that she preferred organizing people for social action rather than reviewing proposals for economic development, Shapin went to work for the Redevelopment Land Agency (RLA), the Urban Renewal agency for the District of Columbia. For the first four months, she did tedious documentation. When responsibility for developing the District of Columbia Model Cities Program (District MCP) was transferred to the RLA, Shapin, who had been assigned to the new program, regarded the move as a stroke of good luck.

Miscues in the District

At the time, a three-person commission appointed by Congress governed the District of Columbia . . . this was about to change. The first step was to have an appointed mayor with mayoral powers and then, to elect a mayor. Mayor Walter Washington was the first appointee and, subsequently, the first elected mayor. The application for Model Cities had been prepared under the old commission in which one [member] was connected to the Army Corps of Engineers. Apparently the corps prepared the first plan that concentrated on developing the Anacostia River basin.

Because the city was the District of Columbia, HUD, [feeling] that it had to, approved funding but rejected the plan. Under the newly appointed mayor, the Redevelopment Land Agency was charged with redoing the plan. But the RLA was absorbed in an ambitious redevelopment project—among the first such projects to include housing rehabilitation—for the Shaw neighborhood located along U Street from Ninth to 12th Street. So responsibility for the District MCP plan was given to the Land Agency. Two RLA people, Bill Dodge and myself, were transferred to the mayor's office and given the job of developing the plan. The new deputy mayor was put in charge.

Our biggest problem was the short time schedule. We had six to eight months. There was no organization, no staff, and no director. A search for the right director was being planned but, in the meantime, we had to decide how we were going to proceed.

Two decisions were made. One was for the mayor to put out a call for civic-minded volunteers, residents from the Model Cities area, which included the Shaw [neighborhood]. From the list of volunteers, the mayor appointed an ad hoc citizens committee. Also, the mayor directed each city department to detail a senior-level staff person to the Model Cities planning effort. The departments sent people who were square pegs—creative troublemakers who challenged the status quo and whom the departments were happy to be rid of. Somehow Bill Dodge and I were to coordinate this "headless horseman" of a planning process. We had subcommittees for each category to be addressed: health, education, environment, public safety, recreation, and economic development, etc. Members were assigned from the ad hoc citizen committee and in each category the loaned staff person was put in charge. Bill Dodge and I floated around the edges; on good days we floated at the top. In this vital time, we swapped ideas by day and had meetings by night. We had one secretary and some space in a building across the street from City Hall.

Was there a power struggle between citizens and the district?

Planning began just after Martin Luther King had been killed. There had been riots and buildings burned along the commercial streets in the Shaw area. However, internal strife on the ad hoc citizens committee was not a problem. The chairman of the committee, a very gentle, well-respected black man named Watha Daniel, kept the group from becoming polarized and dysfunctional. He wanted none of the all too common radical posturing and rhetoric.

Walter Fauntroy, a local leader of the Southern Christian Leadership Conference (SCLC), was the guiding light behind the Urban Renewal project for the Shaw neighborhood. He had envisioned holistic change for the area and transferred his vision to the District MCP. The project was to transform the neighborhood, but, at the same time, we struggled with the how of accomplishing the plan's goals. The tools of Urban Renewal were physical development tools. Layered onto the challenge was the problem of social unrest. Model Cities was now the intended vehicle for addressing all these expectations—the root issues of neighborhood revitalization and changing the social dynamics of poverty.

Was there a strategy?

The categories we established remained intact through the planning process. I preached to the subcommittee that the opportunities were in the cracks. By that

I meant that the opportunities for creative programming were in the areas that blended two or more program areas. The strategy was to weave a set of program responses that bridged categorical areas.

Even though much time and labor had been expended, the first draft was ragged. Contributing to the problem were the loaned staffs' differing levels of competence to write and conceptualize. Finally, the mayor's office hired a director from Los Angeles, California, a man who, I believe, had worked in advertising for an entertainment company. For the brief six months that he stayed, he made one important decision: he hired a deputy director named Ted Greer. The director and deputy director, now in position, searched for permanent staff. The loaned staff returned to their respective agencies. I don't know why, but at that point we began to have strife. Racial issues and challenges to the hierarchy began to surface.

We realized that we needed to hire someone to clean up our sprawling plan—to edit, not just the writing, but to condense and smooth the plan so it could be submitted to HUD. The consulting firm of Marshall Kaplan, Gans and Kahn, which had just finished the Model Cities plan for Boise, Idaho, was selected to do the job. They began a blitzkrieg. The newly hired District MCP staff had no vested commitment to the laboriously drafted plan we had done. To complicate matters, the mayor was now running for election so his attention was focused elsewhere. In the meantime, we had begun a campaign to elect our *official* citizens committee with the slogan "Home Rule comes to the Model Neighborhood." The mayor was unhappy because he felt that our election preempted his election campaign.

Ironically, the same residents—the same people who had been appointed to the ad hoc citizens committee—were elected to the new committee. At its first meeting, someone said, "We're being asked to endorse a plan that we didn't participate in." Nearly everyone agreed, "Yes, this was a plan prepared by the ad hoc committee, not the elected committee!" Somehow we managed to back away from taking a vote and surrendered the plan to the consulting firm whose staff worked with the District MCP staff. In about a month they had written a plan that had almost no resemblance to the original one done with the residents but a striking resemblance to the plan for Boise, Idaho. The plan was big. It was smooth. We submitted it and received funding. Much of the programming that had been so carefully hashed out earlier was replaced by ideas solicited from other places. Some aspects of the plan had funding but no content or, as with the environment category, had insufficient funding to accomplish anything. To me, the plan represented nonthinking and nonplanning.

Did you see these problems as unique to Washington, D.C.?

Many places can make a career of not getting things done. In Washington, D.C., there is no overlay of state government or county government; it's a straight shot from the federal to the district government. I think the explanation is that people in district government model themselves after federal civil servants. There is no sense of urgency and everyone gets paid.

I remember this planner at the Redevelopment Land Agency who looked like Zero Mostel. We were at a meeting with the agency. He had big gestures and expressions and liked to sit by the window playing with the cord for the venetian blind. At one point in the discussion he exploded and said, "I don't know why anybody in the district worries about nuclear attack. If there was a hydrogen bomb on Pennsylvania Avenue and someone lit the fuse, it wouldn't go off. Nothing ever goes off in this city." He was right.

What did you learn from your experience in the district, and is there a legacy?

I learned that local government imposes its own limitations on planning. Model Cities provided an unfettered opportunity to cut across fields and to be imaginative in program approaches. But in any bureaucracy, really talented people are frequently suppressed. I liked the notion of "Send me your bureaucratic troublemakers and [we'll] form a hearty band of creative people," but it was something I never had the chance to replicate.

At the neighborhood level, all too often the community activist can be good at dismantling but not too good at mantling. A lot of energy was misplaced. The legacy of Model Cities in Washington, as in other cities, was that it fixed the expectation that different local agencies would somehow have to connect to one another and that, collectively, they would bear responsibility for making a neighborhood work.

Jan Shapin lives in Newport, Rhode Island. In 1982, she organized, then directed, the Community Development Training Institute (CDTI). Currently she is a freelance consultant specializing in public housing for Jan Shapin and Associates.

Jeff Swain
Model Cities Program Director, Rochester, New York

Jeff Swain, who communicates with the directness of a New Englander, was born in Boston, Massachusetts, in 1943. He attended elementary school on Long Island; high school in Fairfield, Connecticut; and college at Dartmouth College in Hanover, New Hampshire. After two years in the navy, Swain entered graduate school at the University of North Carolina at Chapel Hill where he studied city planning and public administration. By 1968, he was a city planner in

Photo 6: A neighborhood meeting. Man holding book, Jeff Swain.

Rochester, New York. By 1969, he had become the physical development planner for the Rochester Model Cities Program (Rochester MCP), and, following the ouster of two "lame-duck" senior Democratic staff members by the city's new Republican administration, he was appointed the program's director.

An Issue of Control

Rochester was appealing because it had a very strong economy with Kodak, Xerox, and Bauch and Lomb—all were headquartered there. The riots in 1964, [had been] a stunning wake-up call. Rochester, known in some circles as "Smug City, USA," didn't think it had any problems. In the wake of the riots, the religious community—white and black—got together and decided to bring in activist and community organizer, Saul Alinsky.

What caused the riots?

The spark, between teenagers and police, was at a Friday night dance in an area that would [eventually] become the Model Cities [Neighborhood]. It just went from there to major riots on both sides of the river—Rochester is split down the center by the Genesee River. The riots spread from the low-income area on the city's east side to the low-income area on the city's west side. There were a couple of deaths. Then all the issues came pouring out—people without jobs, disenfranchised, and so on. Saul Alinsky organized what became known as FIGHT—Freedom, Independence, God, Honor, and Truth. FIGHT became a highly contentious organization whose major strategy was to go after Eastman Kodak for jobs, even [causing] proxy fights at Kodak's annual meetings. It triggered the development of Rochester Jobs Incorporated—employment opportunities in the private sector for minorities, primarily the black community.

At the same time, there were power struggles in the Community Action Agency. The city [had] begun to experience declining population. Because of in-migration during the postwar era into the 1950s and 1960s with all the growth at Kodak and Xerox, there was a fairly significant black community as well as Puerto Rican/Hispanic community. All had strong roots in what became the Model Cities Neighborhood.

The city took an inordinately long period to determine how residents would participate. Finally the decision was made that there would be elections to determine who would represent the community [on] the Model Neighborhood Council. Half the seats would be residents directly elected from the neighborhood, and the [remaining seats] would be individuals appointed from various service organizations. Putting all that together took six months. The planning of the program didn't start until late in 1968.

At that point, I was a city planner in the city-planning department and separate from the emerging Rochester MCP administration . . . it was obvious that the Planning Bureau was not at the center of real redevelopment activity and somewhat irrelevant. The Planning Bureau—three of us, young and idealistic—lobbied the Urban Renewal leadership, who were managing the Rochester MCP and [who] realized that they had to expand the staff. Essentially we were transferred to the program. The effort to do the first-year plan took us into 1969.

Was this your first involvement in citizen participation?

Advisory committees had been associated with Urban Renewal projects. Rochester had been a significant recipient of Urban Renewal funds so there were several active projects, one of which was in the Model Cities area. [However], this was a new ball game. The city was responsible for a Model Cities Program overlaid on a highly contentious community with blacks, Hispanics, and poor whites—the Model Cities area also incorporated a largely white section [comprised of] Poles, eastern Europeans, and Italians. One vivid memory is of the city manager, Seymour Sher, addressing the Model Neighborhood Council for the first time after the elections. He said, "This is your program." That set the stage for what followed. The question of the city's role, the neighborhood's role, and who had control was always there. The statement was significant. It reflected either no power to design and implement the program or naïveté. I'm not sure which.

What priorities emerged in the development of the plan?

This sets the tone for a combination of trying to articulate priorities as well as suggest some of the lessons learned. We set up individual components—physical planning, housing, economic development, education, jobs, and health. A staff person or agency representative worked with subcommittees of the neighborhood council. Obviously, the ideal was to have a plan that was comprehensive . . . trying to address neighborhood problems. [Rather than] trust in achieving institutional change, the tone from neighborhood representatives was new institutions—an Economic Development Corporation and a Housing Management Corporation, and the incorporation of the Model Neighborhood Council so it could have its own staff . . . [making] it the institutionalized citizen participation activity. As part of the original strategy, these institutions reflected the issue of neighborhood control.

Was there a comparable economic development operation in the city?

[There was] a Kodak-sponsored Economic Development Loan Program, but it was not respected in the Model Cities Neighborhood or trusted . . . therefore it reinforced the we-need-our-own-corporation [conviction]. The overriding thing was to incorporate and fund the Neighborhood Council because that was the manifestation of the control issue. Jumping ahead to the legacy of achievements, we did take full advantage of the presence of Urban Renewal projects and Urban Renewal funds and a few other HUD programs such as Neighborhood Facilities and Open Space to leverage some new community facilities that are still serving the community today.

I must say the "new institution" strategy did not work. In November 1969, city elections resulted in a change in the city's mayor, City Council leadership and city manager at about the same time the first year Rochester MCP plan was approved. There was naïveté tending toward neglect. "Let them have their program and we'll just go along for the ride," was the way some in City Hall would have characterized it. In trying to set up new institutions the level of expertise required to do it, and do it well, was not there. For example, the Economic Development Corporation tended to be reactive, funding retail businesses in the neighborhood, [which] operated for a year or two before going out of business

Another aspect of economic development was that a few banks—[with representation on the] board for the Economic Development Corporation—used the corporation to layer additional loan assistance for some of their small business loans that may have been in trouble. Some businesses succeeded and some didn't, but those banking institutions were not looking at any overall plan. [They] were looking at a means to provide support for their portfolios more than looking at the needs of the neighborhood.

What about social services?

We did have successes—daycare programs in the neighborhood settlement houses provided an additional daycare infrastructure that survives today through United Way funding. But very few if any social services programs survived the transfer into Community Development. In the Rochester MCP, it was more who brought in their proposals and who could muster a majority vote on the Neighborhood Council. A major health center for the Model Cities area was funded independently of Model Cities. That took the pressure off for direct Model Cities funding for health programs.

Clearly, the overriding dynamic was that the Rochester MCP brought blacks, whites, and Hispanics together in a planning and deliberation process for the first time. The senior members of the city administration had no idea how to cope with it.

How did you, a white Anglo-Saxon protestant, get picked to head a program that represented so diverse a population?

Probably the Neighborhood Council was so fraught with its own internal conflict that it couldn't make a case for anyone in particular. [I had] been on the staff for two years, had gotten along with most of the members of the council and was a known commodity. In fact, the president of FIGHT would often ask how it was I was able to function in that environment? At the time my answer was, "Well, that's my job."

I decided to take residence in the Model Neighborhood. One of my vivid memories is of a meeting in a room [filled] to standing room only with members of the Neighborhood Council, a group in the back of the room [displaying] a Puerto Rican flag, and a mix of blacks and Hispanics all around the meeting table. I was seated at the head of the table next to the chairman who was Hispanic, a "lieutenant" from FIGHT—under somewhat of a peace treaty with the Hispanics at the time. [He] whispered in my ear, "You see this guy over here behind your left shoulder?"

I said, "Yeah."

He said, "Don't worry about anything. He's got a gun and he's here to protect you."

That was the tumult we were dealing with. In that environment, it was very difficult to craft and manage an effective program. [With] the transition from

Model Cities to Community Development, one of the significant lessons—at least as it was applied in Rochester—was that under Community Development there would not be any separate board or committee to provide advice, and there never has been one! The Model Neighborhood Council had become a contentious, vested interest group. [For Community Development], the strategy was to provide open access to all qualified neighborhoods. It was up to the neighborhoods themselves to organize and make their case for Community Development allocations. The program was to be city run with ample avenues and opportunities for citizen participation in public meetings.

Over the years, the minority community has matured politically. And the notion of institutional change rather than new institutions has played itself through in Rochester. In the most significant departure from the original Model Cities Program philosophy, the city grabbed hold and established its own philosophy of citizen participation, not citizen control. Institutional change is the approach in the government sector and the private not-for-profit sector. Community Development money has been used very effectively in working with the United Way and other social service priorities of the community.

Interestingly in 1974, after all the tumult, the elimination of the Model Neighborhood Council was not a big issue. People in the Model Neighborhood had learned that this council did not serve the program well, and others felt disenfranchised. So, it was not a heavy political lift to eliminate the neighborhood council. Probably there was a collective sigh of relief . . . now neighborhoods could do their own thing.

Were there projects that you wanted to do but weren't able to do?

Some days it was just getting up in the morning, going to work and making it home. Obviously some programs failed. We tried to start a building trades program—a housing rehab program with residents doing housing rehab. Little did I realize how tough the construction trades were and how tough . . . to learn rehab skills.

The Economic Development Corporation was funded at a pretty hefty price. When I look back . . . [I ask] why didn't we have a stronger board, a more reputable board of directors, or a better staff?

One of the biggest issues was a [HUD] requirement for a resident employment program. In a city with a population of 250,000 of which 15,000 to 20,000 people lived in the Model Neighborhood area, it was difficult to find capable people to run programs. We all acknowledged that Model Cities had some inherently conflicting objectives. Nobody, from HUD on down, understood how you had to broker different objectives [to] have a successful program to bring the residents into jobs and into positions of decision making.

Today is a much different. What city government learned and what its leadership continues to do is to conduct a far more responsive approach to governance and citizen involvement.

Jeff Swain lives in Albany, New York. He is the deputy comptroller for the New York State Division of Retirement.

Cal Wilson
Model Cities Director: Tuskegee, Alabama

Self-described as "quiet . . . unruly . . . but not a bad kid," Cal Wilson was the one everyone asked to beat up the school bully. If the bully couldn't be found, he just might beat up the person doing the asking. If the "don't-mess-with-me" posture made Wilson a good prospect for high school football, Wilson wasn't interested. Not until his older and smaller, football-playing brother came home one day "beat up and bloody" did Wilson join segregated Ross High School's football team. Thinking, "I'll take care of them," he began to play in his sophomore year . . . so impressively that in 1963, the University of Indiana at Bloomington offered him a football scholarship. Within Indiana's nearly all-white student body Wilson belonged to a core of black athletes who, despite racism on campus, carried the school to the Rose Bowl in 1968.

After receiving a bachelor's degree in marketing, Wilson took a brief look at a career in professional football; however, because of his recent marriage to Kathleen, his high school sweetheart, he moved to Gary, Indiana, to become a system loan officer for Commercial Credit. By August of the same year, he found himself standing in line with 2,000 other Army draftees in a depot in Chicago, Illinois. When he noticed that the line for the marines was negligible—marines were the ones getting killed in Vietnam—Wilson, who had run out of patience, joined the marines.

In 1971, his tour of duty completed, Wilson moved to Tuskegee, Alabama, to be with his wife while she pursued a master's degree at Tuskegee University. When the position of Manpower Specialist opened up with the Tuskegee Model Cities Program (Tuskegee MCP), Wilson, who had been taking odd jobs to put food on the table, seized the opportunity.

Goal to Go

Tuskegee was [like] any other one-horse town in the South . . . nobody planned. We didn't know anything about economic and commercial development. Those that [did] were at Tuskegee University, a whole different arena. Model Cities brought an array of young talent to the forefront. With committees that geared up the neighborhood, the city had gone through a long planning process—"What are we and where do we want to go?"

When you became director of the Tuskegee MCP in 1971, the program was in its third year and had had six directors.

[According to the Regional Interagency Coordinating Committee (RICC)], Tuskegee was a high-risk program. We had a whole lot of findings. We wanted an economic base . . . synonymous [with] a tax base . . . because Tuskegee had an institutional base. Industries were popping up all around in other cities; [however], Tuskegee . . . didn't have the infrastructure to bring business in. What I wanted was to give Tuskegee the wherewithal to [attract] business. As part of our long-range plan we did an infrastructure study. We put in an airport, an industrial park and improved water, sewer, and treatment.

Many businesses could have located in Tuskegee—a more preferred site based on their needs—but they decided not to come. In fact, an article written in the Atlanta Constitution at the time said that several businesses in the surrounding area when asked why they didn't pick Tuskegee responded that the political arena was black—there were just too many black people. So you can't overlook the fact that perception had a bearing on how the city developed. Also, the industrial park was never promoted properly. People didn't really understand how. You need an industrial bulletin board; you need somebody hired to do the job.

Model Cities was the incubator for many small businesses, especially black businesses that exist today. The Incubator Program was affiliated with Tuskegee University. The people who sat on the board were staff members from Model Cities as well as instructors from the university. If there was a new business, expanded business, or existing business, we would sit with them and go through whatever problems they had at the time. For example, we [sat] with the owner of one of the most successful, local restaurants on a daily basis to teach him how to keep books.

What about social services?

The only social service that existed before the Model Cities Program was traditional welfare. Model Cities created a city recreation program; a daycare program for mothers working in town in institutions because we have very little industry; a juvenile probation program; and a senior citizen program. They are all still functioning and are now funded with traditional city money . . . tax money. Model Cities created the social structure of Tuskegee.

Did the infrastructure need attention?

It was undersized. We had water, but we didn't have six-inch mains; we had two-inch mains. We had fire protection, but only in certain areas. We had sewage treatment, but it was overloaded. Some main streets were paved adequately, but most side streets were not. Model Cities just revamped these things completely. Tuskegee has a pretty good system now—a sewage treatment plant that can serve the city for the next 10 to 20 years. All was accomplished through Model Cities and Community Development.

In retrospect, what would you have done differently?

The needs would be the same, but I would have tried to work through a more political process and leaned on private-sector involvement. Many of the boards were jam-packed with politically oriented people. I would have had more people from the private sector on those boards because they knew and understood better the real needs of Tuskegee. More business was the key . . . I didn't see it that way at the time. Now, more than daycare, I'd rather mothers get a job first.

In the last few years, everyone who knows something about planning and development has gone. The emphasis should have been on staff expertise. It should have been on planning and it should have been on developing internal capabilities.

What is the emphasis now?

Surviving from one day to the next. Having enough money to keep the power on in Tuskegee—not overlooking the fact that it takes planning to do that.

Cal Wilson lives in Tuskegee, Alabama. He retired as Tuskegee City Planner in 1997, but continues to work as a consultant.

Chapter 8

Great Aspirations

Fifteen-year-old Mark Tigan and his family leave Rochelle, Illinois, for a new start in California. He becomes a student at San Jose State University where he tries nuclear physics among other majors before settling down to environmental studies. He becomes a student leader in a campus celebration of Earth Day that attracts national attention with the symbolic burial of a car. Following college, he trains in HUD's Urban Technical Services and eventually travels to Winooski, Vermont, to direct the Winooski MCP and the Winooski Community Development Corporation. The city, which is experiencing defunding stress as the Winooski MCP comes to an end, has problems with unemployment and housing and wants to build an industrial park. One strategy for attracting businesses to the city is to promote the city in a trade show in Montreal, Canada. Another is to begin a rumor that Canadian investors are inquiring about the availability of real estate in Winooski. As the city looks for ideas to save money, someone makes a tongue-in-cheek suggestion to place a dome over the entire city to save on heating costs. Within days the idea attracts national attention and is propelled forward by the media. Although the dome is never built, the city hosts the first National Dome Symposium—attended by nearly 5000 people—and with the help of three Urban Development Action Grants the downtown area is revitalized. In retrospect, Tigan observes that gains such as those achieved as a result of the Winooski MCP are lost if administrators do not remain vigilant.

John Sasso works as a housing inspector in Providence, Rhode Island, until the neighboring city of Pawtucket hires him to do a housing study in preparation for an Urban Renewal project. Soon, he is appointed deputy director of the new Pawtucket Redevelopment Agency and next, director of the Pawtucket MCP. Projects include educational programs for children and adults, a lunch program for school children that frees mothers to work during the day, and an environmental program in which workers hired from the neighborhood collect trash so efficiently that residents feel pressured to produce more trash to keep up with demand. A major priority is deflecting the destructive energy of young gang members. Coincidentally, bridges have recently supplanted the need for several state-operated Narragansett Bay ferries, one of which the Pawtucket MCP wants to convert to a youth center. The governor, who has supported the project, expects some good publicity. Despite navigational difficulties the ferry arrives in inland Pawtucket. Unfortunately, the effectiveness of the new youth center is dependent upon follow-through support from the city.

Young architect Maurice Dawson hitchhikes from Chicago, Illinois, to Berkeley, California, to join community activists. In Berkeley, he donates design services to various nonprofit groups, then moves to Oakland, California, to work for that city's redevelopment agency. Kaiser Industries, looking to improve its affirmative action numbers, recruits Dawson. He relates a humorous anecdote about receiving, what he believes to be, a notice of dismissal but is, in fact, a bonus for work well done. Meanwhile, Oakland is accepted into the MCP. Dawson believes that with his planning, design, and community experience and with activist friends such as Huey Newton, he is ideally suited for Model Cities. Within two months of being hired, he is director. Because the Oakland MCP has not responded to policy notices from HUD, the program is without resources. Also, activists want majority control on the citizen board. Police brutality and community justice—two major issues—are made more contentious by the police department's practice of hiring recruits from states such as Alabama and Mississippi. The Oakland MCP initiates a Police Intern Project that pays tuition costs and a small stipend to participants from the Model Neighborhood. Those who complete their studies may apply for a position in the police department; however, many of those who apply mysteriously wash out on the Rorschach test. By challenging the standards for interpreting responses, Dawson proves that the problem is a matter of "cultural racism." On another front, Dawson, who wants planning for the Oakland MCP to be governed by a rational process, designs a method for evaluating every project according to its social, physical and economic impact.

Mark Tigan
Model Cities Program and Community Development
Corporation Director, Winooski, Vermont

By age 12, Mark Tigan had picked asparagus with migrant fieldworkers and worked on construction sites with his father during summers. His father, tired of the construction business, wanted more time with his five children; his mother, who wanted to try her hand at running a yarn shop, wanted less. So, at age 15, he and his family left their hometown of Rochelle, Illinois, for a new start in San Jose, California. Said Tigan, the trip was "like the Beverly Hillbillies." The family loaded a second-hand grain truck with household belongings, covered everything with a tarp, and went west.

After three years, "the yarn shop tanked," and his father returned to construction work. Tigan, who had entered San Jose State University in the mid-1960s, tried nuclear physics, law enforcement, and forestry until, with support from a fellowship, he came to rest in environmental studies, a major that would eventually lead him to Winooski, Vermont.

"Dome over Winooski"

San Jose's observance of Earth Day was about to begin. For credit in Humanities 160, I became codirector and governmental liaison for Survival Faire. (The instructor for the course, John Sperling, went on to found the University of Phoenix and would later write about the fair in his autobiographical, *Rebel with a Cause*.) The fair was a major environmental awareness event that culminated with the symbolic act of burying a brand new car on campus.

The process required that I placate opposing factions as well as run the gauntlet of necessary arrangements with local bureaucrats. The Black Panthers threatened disruption on campus if we didn't donate the value of the car to the unwed mothers of Oakland. We made the donation. Caesar Chavez thought we were ignoring the Farm Worker's movement, so we put grapes and a Farm Workers' sign in the car's trunk when we buried it. We needed permission from then Governor Ronald Reagan to bury the car and help from the Santa Clara County Public Works Department to dig the hole. We also needed a parade permit to have horses pull the car through downtown San Jose. Marching with us were farm workers and supporters of the antiwar movement.

The car was symbolic . . . and very press worthy. It represented a major danger to the environment and, in a sense, the auto was fueling the Vietnam War because of U.S. corporate oil holdings in South Vietnam. The media, including *Ramparts Magazine* and Walter Cronkite, covered the fair extensively.

At the same time, I was searching for grants and loans in order to finish my college education. I was becoming a "money finder," someone who looks for grants and loans where no one else looks. A year later, I began to write environmental impact statements for the County of Santa Clara. Jim King, who taught a graduate-level course I was taking, worked just across the alley for the city of San Jose. He became my mentor and hired me to work in a program named Planned Variations, a citywide expansion of the Model Cities concept.

In the early 1970s, after training with a new HUD program in community development named Urban Technical Services (UTS), I went to St. Bernard, Ohio. Within 10 months, the entire City Council and the mayor who had hired me were voted out of office. I had to sue for my last two months wages. Then someone said, "Vermont. Go to Vermont."

Winooski, a small city bordering Burlington, Vermont, was searching for a Model Cities Program director. The new director would be responsible not only for the Winooski Model Cities Program (Winooski MCP) but also for the recently formed Winooski Community Development Corporation. Ever since working with Jim King in San Jose, I had dreamed about running a Model Cities Program.

What was the plan for Winooski?

The city had three goals that I adopted as my goals. The first was to redevelop a pig farm into an industrial park and cut unemployment in the city. The second was to stem "disinvestment" and blighting and the high crime rate in the downtown commercial district. The third was to rehabilitate, winterize, and insulate housing. As a relatively poor mill town, many of the citizens of Winooski lived in substandard housing and paid high utility bills.

One strategy for accomplishing these goals was consensus building. Winooski had a poor self-image and, like many older cities, the community felt that nothing could be done. After several years of high federal assistance levels under Model Cities, the city was experiencing a "defunding" stress. Winooski needed political visioning and capacity building as it ushered in the Community Development Block Grant Program.

Development for the industrial park was slow to get going. With over 15 landowners involved, the land had to be assembled without eminent domain. It was a nightmare. During the process, we had applied for and been awarded funding for public improvements such as roads and water. Once the land was effectively available, we could write down the price, provide quality utilities and, because of high unemployment, guarantee workers. Attracting industrial investors was relatively easy. In fact we ran a promotional campaign—cocktails, complements of HUD—at a trade show in Montreal. People were convinced that if Rene Levesque, whose campaign platform hinted at nationalizing some industries, was elected premier of Quebec businesses were going to flee. As a result of the trade show we had so many visitors that we sold out the industrial park in just over a year. Over the next few years, the unemployment rate was cut in half.

We were often told that corporations advised their employees against locating in Winooski because the schools were bad and the crime rate was high. The statistics proved otherwise so the staff pulled some guerrilla tactics. We started spreading a rumor in key places like country clubs and real estate offices that investors out of Canada wanted to know about all the available real estate for sale in Winooski. The rumor spread rapidly and, as hoped, local real estate developers bought vacant buildings and waited for the high rollers from Canada to take it off their hands, . . . which of course never happened. Ironically, the developers, knowing they were stuck, began to clean up these properties in order to lease them.

Two successful Urban Development Action Grants turned the downtown around. One grant funded market-rate housing along the riverfront. The goal was to integrate affluent families into a predominately low- and moderate-income neighborhood, in effect diluting the economic and social problems of the area. The other grant effectively completed an earlier HUD Urban Renewal project by funding the renovation of an old mill into a commercial area with boutiques and office space. Nearby, another mill was converted to elderly housing using Section 8 vouchers. Next, the artist community came alive; Winooski was becoming an in spot.

How did Winooski get into the national spotlight?

At one point Winooski was in heavy competition for a Neighborhood Strategy Area (NSA) grant. After we had campaigned heavily in Washington, HUD finally said, "We're prepared to give Winooski the grant, but we want to make a ceremony of the award." That meant we had to get some media coverage.

Only coincidentally, I received a phone call that same day from a producer of the "MacNeil/Lehrer News Report." He'd heard how well the city had done with all the federal grant money it had received. "MacNeil/Lehrer" wanted to do a feature story on Winooski and contrast it with a small city in Ohio that had refused federal money. He asked if we had any award coming up that could be filmed. We did. So I called HUD and said, "We just arranged for some media coverage. How's "MacNeil/Lehrer?" I had just fallen into a mud puddle and come up with a salmon. We got the grant. We received very favorable coverage from "MacNeil/Lehrer" and some personnel notice from HUD, which never hurts.

Explain the "dome" story?

The dome story is a story that just won't die. Here's how the media got involved. The city of Burlington was attempting to dam up the river that flowed in front of the mills we had just rehabbed. The riverbed would be left dry. We brought in a famous energy lawyer from Hartford, Connecticut; we were going to fight the city of Burlington and Green Mountain Power's efforts to dam the Winooski River. One night, after the lawyer had made a presentation to the City Council, the staff wanted to go out for a few glasses of wine. Soon, the lawyer began lamenting about society today: all that demand for more power and no government emphasis on conserving power. We launched into a brain storming session on how government could balance the conservation of energy with the creation of energy. Leaving out the name of the originator to protect the guilty, an interesting concept emerged: the idea of putting a dome over the entire city was put forth. The city was only one square mile; a dome would keep the heat in. We laughed and went on to another topic. At work the next morning, I actually gave the dome idea two more thoughts and then forgot about it.

About a week later I was in Washington, D.C., meeting with Joe Clarke, the HUD intergovernmental liaison dealing with Congress. Joe Clarke was from Baltimore. I mentioned our staff discussion on the idea for a dome over Winooski. He immediately sat up and said, "Bob Embry, the assistant secretary of HUD, used to be the director of Community Development for the city of Baltimore and still lives there. He always said that the only way to preserve 'down towns' was to put them on a level playing field with suburban malls." Embry had wanted to dome Baltimore's downtown. Clarke suggested that HUD might even fund a dome for Winooski.

The [Winooski MCP] staff had a good laugh. But somehow the idea began to snowball. Joe Clarke called to say he had arranged a meeting with Bob Embry. I was to carpool from Baltimore to Washington with him and Embry in two weeks. While riding along, I nonchalantly mentioned the dome over Winooski idea. He loved it . . . and furthermore, he would find some discretionary funds for an analysis of the dome idea. Now I had to worry about how to present the dome idea to the City Council. The city would actually have to submit an application to HUD.

HUD wanted the dome study, but to get the City Council to buy in, I thought we would have to bootleg other more practical projects into the application. The staff prepared a complicated lengthy grant request, which included the dome study, a low-head hydro analysis, a solarization project, and a citywide program for winterizing and insulating houses. I was prepared for a lot of ridicule from the City Council. But, in so many words, the council said, "We don't care about the solarization/winterization/low-head hydro. We love the dome idea." The vote to approve was the only unanimous vote we ever got from the City Council. By the next morning it was front-page news in the *Burlington Free Press,* and by afternoon, it was on the wire services. Our parking lot was full of satellite dishes and news service vans. Dome over Winooski was born.

Bags of letters from around the world and from classrooms doing research on the dome idea came into the post office. It was about the same time that the revolution in Iran made oil supplies problematic. Winooski was getting coverage from TV talk shows, the *New York Times, Time Magazine,* and the *Saudi-Arabian Press.* As best we could figure it out, Saudi Arabia was fearful that U.S. cities, facing an oil crisis and higher oil prices, were going to dome themselves so as not to need home heating oil.

The dome idea was nothing but a concept over a glass of wine. The next thing we knew, the media was building the dome.

They would ask, "How tall is it going to be?"

We'd say, "Well, it can't be over 250 feet tall because airplanes would have to fly over to land at Burlington International. The next morning we would read, 'Dome to be 250 Feet High.'"

The press would ask, "Will it be see through?"

We'd say, 'We think we'll have to open it up." The next day we'd read, "Dome To Have Hydraulic Opening."

They'd ask, "What about cars?'

We'd say, "Well, cars not wanting to stop in the city would go through a tunnel. For intracity traffic, we'd have electric cars." The next day we'd read, 'Dome comes hand-in-hand with new technology for electric cars."

The residents of Winooski were so proud. Relatives called from all over the country to say they had seen the city on TV. We found out that little dome communities were all over Antarctica and the Arctic; dome research facilities were in northern Canada. Businesses were actually in place to do nothing but design and build domes. There was even one in southern Vermont named the Bluebird Dome Company.

Dominic Casavant, a visionary and the previous mayor of Winooski, thought we needed a symposium. We organized the First International Dome Symposium. We called for papers and organized a trade show so that dome companies could put up displays. For a keynote speaker, we invited Mr. Dome himself, Buckminster Fuller. About 5,000 people attended the two-day event. Media coverage continued. In fact, Pierre Salinger covered the event for the British Broadcasting Service.

We submitted the grant application to HUD at about the same time President Jimmy Carter had failed in his attempt to rescue the hostages in Iran. He was up for re-election and wasn't too happy with the dome story, so he called HUD and said, "What are you doing? This thing is going to be on Sen. Proxmire's Golden Goose Awards. The administration is attracting all kinds of negative press because of this crazy town in Vermont." As a result, Bob Embry called to say that HUD couldn't fund the dome study, but it could fund other aspects of the grant application. And as a man of his word, he could offer an alternative: a low-profile "force account" analysis of the dome. Three people out of the Tennessee Valley Authority (TVA) were detailed to Winooski to study the feasibility of a dome.

Photo 7: John A. Sasso at a ground breaking ceremony with then Governor Jimmy Carter (Photo credit: Omi Walden)

Funny enough, the dome was physically possible if the right-of-way could be acquired to anchor it. And it was economically possible if the building material could last 100 years and only if the price of home-heating fuel hit a rate of $1.20 per gallon. To the economists, it was feasible. However, the TVA social scientist concluded that people did not want to live in a dome. The *New York Times* printed an editorial against building domes over picturesque cities in Vermont. The editorial suggested that supporters of the dome idea hadn't thought it through; why would people live in Vermont unless it was to see church steeples and have the ambience?

Here's the point! Old-time Vermonters generally don't like cold Vermont. They'd love to live in Florida, but they can't afford to. It was the recent yuppie immigrants from New York and New Jersey who wanted uncovered steeples and six inches of snow on the ground.

What did you learn from your experience in Winooski?

Winooski went through a major revitalization—a renaissance. As professionals move on, it's important to leave the appropriate training and ethic in place so that improvements are maintained and urban managers avoid complacency. If the administrators and elected officials who inherit the advances aren't vigilant, the advances are lost. If businesses aren't supported and people with low and moderate incomes aren't given a sense of worth and the means and incentive to maintain what they have, social and physical progress become history. When the tax base is increased but not spent on maintaining the investment that increased the tax base, the area reverts back to what it was 15 or 20 years ago. The city has to start all over. The lesson, one that should be built into the revitalization strategy, is the need for a "stay recovered ethic"—a maintenance ethic for community development.

Mark Tigan went on to become director of community and economic development for Santa Monica, California. Currently, Tigan lives in Newport, Rhode Island. He teaches at Clark University in Worcester, Massachusetts, owns Tigan Consulting and Development, Inc., and lectures widely on community development issues.

John Sasso
Model Cities Program Director: Pawtucket, Rhode Island

I grew up in Providence, Rhode Island, an Italian-American who went to Catholic schools and, for no reason I can recall, to the University of Miami in Florida to major in engineering. Soon, I was back in Rhode Island, looking for work. In 1962, I was hired as a housing inspector for the city of Providence. My duties required that I learn the American Public Health Association (APHA) standards for housing inspection. These standards were used to determine areas qualified for Urban Renewal. Pawtucket, Rhode Island, a mill town bordering Providence to the north, needed someone to begin a housing study in preparation for Urban Renewal. Within a year, Pawtucket had formed a redevelopment agency. I was appointed deputy director of the new agency and spent the next three years overseeing demolitions, property management, and site development until joining the Pawtucket Model Cities Program (Pawtucket MCP) in 1968.

A Ferry for Pawtucket

Pawtucket had two Model Neighborhoods, Woodlawn and Pleasant View. Because both neighborhoods had similar needs, the Pawtucket Model Cities Plan called for citizen participants representing each neighborhood to work together on two principal committees, social services and physical development. Each committee and their subcommittees went through a process to identify needs and then worked with the appropriate line agency.

One proposal called for improved trash collection. However, to avoid a conflict with the unionized sanitation workers, we decided, with the blessing of the Public Works Department, to run an environmental program in conjunction with the Health Department. We bought two huge German-made trucks that could do everything. We hired workers from within the Model Neighborhoods. If the city had three workers on a truck, we had five; two to go ahead and make sure the trash was out, ready for collection, and three to load the trash into the truck. After a few weeks, there was a noticeable silence from the chairperson of the Physical Development Committee. Finally, after some prodding, she said, 'Too much pressure. We can't make enough garbage. You crack an egg and there's someone to take the shell. We can't stand it.'

Another proposal called for a school lunch program—because children had always gone home for lunch, many mothers could not hold a job. A third proposal called for a neighborhood adult education program, which would be administered by Roger Williams College. Classes were designed for an older immigrant population, people who had never had the opportunity to pursue higher education. One man, a Portuguese-American who spoke little English, attended a communications class and was so proud of his educational accomplishment that he placed his certificate of course completion in the most respectful place in his home . . . on the mantle, next to a picture of the Madonna.

Not everything worked the way we wanted it to. Pawtucket had a problem with tough teen-age gangs vandalizing the neighborhoods. Coincidentally, a new bridge had just replaced the ferry service between Jamestown and Newport, Rhode Island. With the future of the state-owned ferries undetermined, we thought, "Wouldn't a ferry make a fine youth center for teenagers in Pawtucket?" With help from Rhode Island Governor Frank Licht, we got the ferry. The Architecture Department of the Rhode Island School of Design agreed to make its redesign a faculty project. But first we had to take the ferry to Pawtucket via the Pawtucket River, which hadn't been navigated in years.

The process was very complicated. Because one bridge, under which the ferry had to pass, had only four inches clearance, the river had to be navigated at dead-low tide. And only one person—an 87-year-old captain—had the license to guide the ferry up river. However, the governor wanted publicity. All was arranged. The governor, with fanfare and press coverage, would send the ferry on its way.

Some things don't work out. On the day of departure when the tide was right, the governor was nowhere in sight. The captain said, "We're leaving now."

"You can't leave," I said. "The governor is arriving! The press is arriving!"

He replied, "Time and tide wait for no man."

The ferry began its journey. The governor and his entourage arrived to an empty dock. No publicity photos were taken, and everyone was angry with me. Meanwhile up river and at high tide, the 210-foot-long vessel arrived in Pawtucket to a flag-flying escort of Navy tugboats. Later in the day, the ferry, which had been roped tightly as if to secure its presence and purpose for all time, was seen to lean into the dock as the tide receded. Despite the mishaps, the ferry did become a youth center. However, the follow through—transportation for teenagers to and from—was never completely supported and was eventually stopped altogether. The ferry, once again in search of a new harbor and purpose, was piloted to Portland, Maine where it became a restaurant.

When reflecting on this story, I think of my idealism. My staff and I were trained, disciplined, and reasonably expected programs to work. To a degree, my idealism had to do with a faith in government—resources, common ground, and good people in the right places working cooperatively—a faith that still holds today.

Maurice Dawson
Model Cities Program Executive Director: Oakland, California

Soon after earning a bachelor's degree in architecture from the University of Illinois in Chicago, Maurice Dawson began hitchhiking to Berkeley, California, where he planned to work as a community activist. In Berkeley, to his surprise, Dawson found himself donating design services to various nonprofit groups. Neighborhood playgrounds—"Tot Lots"—were very much in demand.

Dawson, who had been raised on Chicago's South Side, was the oldest of six boys born to parents who ran a real estate business. Dawson loved school . . . loved to draw and paint. Art gave him control . . . gave him freedom. He had always wanted to be an architect and thought of himself as "a Frank Lloyd Wright in color."

After a year in Berkeley, Dawson began to work for a design firm in Richmond, California. However by 1964, he had moved again, this time to Oakland, California, where he could engage in community activism while working for the Oakland Redevelopment Agency. Most of his energy was spent exploring methods for producing lower-cost housing. During this time, a project named Operation Breakthrough attracted the interest of Kaiser Industries. However, Kaiser who wanted a contract for the project, was excluded from consideration because of its low affirmative action numbers. Seeking to correct its numbers, Kaiser contacted the University of California at Berkeley and obtained the names of two prospective recruits, one of whom, Dawson, always curious before a new experience, said yes to Kaiser's offer.

At the time, Kaiser Industries was comprised of 60 wholly owned corporations. Coincidentally, in the corporation for which Dawson worked, one lone salesman had been trying, unsuccessfully, for three years to get a contract in Denver, Colorado. Architectural renderings were deemed the solution; however, could the new man do the job? Dawson produced the drawings in 30 days. They were sent to Denver, and, to management's delight, Kaiser soon had a lucrative contract to put its products into 600 homes in Denver.

Shortly thereafter, Dawson's superior said, "Maurice, I want to talk to you. Be in the executive suite at 11 am today." When Dawson entered the room, several corporate administrators were present, including the president and vice president. They handed him an envelope containing $1,000 in cash:

I dropped the envelope, walked to my office and began drawing feverishly.

The manager followed me and asked, "Maurice, what's going on with you?"

I replied, "I didn't want this job in the first place. Now you're going to fire me. I read that this is how it's done in the private sector. First, you jack the guy up and then you pull the rug out from under him."

After some calming words from the manager, Dawson realized that he had just been given a cash bonus. Further, to show the corporation's appreciation, the manager asked if there was anything Dawson particularly wanted to do? Dawson replied, "I don't know a damn thing about corporations. I'd like to interview the president of each corporation. All sixty!"

The Rorschach Challenge

In 1968, Oakland was touted as receiving more per capita [in] federal grants than any other jurisdiction in the nation. At the same time, the Community Action Agency seemed to be in the newspaper three or four times a year for fraud, waste, and mismanagement. When the Demonstration [Cities] Act of 1966 was announced, I had this notion that someone with a sense of rational planning and a commitment to the community could make it work. I had a background in planning, community activism, and campaigning, and was known as a black architect. So I applied [for the position of director of the Oakland Model Cities Program (Oakland MCP)]. I came in second and decided to remain with Kaiser. But two weeks later I was [offered] the position of deputy director. I said, "Hell yes. I'd love to be part of the action."

Two things stick in my mind about the first four weeks. One was that a two-foot pile of letters and regulations had come in—[policy notifications from HUD for various issues]—to which no one had responded. The other was the acrimony of community politics in the West Oakland neighborhood and in the Community Action Agency.

How did that affect citizen participation?

Two well-known activists had come into the Oakland MCP from the Community Action Agency. They had gone to Saul Alinsky training in Chicago and wanted people involved, not just in electoral politics but in program planning and decision making. Oakland's Planning Department was writing most of the development plans, so community participation was not a concept. The activists wanted residents in the majority position on the policy committee so they could pound the tables on land-use issues, job training, housing, and the like. Citizen activists [had been in the habit of] storming the City Council when a recommendation came forward that they didn't like. As a result, the city of Oakland took no action in response to HUD regulations. And the activists had no resources, nor the responsibility to respond to HUD's requirements. Everything was at a standstill.

At the regional meeting of Model Cities Program Directors, a liaison officer from HUD who had been assigned to Oakland said to me, "Washington thinks the situation in Oakland is horrible. With 51 percent of the policy committee being residents, they just don't believe Oakland will ever submit its application on time."

Meanwhile, after two months, the first director of the Oakland MCP left to take a job with the Department of Labor in Washington, D.C. I became his successor. With my background in architecture, and because I knew many community activists, I was considered a good "fit." In fact, Huey Newton and I used to debate Black nationalism and the role of the Nation of Islam. He and other activists had [organized] the Black Power Party for Self-Defense and had started a community newspaper. And because of the police brutality heaped on young black men in the West Oakland community, Huey had carved out a niche [within] the party to influence 18 to 25 year olds.

[Even though] Huey had dyslexia; he was motivated to read about the law, citations, and the penal code. He bought a police band radio and by monitoring police activity in West Oakland, a carload of party members could be on the spot almost immediately to observe and cite the rights of the individual being apprehended. That tactic prevented a lot of folks from getting beat up and from going to jail.

Concurrent with the escalating unrest was HUD training in strategic plan development—program planning and base budgeting. I loved the training. After it was finished, the Oakland MCP sent subcommittee members out into the neighborhood to cover various topics. Police and community justice were ongoing issues.

By 1973, the program had initiated a Police Intern Project. Huey, out of jail only two months before, called me wanting to know about the "pig" project. I went to see him—bodyguards all around—at his eighth floor apartment overlooking Lake Merritt and the courthouse he had just come from. We knew that police brutality was not limited to West Oakland. White flight had started to take place and [black] families, those who could afford to, were moving into East Oakland. Police brutality was following along. The police chief had initiated a policy of advertising for police recruits—and the attitudes that came with them—from Alabama, Mississippi, and Georgia. We needed a Trojan horse strategy.

The intern project financed the cost of tuition and books to Oakland Community College and also provided a monthly stipend for young men from the Model Cities area. With an associate's degree and Police Academy training, they could apply to the police department. I told Huey that even if no one joins the department, I didn't care; because we will have young men with an associate degree and a different scope on what their lives can be. However, if they can go inside the belly of the beast, their presence and knowledge of the law can transform the department from within—like the legendary Trojan horse.

During the implementation phase, we financed a trainer and a [police] lieutenant who was assigned to the trainer and who would be the eyes and ears of the police chief. After about nine months, we looked at evaluations and reports. Something was wrong. The police department had actually processed about 112 applicants, but only eight were from the intern project. I called the trainer and said, "What's with these damn numbers?"

He said, 'Maurice, 'The Rorschach test . . . that's where they're washing out."

I said, "This is cultural racism. It's fundamentally biased."

I called the lieutenant whose salary we paid and said, "I want a meeting with the shrinks who do the testing."

They were a married couple who lived in Berkeley Hills. We set up a meeting—the lieutenant, the deputy, the trainer, and the chief. We were all there. I said to the shrinks, "We've got a problem and I want you to help us resolve it. I want to know what kind of conclusions you're drawing from the applicant responses to the Rorschach Test."

And indeed, the answers that the applicants were giving were counter to the general culture. Yet their interpretations were from a sane and rational perspective, [which] this person with a Ph.D. had never heard before. I was able to convince him and his wife that they were drawing different cultural conclusions than what was meant by the African-American applicants living in the Model Cities neighborhood. As a result, all 25 police intern slots got filled. The Model Cities applicants went into training with two other regular-recruit classes. At the graduation exercise, the valedictorian for all three classes came out of the Police Intern Project. And that made everybody believers. One became the first African-American motorcycle cop, one joined the FBI, and another became an accountant with Paine-Webber.

What were other aspects of your experience in Oakland?

I was enamored with the concept of rational, systematic, comprehensive planning. Each planning area—social, economic, physical, and housing—was analyzed "three-dimensionally." If a project addressed a social issue, we would consciously look for the economic implications and opportunities as well as the possible spin-off from physical development. Each program had to look at the secondary and tertiary benefits that could be factored in to a revised design of the primary project. That idea—three-dimensional planning—and majority citizen participation were the hallmarks of the Oakland MCP. In fact, in 1972, the National League of Cities and the U.S. Conference of Mayors asked for our perspective on how that concept enhanced capacity and if, as a new style of management based on the Model Cities Program, it could be applied to cities across the country.

Were citizen participation meetings confrontational?

We had the community-elected West Oakland Planning Committee with its 51 percent citizen majority; we had the committee's separate staff to keep an eye on the program staff; and we had the program staff. All were housed in the same building. The building had a huge conference room that I had painted powder blue. A symbol! "Keep your eyes to the skies. Keep your eyes on the prize." But another reason was to cool passions, which tended to flare up in our discussions of various aspects of the Oakland Model Cities Program. One bizarre incident occurred after the Black Panthers won five of the 15 seats on the committee. A gang named the Snipes decided to stage a coup. They came, seven strong, to a meeting in the powder-blue room. With nine-millimeter guns pointed, they attempted to oust the five Black Panther committee members from their seats. I motioned to someone to call the police on a special hotline and with that the confrontation ended peacefully. All guns went into a paper bag, which was hastily removed from the building and turned over to the police. The meeting continued.

In the end, because of the Oakland MCP, many social services such as legal aide and social security remain in the community today. One important legacy of the program is the presence of a comprehensive, community service building with a new branch library. When the program began, West Oakland needed a community center and the existing library was nothing but a storefront with a pot-bellied stove and used paperback books. The Community Action Agency actually had initiated the project idea and had applied for a Neighborhood Facility Grant; however, the changeover to the Model Cities Program was in progress. The agency didn't have the capacity to produce the final application or the drawings. When I approached the city architect, he said, "You know, that idea has been around for a long time." He had plans dating back 10 years. After seeing the preliminary drawings, I became even more determined. I shut myself in my office for two weekends and produced the architectural concept drawings. We submitted the plan, got the grant, and added Oakland MCP funding to make it a $1.2 million development. The construction bid came in under budget. The extra money was used to improve covering and finish materials. The final product was gorgeous and it's there—18th Street and Adeline Avenue in West Oakland.

In 1975, Maurice Dawson became an urban program manager for the state of California. He next worked in community development for San Mateo County where he led the county's Housing Authority. After 22 years, he retired and now lives in San Leandro, California.

Chapter 9

Enlightened Good Intentions

Omi Walden's effort to secure a position for her husband, who is stationed in Vietnam, with the MCP in Alma, Georgia, unexpectedly results in her own employment. Because she knows the community and knows farming, she is valuable for public relations. The program embarks on several projects uniquely adapted to conditions in the area. One is the complete revamping of the entire school curriculum—possible because the town has just three schools, all having been integrated without problem. Another introduces the cultivation of blueberries as a new cash crop for local farmers. Collaboration with a retired University of Georgia researcher—who, for 40 years, has been developing a blueberry species suitable to the area--and an effective promotional campaign aimed at local farmers, produces an economic success that is duplicated in other southern states. Walden credits the program's success to professional team effort and planning out a project "completely."

Hank Dishroom, age 15, moves from Louisiana to California and attends his first integrated school where, to his amazement, every student in class has a microscope. In college, he discovers political science, and, later, while working for Alameda County as Business Manager for the County Health Department, he is intrigued by a collaborative effort between the department and a Community Action Program to secure jobs for low-income people. Soon, he becomes director of the MCP in Richmond, California, where the city's population, once 120,000 during WWII, is now 70,000 and beginning to climb, however, housing, built for the war industry, has been torn down. Also, waterfront shipyards have been abandoned and the buildings that remain don't have utilities for the 1960s. Dishroom believes that the city, because it is among the first to involve citizens in the MCP application process, benefits because the citizen board has experience and can tolerate outsiders—city appointees—on the board. With the emphasis on housing, the Richmond MCP sets up a nonprofit housing corporation and Renters Assistance Program; however, landlords abuse the Renters Program and it is dropped. Another project addresses the city's reoccurring problem with flooding by constructing a citywide storm drain system. Dishroom reflects that unrealistic expectations caused residents to demand better housing than the program could deliver and better jobs than they had skills to perform. To counter the latter problem, the Richmond MCP does not place people above their qualifications but provides on-the-job training for advancement.

Design engineer Richard Pline comes to New Bedford, Massachusetts, as a city planner and makes a career change when he is hired by the Community Action Agency to direct a CEO-funded Small Business Development Center. Other antipoverty programs in the city are under media fire. Also, the failure of Urban Renewal to build replacement housing has contributed to a severe distrust of federal programs. Nevertheless, New Bedford applies to HUD and is accepted into the MCP. Because the Small Business Center has not drawn criticism, Pline is appointed director of the New Bedford MCP. His goal is to build capacity in city government. As a sign that the MCP has gained the trust of residents, Pline notes that, unlike previous Urban Renewal projects, the project-site sign identifying a New Bedford MCP mini-renewal effort is not vandalized. Pline believes that a successful component in the New Bedford MCP is its public education initiatives—solving the problem of racial imbalance in schools, establishing a curriculum and training center, and starting a breakfast and lunch program. He learns that staying out of the limelight is the best way to get things done.

Omi G. Walden
Director of Public Relations, Model Cities Program: Alma, Georgia

Omi G. Walden was born in rural Georgia on December 25, 1945. She was a farmer's daughter in a family that was among the first to try vegetable and truck farming in the Southeast. Her parents, who enjoyed searching for innovative solutions to problems, instilled that same enthusiasm in their daughter.

In 1969, when Walden returned home to Alma to help care for her terminally ill mother, she had a degree in journalism with a major in public relations from the University of Georgia. Her husband Ralph, who was an army engineer, was on duty in Vietnam. Neither had plans beyond his return home. However, when an article in the local paper said that the Alma Model Cities Program (Alma MCP) was looking for a project engineer, Walden set up an interview with Jim Williams, the program's executive director. She went, with her husband's resume in hand, determined to secure a position for him upon his return from Vietnam.

Williams had his own agenda. He needed a public relations person—someone to work in citizen participation and to bridge difficult relationships, especially with the school system. When asked by Williams, "What do you do . . . it would be great to find someone who knows the town . . . who do you know?" Walden answered, "My brother is principal of the elementary school and his wife is director of the Vocational-Tech Department at the high school." Williams was so happy with the answer that, according to Walden, "he almost passed out."

Walden joined the Alma MCP staff the next day. The first-year plan had already been submitted and some projects were underway. Upon his return from Vietnam, Ralph became Construction Projects Engineer for the program.

Forty Years of Blueberries

Bacon County, one of the smallest counties in Georgia, had a reputation for being progressive. Alma was unique; the schools had been integrated without any problem whatsoever. The size of the county allowed for simplicity—there was one town with three schools: an elementary school, a junior high school, and a high school. The population, which was predominantly white, included a black minority. The leadership, which had a history of involvement in state and local government, was strong. The mayor, Henry Bishop, was the youngest mayor in the history of Georgia. Everybody knew everybody and understood the importance of working together.

At the time it was selected for the Model Cities Program, [the] county was on the verge of bankruptcy. Interstate 75 had by-passed Alma, negatively impacting the economy. The financial and professional resources of the Alma MCP supported the community's effort to reverse the erosion of its tax base and the out-migration of its people.

I've heard it said that more money came into the county from Model Cities than was in the county budget.

Absolutely! When all the planning and coordination got to be too much, we would jokingly debate whether to park the funds in the bank and give everybody—about 3,000 to 4,000 people in the entire county—an interest dividend, or just divide the $7 million equally. The beautiful thing was that you could use Model Cities funding for the local funding match-requirement for other federal grant programs. For the first three years of the program, an average of about $6.7 million came into the county per year. Our comprehensive plan provided a balance between education, health, open-space planning, industrial development, social services, infrastructure, and even agricultural planning and development.

What kinds of projects did the Alma MCP develop?

Our Blueberry Program was the most famous. Jim Williams called me in one day and said, "You know all the farmers; you grew up on a farm. The farmers aren't satisfied with what we're doing. They think we should be doing more in the agricultural area directly. Corn and tobacco are diminishing as primary crops and they would like a replacement crop."

I laughed and said, 'The last time that happened, the boll weevil did it for us. Finding a substitute crop is highly unlikely, but we'll certainly investigate the possibilities."

Al Dowdy, who had come to Alma from Michigan to manage a cattle farm, suggested that we inquire about blueberries. He said, 'In Michigan, blueberries are a major cash crop, and they grow wild in this area." That got my attention. I had wonderful memories of picking wild blueberries as a child.

The University of Georgia directed us to a retired gentleman, Dr. Tom Brightwell, who still did some work at one of the university's extension services in Tifton, Georgia—about 80 miles from Alma. For over 40 years, he had been with the University of Georgia researching the development of a species of blueberries for growth in southern Georgia and northern Florida. No one had shown any commercial interest in his work. When we told him what we wanted, it was as if the "long-lost daughter" had come home.

Dr. Brightwell did everything to assist us. He gave us cuttings and helped us set up the rooting beds. We got an Economic Development Agency (EDA) grant to set up a berry processing and marketing co-op. In the meantime, we were rooting hundreds of thousands of blueberries and sending Model Cities staff, and community volunteers to Tifton to take plant cuttings.

With help from the Rural Development Center in Tifton, the local extension services, and the University of Georgia, we formed the Georgia Blueberry Association. To pitch our trade association, we went to the most successful farmers and said, "We've identified a new cash crop. The nursery operation is well underway and we need your leadership. We'll publicize your leadership if you will plant five acres of blueberries in a very visible spot and promote blueberries as the greatest thing since sliced bread." We trumped around town and got 25 farmers to sign up . . . and gave them enough cuttings for five acres each. Within 10 years, Georgia became the third largest blueberry producing state in the nation. Now, blueberries are a major cash crop from Texas to North Carolina.

In education, every book and every piece of lab equipment was taken out of all three schools, and the curriculum was completely revamped. The elementary school implemented a computer-assisted learning curriculum [that had been] developed by Westinghouse Learning Corporation. Children were free to move from classroom to classroom in individualized learning programs, without teacher supervision. This was revolutionary. To help alleviate teacher resistance, all teachers were required to obtain a master's degree and participate in continuing education programs.

Our most endearing initiative was the Early Childhood Development Learning Program, with all the 3, 4, and 5 year olds in the county voluntarily participating. The program attracted a lot of attention. Governor Jimmy Carter was particularly interested and very supportive. U.S. Sen. Hubert Humphrey [of Minnesota] brought the Agricultural Subcommittee on Rural Development to look at Alma-Bacon County as a model for developing the U.S. Rural Development Act. And even though Lester Maddox, [former governor of Georgia], branded the program as communist and threatened to come down and run picket lines, our early childhood program became the model for the state kindergarten program initiative.

Why was education a major component of the Alma MCP?

Because of the area's simplicity . . . it was natural. Before we had three centralized schools, we'd had neighborhood schools, which were focal points for community life and leadership. The idea that education contributes to a better quality of life was ingrained in community leaders. We formed citizen participation task forces around these neighborhood boundaries. Each neighborhood task force had representatives on subject-based or planning area task forces whose representatives, along with certain City Council officials, comprised the Model City Commission—in effect, a board of directors for the Alma MCP. It was a grass-roots initiative and ensured education as a top priority.

Describe the program's leadership.

The executive director, Jim Williams, the senior planner, and the program manager all came through the HUD Intern Program. We were new to the community. People listened. The dynamics were incredible. Ideas came from the people, but having the professional team to follow through on the details necessary to plan, fund, and carry out projects of significant scale was essential. Having the community, business, and elected leadership support the professional team was an absolute necessity.

I believe in team management . . . and in comprehensive planning. No matter how small the project, you sit down and plan it out completely . . . and that may have come, in large part, from my experience as a member of the team. It also showed me not to be afraid of bold vision, that all things are doable.

Following the Alma MCP, Omi G. Walden worked in state government, first for Governor Jimmy Carter and then for Governor George Busbee. During Carter's presidency, she was appointed assistant secretary for Conservation and Solar Energy for the U.S. Department of Energy. Currently, she lives in Hilton Head, South Carolina.

Hank Dishroom
Model Cities Program Director: Richmond, California

During World War II, Hank Dishroom's mother and stepfather moved to California to work in the war industry. Dishroom remained in Monroe, Louisiana, until 1945 when, at age 15, he traveled to California to join his parents. For Dishroom, California was a New World. In Monroe, he had attended a segregated Monroe Color High School where graduation followed completion of grade eleven and one microscope had to do for an entire class. In Oakland, California, every student had a microscope. In Monroe, there was one Chinese family and a few Jamaicans who, according to Dishroom, were the only "foreigners" in town. In Oakland, the school population was about three percent black and about 10 percent Chinese and Japanese.

When World War II ended his mother and stepfather used their savings to open a laundry and dry-cleaning business. Dishroom learned the cleaning business, then worked in the post office as a letter carrier until he was drafted for the Korean War. He attended infantry school in Fort Benning, Georgia, was commissioned a second lieutenant and subsequently assigned to Fort Ord, California, where he taught infantry tactics until his discharge in 1954. He soon married and a few years later realized that he had had enough of the post office. Said Dishroom, "I quit and went to college."

Dishroom found his calling in junior college and soon transferred to the University of California at Berkeley, where he studied political science. After Berkeley, he began working for Alameda County as a personnel analyst and then as the business manager for the county health department. At the time, the health department, in collaboration with a Community Action Agency named New Careers, provided entry-level jobs for low-income people. That collaboration stirred Dishroom's interest and influenced his decision to apply for the position of director when, coincidentally, the city of Richmond in neighboring Contra Costa County was searching for someone to run its Model Cities Program.

A Pragmatist in Public Service

During World War II, Richmond's population had doubled from 60,000 to about 120,000 people. By 1968, at the start of the Richmond Model Cities Program (Richmond MCP), the population—about 15 percent Mexican-American, 33 percent black, and the rest white—had gone as low as 70,000 but was building up again. The hills surrounding the city were covered with oil tanks belonging to Chevron and Union 76. Housing built for war industry workers had been torn down, and the waterfront area, shipyards during World War II, was abandoned. The few remaining buildings, built in the 1940s, didn't have the utilities needed for the 1960s.

Richmond was a liberal city and had elected a black mayor in 1962. [Also], two members of the nine-seat City Council were black. Prior to Model Cities, the Planning Department had established neighborhood jurisdictions and set up neighborhood councils. Three of those districts comprised the Richmond MCP target area. I hired the planner who had [earlier] worked with the Planning Department to set up neighborhood councils and had then worked with the councils to develop the city's Model Cities application—making Richmond one of the few cities to have citizen participation in the application process.

For the planning process, I hired a neighborhood council member and activist. That connection gave me quick contact with key neighborhood people who could serve on the permanent Model Neighborhoods Citizens Board. An election was the final selection process for nine board members—seven more members were city appointees representing significant city organizations such as the Chamber of Commerce, the Industrial Council, and the Central Labor Council. I had an advantage because the citizen members had some experience. They weren't opposed to having outsiders—city appointees—on the board. Although I did spend time educating the citizens on how to deliberate with appointees who knew how to get what they wanted and who all had contacts on the City Council. Interestingly, some of the more important people around town were happy to accept appointments to the Citizens Board.

Our heavy emphasis was on public works and housing. One program was the Housing Neighborhood Improvement Center. The program provided owners with a small grant or loan to repair their houses. That program is still going on. Now, the Community Development Block Grant Program awards the grants and banks make the loans.

We set up a nonprofit Housing Development Corporation that continues today and is housed in an office building built with the assistance of the Economic Development Agency (EDA). However, we had to drop the Renters Assistance Program, which paid the first and last month's rent and the deposit for people who couldn't afford the initial outlay, [because] landlords shopped around until they found someone who was eligible for the grant. [Then] they made deals . . . which stopped other people from getting housing.

[Other] programs helped residents take advantage of existing systems. For example, the city had a program under state law wherein if more than half the neighborhood voted to put in sidewalks, curbs and gutters, the city would do the work and charge the individual homeowner on his tax bill. Even though the home ownership level was very high in the target area, few residents had the money to elect the program. With Model Cities funding, low-income homeowners were free to elect a program that benefited the entire neighborhood. That was a big deal, because Richmond was a city that flooded—water runs from the surrounding hills through Richmond's lowlands and into the bay. With the cooperation of HUD, the Richmond MCP put a storm drain system throughout the city. Richmond hasn't flooded since.

In retrospect, would you have done anything differently?

I would want to have more realistic expectations. People expected housing for low-income families to match more affluent housing. Consequently, neighborhood residents resisted housing that would have been standard in a middle-class neighborhood. Residents expected Model Cities housing to be ideal, not average.

More troubling, were the employment expectations. In our Concentrated Employment Program, we found that many people didn't understand the requirements for job advancement. They wanted jobs in which advancement was available and automatic, but they didn't understand that advancement was tied to the quality of work a person did. Orientation for enrollees in the program addressed the competitive nature of the "world of work." Other job-related issues were taken care of—medical, dental, and legal problems that could lead to illness or removal from a job-site on an outstanding warrant, but the conditions for advancement weren't driven home.

Few minority directors were able to make the transition from Model Cities to the citywide Community Development Block Grant Program. Why were you successful?

One of the decisions I made as director turned out to be very fortunate. I could hire any way I wanted as long the advisory board was satisfied. We didn't hire people above what they were qualified to do. If we hired someone to be a planner, we trained that person under a professional planner. We encouraged trainees to go to college—many went on to get master's degrees. When Model Cities made the transition to the Community Development Block Grant Program, many of those employees made the conversion to civil servants.

Model Cities had added programs to the city's responsibilities; city management had become unwieldy. A consulting group did a management study that advised hiring another assistant city manager. I applied for the job and was hired in 1974. As assistant manager, I was put in charge of community development, the employment program, the Redevelopment Authority and Port Authority. We were able to keep Model Cities staff, [and], by negotiating the civil service conversions with the unions, we could get regular city employees. City departments absorbed parts of community development—the housing program is part of Public Works. The Chief Housing Inspector for the city once ran the Inspection Program in the Richmond MCP. Community development just became part of the city and was accepted.

In 1979, Hank Dishroom became San Francisco Regional Manager for HUD. He retired in 1995 and lives in Richmond, California.

Richard A. Pline
Model Cities Program Director: New Bedford, Massachusetts

In 1964, Richard A. Pline was a design engineer who had a bachelor's degree in physics from Case Institute of Technology in Cleveland, Ohio. He had recently made the third move in a 10-year career, which took him to New Bedford, Massachusetts. In New Bedford, the city planner had the ability, in Pline's words, to "wave a magic wand over people" and transform their careers. Knowing that the city was about to become involved in several antipoverty programs, the city planner suggested that the community-minded Pline interview for a position.

Pline was interested, but he was also wary because of the negative press that surrounded New Bedford's Job Corps Program. Pline decided to interview with the Community Action Agency but was told that he didn't have the right degree and dismissed. However, a year later, the agency set up a Small Business Development Center, which would be funded by the U.S. Office of Economic Opportunity, and asked Pline to be the director.

Even though the small business center operated as a separate corporation, Pline knew that both Job Corps and the Community Action Agency had had a significant impact on attitudes in the community. The agency, the object of critical editorials in the local newspaper, was experiencing political problems. Further, a Concentrated Employment and Training Act Program (CETA) was complicating community relations, and Urban Renewal, which had been involved in "clearance" since the early 1960s, had, so far, constructed no replacement housing. In New Bedford, federal programs were viewed with distrust if not outright hostility. Nonetheless, New Bedford was in the application process for the Model Cities Program.

The Facilitator

The city had applied in the first round and been rejected. We failed because HUD said that the [New Bedford] Redevelopment Authority—[the agency which submitted the application]—could not run the New Bedford Model Cities Program (New Bedford MCP). The program had to be run by the mayor. Another objection was that there had been next to no citizen participation in the preparation of the grant application.

Then, on the way to the second round, the city, using the Community Action Agency, elected a New Bedford MCP planning council of 12 people. That election and the efforts of Senator [Edward] Kennedy of Massachusetts got us funded in 1968. In fact, New Bedford was one of eight cities funded between [the first and second rounds].

In the meantime, the Small Business Development Center had kept pretty much to itself. I had a good staff and there was almost no controversy about what we did. The city's new city planner said to me, "I'm going to recommend you to the mayor for the position of Model Cities Program Director. Are you interested?" I liked the idea.

What did you want the New Bedford MCP to accomplish?

The main thing was to build capacity in city government—to do things that weren't categorical. That is: to avoid the turf-based Urban Renewal approach and avoid so much concentration on community organization . . . which I never thought would get anywhere unless it was highly focused and we provided some means [for] implementing objectives. There weren't enough resources in city government to let Mayor Edward Harrington do what he needed to do. There was hardly enough money to pave the streets.

What were the dynamics of citizen participation?

The 12-member [New Bedford MCP] planning council was, by and large, an agreeable bunch. They had to approve everything . . . even my hiring. They were ordinary citizens except that about a third of them had been very active in the Community Action Agency or in neighborhood centers. I was worried . . . because that overlap might bring the same problems, such as negative press, that the Community Action Agency had experienced. However, the Model Cities staff and the mayor worked hard to have the planning council develop its own identity.

Interestingly, one morning in the spring of 1970, a group calling itself the Model Cities Ten took over my office. They didn't want to talk to me; they wanted to talk to the new mayor, who didn't know the program. They were not threatening or disruptive. To get to the mayor, they were making an end-run around the elected planning council. [However], the council said that the protesters should have taken their grievances to them first . . . and that weakened the Model Cities Ten approach.

What did the New Bedford MCP accomplish?

The program laid the path for the development of capacity in the executive branch. [For example], under Model Cities, the city did a mini-renewal project. We bought three acres of a highly deteriorated part of the neighborhood—a former strip commercial district along South Water Street. We paid fair market value for the properties and we paid for the relocation of residents . . . and we demolished everything. From the minute the clearance started, until the new housing was constructed, the project sign on the site was the only sign in the city without graffiti and without rock marks—people weren't discouraged: they regarded the project as something that would happen. We turned the land over to the housing authority, which developed 58 units of public housing in two years. The housing was well maintained and a source of pride to the Puerto Rican community, which it principally served.

Probably the most successful New Bedford MCP component focused on the public schools—at the time, there was a lot of ferment in favor of open classrooms and individualized instruction. We brought in teacher aides and a breakfast and lunch program—which later grew to be citywide—and we established a curriculum development and training center.

The school department had a serious racial imbalance problem in four of the seven schools in the neighborhood. The way out was to build a new, bigger school that would draw from a larger area of the Model Neighborhood. We paid the local share of a Neighborhood Development Program grant, which cleared the site. Our educational initiatives influenced the new Alfred J. Gomes Elementary School, which became the model for three other schools the city built soon after.

What survived of the New Bedford MCP after the transition to the Community Development Block Grant Program in 1974?

The program's major contribution was how to identify and build capacity in city departments. Through the Information and Evaluation Program, developed [to provide guidance to individual] Model Cities, we involved the Planning Department and designated a new department [named] Management, Development and Evaluation. As a result, we had a very effective team—city planner, management and development, public works and water.

What lesson was most valuable in your experience with the New Bedford MCP?

That to be a facilitator—not a manipulator—was absolutely wonderful.

Like conducting an orchestra!

Finding a way to convince people, getting them to own an idea, and not being in the limelight myself. I think that was the message the National Model Cities Directors Association (NMCDA) delivered, and what HUD set out to do: to get the chief executive—the mayor—to make things happen. In the early days of the program, I had difficulty with some members of the City Council. We learned to present proposals to them as the mayor's package. Anyone who had anything to say had to see the mayor. This resulted in a more productive environment for the Community Development Agency and preserved the integrity of the annual plan, [which was] developed with citizens.

In 1974, Richard A. Pline became the mayor's assistant in charge of New Bedford Community Development. In 1986, he resigned to enter law school, and in 1989, at age 58, he passed the bar.

Part Three

Lessons Learned

"You've got to go to the people who have the money and make them creative . . . or throw them out. It's the old Rubik's Cube. You've got to turn the
sucker a dozen ways until it fits."

Carlyle Cox

Innovations that grew out of the Model Cities Program arose from a collaborative effort among citizen groups, Model Cities Program staff, and city
officials to identify needs and to plan strategies so as to arrive at a cohesive plan
for solving a community's problems. However, the price of innovation was often condemnation by critics because of the unintended consequences of experimentation. Nonetheless, the principle established in Model Cities, of bringing
federal, state, and local resources together as an effective tool for solving complex social, physical, and economic problems in cities and counties continued on
and inspired the Community Development Block Grant Program (CDBG).

Part Three follows the path of transition. Many of those interviewed began
careers in Model Cities. Having tested the tenets behind the program and learned
in the process, they continued on in Community Development. Their recounted
experience begins with political obstacles that required deft negotiations with
congressional leaders in order to establish the Community Development Block
Grant Program and extends to practitioners who creatively utilized the resources
of Community Development to make significant improvements in the communi-

111

ties they served. Several express their concern for the bureaucratization that increasingly characterizes the 30-year-old CDBG Program.

Chapter 10

The Baby in the Model Cities Bath

Floyd Hyde, who is HUD assistant secretary for Community Development when discussion of the CDBG begins, is committed to building on the experience of the MCP. As a result of reorganization, six HUD categorical programs are placed under Community Development but each program has its own intent, making administration impossible. Hyde suggests putting the six programs into a single block grant that will cover the activities of all. When the Office of Management and Budget agrees but raises the question of "automaticity"—meaning a politics-free application process—Hyde tries to work out a formula for the fair distribution of funding to cities. One of the problems to be solved is the need to guarantee steady funding to cities for the duration of a multi-year plan. Other problems include deciding how to distribute funds—to states, cities, or both, and whether to include small cities and/or counties—and how to deal fairly with cities whose funding will decrease as a result of the formula. Yet another problem is the rivalry between cities and states for control. Nixon is so taken with the concept of block grants that he proposes six block grants for domestic programs in his 1972 State of the Union address. In 1974, only the CDBG proposal passes Congress.

Because eight, extensive housing bills have gone to the House between 1961 and 1970, George Gross, counsel to the House Subcommittee on Housing and Community Development, suggests to the chairman, Rep. William Barrett of Pennsylvania, that it's time to do some oversight. The committee sets up panels and invites papers but imposes two rules: no public hearings and no presentations by public interest groups. With John Zuccotti, who prepares contributions for publication, Gross identifies three requirements essential to a federally funded community development program—funding every year, flexibility to use funding to meet broad goals, and enough money to avoid constant lobbying. These requirements underscore the House bill, which, if passed, will create the CDBG Program. The Senate has its own version emphasizing objectives. To resolve differences between House and Senate, Rep. Thomas Ashley of Ohio, a member of the House Subcommittee on Housing and Community Development, is willing to negotiate anything as long as the program's basic priorities remain intact.

Dave Garrison, USCM and NLC lobbyist, recalls that the redevelopment lobby supports the Senate version in which funding goes to independent authorities within a city. In the House version, funding is determined by formula and goes to the city. The formula prevails; however, its use will cause a huge drop in funding to some cities necessitating a "hold harmless" clause to correct discrepancies.

The use of a formula appeals to the Nixon administration's New Federalism. Warren Butler, HUD deputy assistant secretary for Model Cities, relates a humorous anecdote about an unsuccessful effort to rename the MCP. Instead, Planned Variations becomes the designation for an experiment in approximately 15 cities in which the MCP is expanded citywide. The experiment, a prelude to the CDBG, preserves the MCP focus on low-income activity and broad development in areas such as social services and transportation.

Butler, Gross, and Garrison discuss the difficult process of getting proposed legislation to Congress. The funding formula for the proposed CDBG Program must satisfy cities and political interests but not raise the ante too high. Also, there is pressure to act quickly before amendments to Urban Renewal preempt the thrust of community development legislation. And there is fear on the Hill that a formula will eliminate congressional control and rob members of credit for community development projects undertaken in their districts.

A journalist for the Housing and Development Reporter, Barry Zigas covers issues surrounding the Housing and Community Development Act of 1974. Dissatisfied with reporting and wanting involvement in policy, Zigas begins working for the USCM and next, the National Low Income Housing Coalition (NLIHC). He encounters and is impressed by professionals, who inspired by earlier experiences in, and commitment to, the MCP, act as advocates for the community. However, Zigas perceives that the connection "between people in community development and federally assisted housing programs" is weak. While the MCP initiated the process of institutional change in city government, the decentralization of funding during the Nixon administration furthered the process. Yet, people new to the field of community development find it increasingly institutionalized and bureaucratic. In a comparison of the MCP to Tammany Hall, Zigas posits that both used money to co-opt community leadership into a system of controlled "patronage and revenue sharing." He notes that prior to the MCP, Congress had feared the corrupting influence of city government; thus funding through independent housing authorities was the federal government's attempt to bypass city government.

In the mid-1970s, the CDBG relocates responsibility for housing—not with developers as mayors used to do—but in places more responsive to community needs. Zigas recalls the tension that existed between neighborhood groups, who distrusted the good faith of cities, and cities, which did not want additional targeting requirements affecting the use of CDBG funds. By 1985, the Reagan administration has eliminated nearly every direct-production subsidy program in the housing arsenal. An alternative idea, tax credits, begins to take form; however, the NLIHC is ideologically opposed to any tax advantage for use by private developers. Nevertheless, the NLIHC decides to push the concept forward and set the terms of the debate. After some hardball negotiations with private developers, the tax credit subsidy, with set-asides for non-profits, passes Congress.

Originally from "gritty old" Manchester, New Hampshire, George Karras first works for the Bureau of Labor Statistics and, next, for the International Labor Union. In 1961, he begins working for the Area Redevelopment Administration (ARA), which, because it deals with "distressed areas and chronic unemployment in older northern cities," anticipates the MCP. Also, the ARA is predecessor to the Economic Development Administration (EDA), created in 1965 and having programs in many MCP cities. Although EDA and MCP programs are coordinated at the local level, their relationship at the national level is limited because, according to Karras--now Commerce Department deputy assistant secretary of Operations--the MCP had a short life span and the program could not be defined. After Reagan, who wants to "kill" the EDA, takes office, Karras quits Commerce "for his own sanity," and works with Rep. James Oberstar of Minn., to put together a report demonstrating the value of the EDA. When the Reagan administration threatens the CDBG, Karras conducts a survey on the CDBG, which identifies "the real constituency" as sub grantees who receive funds at the local level and "who run programs benefiting millions of people." To build support for the CDBG, Karras shows members of Congress how the CDBG benefits their districts and how they, in turn, may enjoy the political benefits of identifying with the program.

Floyd Hyde
HUD Assistant Secretary for Community Development

By 1970, the transition to the Community Development Block Grant Program (CDBG) was underway. However, the success of the program, in its formative stage and with a politically uncertain future, depended on placing the right person in charge. After some deliberation, George Romney, secretary of HUD, gave the job to Floyd Hyde.

The Block Grant Solution

I was committed to building on what we had learned from the Model Cities Program. When Governor Romney reorganized HUD, he put six individual [categorical] grant programs all under HUD jurisdiction—into one place—into community development. The problem, which became apparent, was that each program had its own intent and purpose and might not mesh with another. It was a mish-mash for cities.

I told the president's cabinet a story that illustrated the problem. I had spent three years getting a neighborhood facilities grant through HUD for a black community that had wanted it for 10 years. I finally got it approved. Then HUD said, "We don't have any more neighborhood facilities money, but you can apply for an open space grant" . . . the whole application process would have to be repeated! The cabinet members just shook their heads.

To begin, I brought in a consultant to work with my staff: Warren Butler, John MacLean, John Tuite, and Don Patch. We put charts all around the conference room trying to figure out how to make one thing mesh with another. I wanted to create a block grant with these six disparate programs and work out an annual arrangement with a city—an annual appropriation that was sensitive to a three-year plan. If we could bring the six programs together as a block grant, cities would have a variety of options. Model Cities Program [MCP] money, being more flexible, would be "the glue at the top." [MCP money could pay the costs incurred by a city department for the administration of a federal grant.] However, we didn't have the manpower. We had some "gung-ho" administrators, but under the categorical system of reviewing and selecting, what we had tried to do couldn't be done administratively. In a memo to Richard Van Dusen, undersecretary of HUD, I suggested the possibility of developing a single block grant covering all the activities originally included under the six programs.

Right after that, Romney took us to Camp David for a brainstorming session. We were still thinking of something for which cities apply: [i.e.,] if the standards were met, the city got a block grant. Romney liked the idea and said,

"OK, start working on it." We came up with an outline and went to Dick Nathan at the Office of Management and Budget (OMB) to lay out the plan.

Dick was a cautious type. He said, "What about 'automaticity'?"

"What was that word?"

"Automaticity."

I said, "What?"

He said, "It's got to be automatic so there are no politics in it."

It made a hell of a lot of sense. So we went back and tried to work out formulas. That went on and on. Finally we got a formula that seemed to work. It factored in poverty indices—age of housing, population, growth, etc. . . . I had a minor battle to get citizen participation included. Also, we needed a provision for loan guarantees so cities could use their future block grant money as collateral against a loan from HUD. A project could take two, three, or four years out—the problem with an annual grant is that nobody's sure if Congress is going to approve funding for the following year.

I give Erlichman credit. He became a supporter.

Also, funding could now go to suburban communities with a population exceeding 50,000. This was a political pay-off to Republicans because many of these communities had Republican mayors.

Some of the big, old-time Democratic mayors wanted competition. Each thought, "If it's competition, I know I can get more than my share of the pie." We had to cover that aspect with "Hold Harmless," a three-year provision that no city would receive less under the CDBG Program than it [had] received from all HUD categorical programs on average for the previous three years. For example, New Haven, Connecticut, [had received] $22 million for Urban Renewal, [but] under the formula, New Haven would receive just $4 million. Because President Nixon and Secretary Romney wanted the program to work, their attitude was, do whatever it takes within reason.

We thought the states had a role to play. We had made inroads into getting state government involved during the Model Cities Program. Because funding for many social programs went to the states, we wanted to find a way to leverage some of that money into Model Cities, so HUD funded state coordinators at the governors' level. They were to get a handle on various federal monies and get some office within the state administration working with cities.

With CDBG, 20 percent of the money went to the states—earmarked for cities with populations less than 50,000. [However], cities didn't want the state to have any say in community development funding, while governors thought all money should come to the state, then the state would administer it to the cities. During a presentation to the National Governors' Association (NGA), this argument went on for half a day. Finally I said, "Okay gentlemen, it's all or nothing. Continue arguing, and it will be nothing."

Initially, counties were not included because some counties are nothing but a place on the map—it didn't make any sense to give money where it wasn't

Photo 8: Installation of sanitation modules developed by the Tucson, Arizona Model Cities Program

needed. But then there are counties like Fresno, which run all the social service/welfare programs. Once you dealt with it, there was an answer. Counties could be included if they met a minimum population requirement.

I wish I'd kept a journal detailing how events played out—the actors, the interest groups . . . what they did. It took us at HUD totally by surprise; apparently, we had convinced the White House. In 1972, when the State of the Union address came up, I was with the mayors at a conference in San Juan, Puerto Rico. We got a call from George Romney. He said, "The mayors have got to listen to that speech. There's going to be some great stuff." In that speech Nixon announced his proposal for the six, special revenue sharing packages—six block grants for domestic programs such as mass transit and employment training. Of the six, only the Community Development Block Grant Program made it through Congress. But what the program has done is not just keep the cities in some kind of balance, not just provide basic assistance, but build those structures with citizen participation. The program has survived.

Warren Butler, George Gross, and Dave Garrison: Equal Opportunity Funding

Warren Butler, HUD Deputy Assistant Secretary for Model Cities, George Gross, counsel to the House Subcommittee on Housing and Community Development, and Dave Garrison, housing and community development lobbyist for the National League of Cities, were key figures in the design and development of the Community Development Block Grant Program.

Gross: In 1969, we had a housing bill that was 100 pages long. In 1970, the Housing and Urban Development Act was 150 pages long. We [had] also passed the biggest mass transit bill in history—$3.1 billion—and an emergency mortgage credit bill, which set up Freddie Mac and gave Fannie Mae the right to purchase conventional mortgages.

Since 1961, there had been eight big housing bills. I proposed to Representative Barrett that we couldn't keep going on with these bills and that we ought to take a break and do some oversight for a year or two. So in the fall of 1970, we set up three panels—one on community development, one on housing demand, and one on housing production. There were only two rules for these panels: there would be no public hearings of any kind, and there would be no presentations by any interest groups.

We commissioned papers—at $1,000 a paper—on various subjects from experts around the country. The papers went into one big book that we published. In the fall of 1973, we hired John Zuccotti, who had worked under Bob Wood at HUD, to see that these papers were relevant and constructive. I remember musing with John Zuccotti: if we were mayors, what would we want out of the federal government? We came up with three primary requirements.

1. We would want the assurance of knowing that we were going to get money every year.
2. We would want the flexibility to use the money to meet broad goals.
3. We would want a reasonable set amount of money [so we can] avoid spending our time, the mayors' time, the National League of Cities' (NLC) time and the U.S. Conference of Mayors' (USCM) time constantly lobbying for more money.

These requirements became our goals for community development.

Four years later with two bills, House and Senate versions, we finally approached a conference with the Senate. The Senate version was the last housing bill of Senator John Sparkman of Alabama, a gentleman and the long-time chairman of the Senate Subcommittee on Housing and Urban Affairs. Representative Ashley told me that we should see Senator Sparkman before the conference. After the meeting, when we were walking back to the House, Representative Ashley said, "What I want you to do is give the Senate everything they want that doesn't affect our basic priorities."

I said, "Not the declaration of Purposes and Objectives section!"

Representative Ashley said, "Give it to them."

Here was the difference. The Senate version had several pages of what the CDBG Program was expected to achieve in the broadest possible terms. The House version had three relatively specific sentences calling for steady funding with a reasonable distribution formula, the consolidation of programs, and the flexibility to use funds to meet national goals. We traded three sentences for several pages of objectives.

Garrison: When I began as a lobbyist in 1970, one of my first meetings was with staff of the National Association of Housing and Redevelopment Officials (NAHRO). They were working on the Senate version of the bill with Carl Coan Sr., staff director of the Senate Housing and Urban Affairs Subcommittee. The Senate version was more traditional and grounded in the existing program delivery systems. The redevelopment lobby, which supported the Senate bill, did not want local government to be in the middle. Neither did Carl Coan, Sr., who was more comfortable with independent authorities running Urban Renewal systems.

My involvement began late in 1972 when the NLC and USCM were fighting tooth and nail to get in on the conversation. When the draft bills were finally on the table, it was exciting to work from the Senate perspective and then go to the House and find everyone coming from a completely different place. The House version scared the hell out of the Senate by insisting on the use of a formula for distributing funds annually. The administration wanted a formula, but the Senate wasn't ready; that was the critical matter. In 1972, the significant moment was the Senate's agreement to the House position. That issue wasn't actually resolved until the 1973-74 session of Congress when the administration's proposal was recast as one of Nixon's Special Revenue Sharing bills, the Better Communities Act—precursor to the CDBG Program. Agreement on the use of a formula for providing discretionary grant funding to cities was the watershed event that changed the conversation.

Gross: In 1971-72, even if people agreed that a formula based on a population/poverty ratio seemed reasonable, the problems were huge. Some cities got too much, others too little. As a result of the formula, cities like New Haven would get far less than they had been getting from various HUD programs.

I argued with Representative Robert Giaimo of Connecticut, that Bridgeport and New Haven—two cities, similarly sized and in roughly the same economic condition—got vastly different funding from HUD. New Haven received about $24 million annually and Bridgeport, about $3 million. Maybe New Haven had better people making the applications, but from a federal point of view, can you justify such a disparity? He finally gave in.

Butler: In 1970-71, the Nixon administration wasn't sure that it wanted to go forward with any kind of program. In one of those years, when Model Cities money was zeroed out, there was a move to put the money not being spent into a school-desegregation pot. These appropriations and budget level questions were going to impact whether there would be any further forward movement.

The spending of allocated funds was often delayed because negotiations took time. The elements of a MCP plan necessitated bringing program resources together with local government—as in education or to create a new entity such as daycare. Hanging over everything was a historical distrust between citizens and government that had to be worked through.

Butler: There was a fair amount of guerrilla warfare going on from our offices. Floyd Hyde's idea was to come up with something that appealed to the New Federalism approach within the administration, one being General Revenue Sharing—the allocation of money to cities by use of a formula. These issues were coming from the administration, and we were trying to figure out what, in Model Cities, could be made to appeal to these circumstances.

We knew we needed to move beyond the association with the previous administration. The Blair House meetings had started—run by John Erlichman, counsel to President Nixon on Domestic Affairs. George Romney, Elliot Richardson, and Floyd Hyde, and others were there. I asked Floyd how things had gone. "You won't believe it," he said. "We spent the first two hours talking about the name of the program." Before the meeting, [Floyd explained], Erlichman had said to President Nixon that Model Cities had a lot in common with the administration's thinking on the New Federalism. Then President Nixon said, "Well, OK, but see if you can come up with a different name." And so there they were, these high-powered members of the Nixon administration sitting before a blackboard with Erlichman wielding the chalk, trying to find a new name for Model Cities in order to satisfy the president's need for change.

They couldn't come up with another name. But Model Cities could change its focus to something larger than the neighborhood. We were going to add money so that 15 or so cities already in the program, could take the process citywide. The idea—[named Planned Variations]—was a prelude to what became Special Revenue Sharing and eventually the Community Development Block Grant Program. Our effort was aimed at moving the Nixon administration toward something other than a formula program like General Revenue Sharing. We wanted to preserve that aspect of Model Cities focusing on low-income activity and a broader range of development including social services and transportation . . . and this was before anyone was thinking about putting programs together at the administrative level.

By then, at HUD, all the physical development programs were being brought together in one place. At that point, we knew which way we wanted to move. We set up regional desks staffed with a fairly junior person from Urban Renewal—someone who wasn't steeped in the tradition of renewal so that that person could be retrained and could put together programs such as Water and Sewer, Neighborhood Facilities, and Open Space.

[In] 1972, long before the CDBG Program became an actuality, we were already internally organized and poised to develop the regulations and the final approach to the program itself. The formula would take more time, but we had scared off some of the old bureaucrats. One of the key things we did was achieve the ability to gather data—statistics on poverty and populations—that affected formula allocations.

Garrison: And because of that data capability, we could analyze information and suddenly, bingo, we were in business.

I remember that James Lynn, secretary of HUD and successor to George Romney, played an important role. He didn't know anything about the program and probably didn't care, but he was a closer.

Garrison: He loved the battle.

Butler: One reason the CDBG Program succeeded was that Jim Lynn came to HUD from Commerce where he had been the general counsel. He was a Nixon person with credibility within the administration, and because he could talk to the administration, he had credibility on the Hill.

Gross: In fact, we could talk to Lynn as well. He couldn't be kept away. He was everywhere, in Representative Ashley's office and in everyone else's office. The biggest difficulty with the administration bill was that the Democratic House approach was a block grant; HUD's approach was Special Revenue Sharing, a version of General Revenue Sharing. The big issue was about federal standards. The administration didn't want those standards, but it was hard to argue against them because we certainly had the votes in the House.

In reality, there were two formulas. The second one, devised in 1977, was the key to making the CDBG Program work because cities could choose to use either formula, whichever yielded the better result.

Butler: Jim Lynn was looking for three things. One, he wanted a formula that would satisfy the cities and the various political interests on the Hill but not raise the ante to the point that he couldn't sell it over the objections of the White House. Two, he needed to have some agreement on the housing . . . Section 8— that was part of the mix of agreements with Representative Ashley. And three, he wanted to move quickly because we still had the old programs out there. There were amendments for Urban Renewal that covered things we were trying to do. He could hold on just so long politically. He had to get a deal. These discussions had been going on for several years, so he was willing to go with whatever seemed to bring all the pieces together and could be sold in the White House.

Then he left for another job. It really didn't matter to him. He was a mechanic, but he had a good political demeanor.

Butler: Exactly! We had some training issues after the Community Development Act took place in 1974. The MCP staff in San Francisco used to drive us crazy because they were young and wanted to do things their own way, but this same staff turned out to be the easiest to retrain for the changes brought about by the CDBG Program. On the other hand, people who had worked in Urban Renewal were going crazy because they didn't know whether they were going to have a job again.

Garrison: The same tension was present in our discussions with people from the National Association of Housing and Redevelopment Officials. They were used to the independently run Urban Renewal Agencies, and were not at all comfortable that elected officials were going to run this program. They believed themselves sound professionals . . . and were offended by the bad rap that Urban Renewal had gotten over the years.

How successful is the Community Development Block Grant Program?

Garrison: CDBG is the one and only major-scale federal program of this sort that has remained intact with the same basic concept for 25 years. It remains the most flexible; [however], because the program is run as a ward-based undertaking in many cities, some of the original functionality has been lost. But in broad outline, CDBG is still the single most important federal grant program for city government in this country. There was a lot of luck in the timing of its enactment, and much of the explanation of its staying power has to do with the second formula, which was introduced in 1977 at the beginning of the Carter administration and approved by Congress shortly thereafter.

To those of us working for the NLC and the USCM it was clear that the start of the Carter administration presented a brief, but important, opportunity. We needed to do something to deal with the significant cadre of older, most depressed, East Coast and Midwest cities to bring them higher formula allocations or the program would begin to lose support.

The decision to put extra money into CDBG was made by the Carter administration. Ron Gatton from the USCM, Carl Reidy, then Washington representative for the mayor of Detroit, and I, worked as a transition team for Pat Harris, the newly appointed secretary of HUD. We made a presentation to her on two proposals: one was Urban Development Action Grants (UDAG) and the other was on the second formula for CDBG.

Secretary Harris recognized that she had an opportunity to come into office with a legislative package in hand. She was savvy and realized that she might actually be able to sell it in the early moments of the new administration. And she did. It became the only urban legislation President Carter would get passed in the entire four years of his administration.

Butler: The two formulas provided an opportunity. The first formula benefited those cities whose populations were growing. The second formula addressed the problems of urban decay. Having two formulas was a political compromise that gave parity in funding to two different urban problems.

Garrison: The formulas gave up the idea that there would be a discretionary decision made by the federal government on each and every grant—whether the plan was good, bad, or indifferent. That was a sea change. We were uncertain because it sounded like we were going on automatic pilot. CDBG was enacted against the background of the 1972 General Revenue Sharing Program, [which] provided totally unrestricted formula grants to states and local governments annually. Providing such unrestricted funding was a new experience for Congress, [and] from its inception, the concept engendered some significant discomfort on the Hill.

Gross: The reason was that Congress was not sufficiently involved in the program.

Which was a death wish for General Revenue Sharing . . . because without regulations and without targeting money toward poor people, the program could not exist.

Gross: But remember, one reason General Revenue Sharing ended was, as Tip O'Neill, Speaker of the House, would say, "Those damn states passing proposals saying we need to have a constitutional amendment to balance the budget. We'll fix them." So Congress took away $2.3 billion from the states and, eventually, another $4.6 billion from cities and counties during a later budget crunch.

Garrison: Since General Revenue Sharing was not targeted to specific needs, members of Congress could not identify themselves personally and politically with the activities being funded—a fundamental political flaw.

In contrast, the National Community Development Association has handled its end of the CDBG Program by helping members of Congress become associated with what is funded within their own district. It is the way our government structures function. When the budget crunch happened, Congress had to listen to local cries to save the program.

What has been the significance of the Model Cities Program and the Community Development Block Grant Program?

Butler: Community-based activity. I was not fond of the old programs in which physical development aspects per se were important: I saw them as isolated and not really doing anything. Urban Renewal Agencies could buy land. They didn't know how to sell it, and they certainly didn't know how to plan for developing it. HUD had $4 billion outstanding in guaranteed loans that weren't backed by any value that we could see in the property itself.

I came from the Hill, from the Republican side. There is a certain anti-aspect, a suspicion of civil servants and of bureaucracy. I take pride in the way CDBG was carried out. We have maintained high professional standards in the carriage of the program, and empowered elected officials at the local level. For 25 years, since it began, the program has attracted little criticism. Job training has been reinvented. Other HUD programs have been criticized, including housing programs, but it is gratifying to know that our approach had local impact and kept community people involved.

Gross: The fact that the same idea started in 1971 in the House Subcommittee on Housing and Community Development and at HUD, yet took four years to get through Congress, shows that a lot of constructive and agreed-upon political forces were in play.

Barry Zigas
President, National Low Income Housing Coalition (NLIHC)

Barry Zigas wanted to be a journalist. From Grinnell College in Iowa, where he had been a student activist, he traveled to Washington, D.C., eager to write about public affairs. After joining the staff of *Housing and Development Reporter* (*HDR*), a national publication on housing issues, he began to cover deliberations in Congress concerning the Housing and Community Development Act of 1974. After three years of writing detailed reports on topics such as Section 312, the Home Loan Repair Program, he acquired an in-depth knowledge—exceeding that of the legislators whose opinions he reported—of the elements that would become the core of the Community Development Block Grant Program.

No longer satisfied with reporting, Zigas, who wanted involvement in policymaking, began working for the U.S. Conference of Mayors. At the time the

USCM, which was committed to goals such as affordable housing, was in the final stages of competing for HUD-issued, technical assistance contracts—helping cities develop a housing assistance plan. For Zigas, working for the USCM revealed how weak the connection was "between people in community development and federally assisted housing programs, how little information they had on the programs, and how little influence cities had on these programs."

Meanwhile, Zigas had begun working with people who had started their careers during the Model Cities Program. Zigas found them a racially diverse group who, despite heated disagreements, "seemed bound together by common experience and a commitment to one another."

Lineage of a Legacy

My perception is that people who had been involved with Model Cities found themselves both fomenting and being carried along by a tide that fundamentally changed political and social alignments in cities. Those who moved into community development brought with them a spirit of advocacy on behalf of the community. They were about converting people to the right way . . . to help disenfranchised populations gain the ability to control and influence the allocation of resources. Not everyone in community redevelopment had experienced this kind change. A real tension sometimes existed between the traditional redevelopment authority people and those who had been through Model Cities.

Because of citizen participation in Model Cities, people became influential in their community. But as that first generation of people aged out of the field, new people coming in found the Community Development Block Grant Program increasingly institutionalized. Running the program was more about technocrats than about champions representing communities.

The Model Cities Program precipitated a change in mind-set that led to institutional change. But no matter what we thought, when President Nixon proposed the New Federalism and the decentralization of funding in the mid-1970s, that also was an impetus to institutional change. The more resources you put at a city's disposal, the more change for elected officials, who then found themselves in conversations about issues that they were ultimately responsible for. It is the mayors who must confront the murder rate, the unemployment rate, successive waves of immigration, and the wrenching social change that results. In a very real way, the creation of the USCM in the 1930s by mayors of big cities beset by social problems was about having to speak up . . . if for no other reason than for political survival.

An urban historian might argue that Model Cities, in some aspects of its administration, was the natural inheritor of the traditions of Tammany Hall—a governmental structure of big city political machines and ward heelers during an era of ethnic change. Money was used to help communities or co-opt their leadership into a system of patronage and revenue sharing that was strictly controlled. The creation of funding streams through independent/state agencies like housing authorities, was an attempt by the federal government to bypass the political structure in cities. Congress and federal administrators feared the corrupting influence of a city government as it occurred in Kansas City, Missouri, for example, when it was controlled by the Pendergast organization, which spent money on whomever it wanted to. Model Cities changed that dynamic.

These things go through cycles. The New Federalism was actually created for the wrong reasons . . . in the sense of getting the federal government out of social programs. Perhaps an intended effect was giving cities more control over resources, thus making resources more accessible to people with real interests rather than [their] having to deal with federal grants from a faceless bureaucracy thousands of miles away. That was always the rhetoric . . . whether anyone believed it or not. Most mayors had been content to leave housing in the hands of developers. When the CDBG came into being in the mid-1970s, a very long process began to relocate the responsibility of housing to places more responsive to community needs

What I found frustrating, as a lobbyist for the USCM, was that nonprofit housing advocates were conditioned to the idea that anyone representing cities must have bad interests. They saw issues as one-dimensionally as they probably thought we did. But I also found that a real connection with people generated a lot of synergy. For instance, with the Community Reinvestment Act of 1977, HUD officials were shocked to find city officials open to working together to get banks more focused on reinvesting in the community.

At the same time, you became a board member, and eventually president, of the National Low Income Housing Coalition.

I had been with the USCM for eight years. I was restless and thinking about what I could do on my own. Then, serendipitously, the NLIHC was in need of a new president. This was an organization whose ideals I was completely aligned with. I left a comfortable office at the USCM in 1984, took a short vacation and returned to Washington, D.C., to the offices of the NLIHC on Capital Hill. I remember standing in front of a small, dilapidated townhouse, reaching for the doorknob, and thinking, 'What have I done?" Then I walked in and got down to work.

The next nine years, 1984 through 1993, were wonderful. At times I'd find myself on the opposite side of my friends in the city lobbies. With city hall on one side, and community groups on the other, common ground was hard to find. Each side had an entrenched position around the issues of community development and neither side would retreat. Cities were unwilling to accept even the slightest additional targeting requirements in the legislation and neighborhood groups were completely unwilling to accept the good faith that many cities brought to the table. A constituency of mayors, cities, and states is a very large mass to move. As a consequence, while Congress might have sympathized with the issues raised by community advocates around the use of community development resources, the tenor and quality of the program changed. Rather than innovative and daring, community development became passive and straightforward.

Although none of us disagreed about what ought to happen, our interests had shifted . . . cities weren't represented by people on the grassroots level; the grassroots level wasn't represented by people with the same passion that characterized those who had been in the Model Cities Program. Cities were being represented by bureaucrats who did not want the federal government telling them what to do with federal money.

It's very much like sociologist Max Weber would describe the growth of a bureaucracy. An idea is promoted, cash is put into it, and an organization put around it, which then creates a bureaucracy with rules and regulations that kill the very idea that led to the organization's creation.

What was the focus of the NLIHC?

The first big issue—and one I least expected—was tax legislation. In 1985, the Reagan administration had eliminated just about every direct production subsidy program in the housing arsenal such as project-based Section 8. The only real engine left to do redevelopment in city neighborhoods was tax-advantaged real estate investment—especially Section 312, the Rehabilitation Loan Program, and 167K, the Accelerated Depreciation Provisions for Rehabilitation. People who had been all around the business, began to drop out leaving behind city governments and community-based nonprofit organizations, many of which had been formed during the Model Cities Program. The nonprofits had begun to occupy crevices left behind by the private sector and to develop housing on a community scale that was cost effective.

Many people on my board felt that for ideological, political, and personal reasons, any tax advantage for development subsidy was a terrible scourge, inefficient and not well targeted . . . and besides, the board just didn't like people who used them. Tax credits shouldn't be the tool of the developer. On the other hand the NLIHC was representing community-based organizations. Not taking advantage of tax credits would mean their going out of business. We couldn't walk away from the only subsidy left, but we could try to set our own terms to the debate. The board reluctantly agreed to move ahead. We created a universe around us based on what we thought the right way to distribute tax subsidies should be. We immediately made enemies of everyone else in the field.

The House, more accustomed to support for housing through federal programs, was slow to the idea of tax credits for low-income housing and allowed the real estate industry, with just a few nicks, to get away with the status quo . . . which didn't help us. In 1986, we testified to the Senate and, to our amazement, actually got U.S. Senator Robert Packwood of Oregon, interested in the idea of a tax credit. After the Senate meeting, I met with Chuck Edson, a legal representative for private developers. I told him we were trying to keep tax credit eligibility to those who earned 50 percent of the medium income.

He said, "Oh, that's just horrible."

I said, "We're considering 30 percent of medium income."

He reconsidered and said, "We can support 60 percent," and suddenly we had a deal. The bill passed pretty much as we wrote it. Initially, we had to bludgeon people to support the bill, but, when the Senate and then the conference committee considered it, the whole broader coalition pitched in to get it adopted.

Of course, after it passed and in subsequent years, everyone claimed to have invented the concept. The tax credit subsidy was a whole new way to do business. The status quo, unable to see the opportunity in front of its eyes, had nearly killed the goose that wound up laying a big golden egg.

We were able to put set-asides into place—15 percent of the tax credit subsidy would be allocated to projects sponsored by the nonprofits. Because of this set-aside, the nonprofits would not have to compete with highly capitalized and well-connected for-profit developers. This protected environment resulted in an absolute explosion of activity in housing developed by nonprofits.

During the Reagan years, there was the issue of transferring more control to local government. State governments made their future in housing with the tax credit and the ability to allocate it. The Rouse-Maxwell Housing Taskforce of 1989, the National Affordable Housing Act, and the creation, finally, of the Housing Block Grant were all modeled on, but separate from, the Community Development Block Grant Program. By formula, states and communities received money to develop affordable housing. For the first time, city government had control over federal housing subsidies. People in community development had their first taste of controlling housing resources . . . and they couldn't get enough. The difference was in how community development people were able to think about community planning. Now, organizations like the NLIHC could work with city councils, state housing agencies, and housing veterans at HUD and the USCM to really prepare the Housing Block Grant. The Housing Block Grant in 1990 and the Community Development Block Grant were the two mainstays in the work of people who had inherited the legacy of Model Cities.

Barry Zigas lives in Washington, D.C. He is senior vice president of Fannie Mae.

George Karras
Deputy Assistant Secretary for Operations,
United States Department of Commerce

Born in 1926 to Greek immigrant parents, George Karras was a Depression era child, who grew up, in his words, in the "gritty old textile mill city" of Manchester, New Hampshire. When World War II ended, Karras, earned a master's degree in economics from the University of New Hampshire, before moving to Washington, D.C., where he worked for the Bureau of Labor Statistics until 1953. From Washington he moved to Philadelphia to work for the Upholsterers International Union until his return to Washington in 1961.

During the Kennedy administration, Karras began working in the Area Redevelopment Administration (ARA), which dealt with distressed areas and chronic unemployment. The ARA, passed into legislation in 1961, preceded the Economic Development Administration (EDA), which was created in 1965. Both programs set the precedent for legislation that would introduce the Model Cities Program in 1966.

The Real Constituency

As chief of the Appalachian division of the ARA, I was responsible for implementing the program in West Virginia, Kentucky, Tennessee, and Virginia. An applicant to the Area Redevelopment Administration could be a state, a city, a county, a township, or any private or public nonprofit corporation. We made public works grants or loans to help local areas attract private-sector investment and thereby, create jobs. Bear in mind that we didn't have very many nonprofit development corporations in 1960 and 1961.

Later on, we got into the "War on Poverty." We helped put together Community Action Programs. These were private, nonprofit development groups carrying a variety of OEO programs. Prior to OEO, the ARA had gotten a lot of nonprofits started in cities and communities. The ARA required the applicant to prepare an overall economic development plan, which focused people's attention on the planning process and job creation.

Was the ARA involved in the Model Cities Program?

It was a peripheral involvement. Not only was the Office of Economic Opportunity already doing its thing, but also the Public Works and Economic Development Act had been passed in 1965. [The act created the Economic Development Administration] and the successor to the ARA. The transition was important because [the EDA] was a larger program and able to reach more communities.

When you get to Model Cities, we did not have much involvement. After all, we had 68 percent of the 32,000 counties in the United States in our program. We had the turf. We didn't always have the money. We were already in the cities designated as Model Cities. We did coordinate our programs through the local planning process, but at the national level our relationship was limited . . . what was a Model City? How could you define it?

One of the problems we had in the 1960s was that we came up with these fancy names: War on Poverty, Model Cities. Well hell . . . you either win or lose a war, right? We didn't win any war on poverty in the 1960s and we still haven't. The choice of terms was poor. They suggested things that were not achievable. The program didn't have a life span. After all, Model Cities folded into the Community Development Block Grant Program. Our closest relationship with HUD was with the Urban Development Action Grant Program.

Many programs were lost under the Reagan administration in 1981. I asked you for help because the Community Development Block Grant Program was among those threatened.

There is a step before, which is important. When Reagan arrived, I decided to resign from the Commerce Department. Representative Jim Oberstar of Minnesota, chairman of the Economic Development Subcommittee, asked me to help him prepare legislation to upgrade the Economic Development Administration. One important part of that work was the survey we conducted of all EDA applicants. We prepared a report that demonstrated the value of the program at a time when President Reagan was trying to kill it. The report had excellent public-relations value in the Congress and demonstrated the importance of EDA programs at the local level.

When we met, we talked about evaluating the Community Development Block Grant Program the same way. What we learned was that the important constituencies of the CDBG Program were not just mayors but also the subgrantees at the local level, who received CDBG funds and carried out programs that benefited millions of poor people across the country. Survey the organizations [that] got the money and [that] carried on the program . . . because they have members who reach hundreds of people. When you have thousands of such organizations, you're talking about a political force that can affect legislation.

One of the things [we] did after the survey was target certain members of Congress to show them how important the Community Development Block Grant Program was in their district. One of the Congressmen—we'd shown him all the organizations, about 30 of them in his district that received CDBG money through the city—said, "Yeah, I vote for the program all the time. How many mayors vote for CDBG?"

It's obvious. Mayors don't vote for CDBG; congressmen do.

Then he said, "That's why I like the EDA and UDAG. I can identify with a project . . . and before a project is made public, I receive notification so I can make the announcement."

But up to that point, Congress had had no role in awarding CDBG Program grants. We were naïve. The city of San Francisco, alone, funded 237 different agencies, including Boys' Club and YMCA, and Congressmen knew that these agencies were important to them.

Correct! We recognize[d] the political value in thousands of organizations representing millions of people who received assistance from CDBG grants. And that's when the National Community Development Association structured a Community Development Week with ceremonies through which members of the House and Senate could be involved in the CDBG Program at the local level.

George Karras is retired and lives in Rockville, Maryland.

Chapter 11

Working the Legacy

As a student during the 1930s at Bethune-Cookman in Daytona Beach, Florida, Jimmy Huger attracts the notice of Mary McLeod Bethune, a champion of black education, who decides to oversee preparations for his career. Every time Huger diverges from Mrs. Bethune's approved path—for example, during WWII, Huger seeks independence in the Marines—she finds a way to coax Huger back on track. By the 1950s, he is back in Daytona Beach and the sole black on the Urban Renewal advisory board. Even though the black community is angry about the failure of Urban Renewal and the dilapidated housing residents must live in, Huger, who runs for a seat on the city commission, is elected owing to the white vote. However, Huger is a politician and strategist who knows how to use federal resources effectively. Because his housing projects yield results benefiting many in the black community, he wins black support. In the 1970s, Huger becomes director of Daytona Beach Community Development, and although he must face many of the same problems that existed during Urban Renewal, he is able to significantly improve housing in many parts of the city.

Born in 1934 in St. Louis Missouri, Martha Brown Hicks is raised with the idea that "college is supposed to happen." She briefly attends Howard University in Washington, D.C., before traveling to California in search of a job. Despite a perfect score on a clerk's test, her position on the hiring list is below less qualified white women. However, Dora Davis, a black woman and a future mayor of Compton, California, convinces her to take a position at a lower salary thus becoming Compton's first black female Civil Service employee. She rises rapidly, studies urban planning at the University of California at Irvine, and becomes director of the Compton MCP. Suspecting corruption in the program, she resigns to takes a job in Santa Monica, California, where she is the first black to become a city department head. Meanwhile, Hicks, who lives in Los Angeles, California, is a member of that city's Citizens Advisory Board. The board, recognizing that improving Skid Row is tied to revitalizing downtown, asks Hicks, whose energetic style has attracted its notice, to become director of the Skid Row Development Corporation. Hicks, wanting to change the concept of Skid Row, initiates program innovations—taking people in for longer periods of time, helping them find jobs or get the benefit of social services, and, with the help of EDA funds, creating two commercial industrial centers. One enterprise, the Justice Bakery, employs all Skid Row workers and still continues today.

Young Dwight Robinson grows up in Flint, Michigan, in a MCP neighborhood where residents enthusiastically exercise their first taste of community self-determination. However, he also feels the community's helplessness when, later, much of the neighborhood is destroyed to make way for an interstate expressway. After Robinson earns a bachelor's in urban planning, he works as a rent collector in public housing in Ann Arbor, Michigan, where people aren't paying their rent. Robinson discovers that a cold beer offered in friendship from the trunk of his car on a hot afternoon gains tenant trust . . . and rent money. However, he distrusts the city's motives when it uses the plight of the working-poor to promote its application for CDBG funds. By 1991, Robinson works for Freddie Mac, the Federal Home Loan Mortgage Corporation (FHLMC), for which affordable housing is a primary concern. In a comparison to the movie, *It's a Wonderful Life,* Robinson explains the connection between a saving and loan business and the FHLMC's multiclass securities investment program with the availability of mortgages. Robinson, who becomes a senior vice president, credits Freddie Mac's continuous effort—the FHLMC maintains an enormous data bank—for better understanding of, and improving, the lending process.

Rather than accompany her husband on another career-related move, Diane Voneida chooses to stay in New Orleans, Louisiana, researching zoning petitions. She decides to pursue a master's in urban studies, and by 1976, she is director of Community Development in Gulfport, Mississippi. Prior to her arrival, a commission administers the first year's allocation of CDBG funds. She finds the commission's effort fragmented. For the program to be effective, she must convince commission members to focus funding on housing rehabilitation in the most challenged neighborhoods. Next, the city of Rockford, Illinois, recruits her to become that city's director of Community Development. In Rockford, all activities having to do with development are consolidated under community development, an arrangement that Voneida believes has potential; however, funds are spread over 14 different wards. Further, a river functions as a natural boundary between two racially and economically different sections. The "most seriously challenged" section is also a major entryway to, and the visitor's first impression of, the city. Voneida convinces the aldermen to target funds and develop a three-year plan that addresses a variety of housing problems and establishes a small business center offering a "critical mass opportunity" for businesses that locate there.

Carlyle Cox, former MCP director of Gainesville, Georgia, becomes Gainesville city manager. He continues to follow his unique instincts—developed during the Gainesville MCP—for using federal resources to make investments in the future of the community. His approach is so effective that at times, state regulations "piggyback" Gainesville practices. By comparing the people and systems in community development to a Rubik's Cube, Cox makes this point: make the people who run the funding programs creative; make them turn the program a dozen ways until the pieces fit.

James Huger
Director of Community Development, Daytona Beach, Florida

James Huger first attracted the notice of Mary McLeod Bethune, the well-known champion of black education, during his college freshman year at Bethhume-Cookman in Daytona Beach, Florida. Mrs. Bethune, certain that Huger possessed academic promise, determined that she would personally oversee his career decisions and thus ensure his future success.

It was the 1930s. Huger, whose finances were exhausted, could not afford his sophomore year at Bethune-Cookman. Instead, he took a job, room included, at a nearby hotel. On the first day, his shift finished, he returned to his room to rest. Someone knocked on the door. Assuming that a fellow employee was dropping by to say, "Welcome," Huger said, "Come on in." In walked Mrs. Bethune accompanied by two other women.

Confronting Huger, she said, "Why are you here?"

Huger, feeling the embarrassment of the moment, managed to explain that he didn't have the money to stay in school and would return next semester.

Mrs. Bethune replied, "No. That isn't going to work. You're going back to school . . . now.'

Mrs. Bethune had already located a replacement for Huger. She told Huger to put his things in a bag and go. After hastily scrambling into his trousers and, by now, the object of interested spectators drawn to the scene by Mrs. Bethune's presence, he marched out of the room. Ahead of him marched Mrs. Bethune and her two aides-de-camp. The experience changed his life.

By the beginning of World War II, Huger, having graduated from West Virginia State College, began working for the Department of the Army in Washington, D.C. Not much later, Mrs. Bethune sent a message: he was needed to help run Bethune-Cookman. Protesting that he had a job in the War Department had no impact—Mrs. Bethune had already taken care of the details; he was to return to Daytona Beach and college life. Also, because of his position at Bethune-Cookman, he would have deferment status against induction into the army. However, after watching his friends go into the service, Huger rejected deferment and took his chances with the draft.

The induction notice came quickly. Meanwhile, the Marine Corps had opened its doors to blacks. Feeling that his talents would be put to better use in the marines, Huger headed for Orlando, Florida, to enlist. After completing the physical and mental exams, he was informed that the corps was very impressed but couldn't accept him because he had flat feet. But he should come back in 10 days; the recruiters were going to seek a waver from headquarters in Atlanta.

"No time," said Huger who would be in the army by then. The recruiters rushed into action. They called Atlanta and had a solution by early afternoon of the same day. Headquarters had determined that having flat feet was a characteristic of Negroes and since James Huger was a Negro, no waver would be required. He was now a marine.

In the marines, Huger fought his way through layers of discriminatory regulations for the right to attend Officers Candidate School. When he finally won the battle, he was weary of the effort and just wanted to be his own person. After his discharge, Huger purchased a gas station in St. Petersburg, Florida, a career choice that felt right for about two months. Mrs. Bethune, always aware of his career status, notified him that he was needed in Washington, D.C., to help run the United Negro Fund College Campaign . . . never mind that he had a small business to run. Mrs. Bethune had found a buyer for the gas station. Within days, James Huger, with wife Phannye by his side, was back in the employ of Mrs. Bethune.

In the late 1950s, Huger, who had, by then, attended graduate school at the University of Michigan, Ann Arbor, and moved to Chicago to become general secretary of the black fraternity Alpha [Phi Alpha] was again summoned to Daytona Beach. With the death of Mary McLeod Bethune in 1955, Huger was needed once again to help in the administration of Bethune-Cookman.

The Bethune Effect

When Urban Renewal started, I was the black person appointed to the Daytona Beach Urban Renewal Advisory Board. The attitude of the average black person toward Urban Renewal was negative because it was taking their land and pushing them out. I argued with the black community that the city of Daytona

Photo 9: Henry Cisneros, Secretary of HUD, and James Huger

Beach had not done anything for them—people still lived in mud with bath-rooms on the back porch. I said, "The only way we can live better is for the fed-eral government to put money into the community." No one believed me at the time. I was almost ostracized by the black community because of my stand on Urban Renewal.

When a seat on the city commission opened up, I was urged to run. Even in predominantly black voting zones, no black person had ever been elected to a seat on the commission. At the same time, a group of blacks had brought a suit against the city naming me as the corespondent—they were going to stop Urban Renewal. The ruling was that the city had to be redistricted, which meant that I would be running at-large.

Considering that 14,000 black people and 40,000 white people made up the city, my supporters felt that I would not get the votes. I said to them, "I've never asked anybody to vote for me because I'm black. The only thing I've asked any-body to do is to trust me, to trust my ability to do a good job. Elect me because I'm qualified to do that job." We went ahead. In the end I got the second highest number of votes, most of them from white people. The argument from the black community was that I never stood up and said I was black. I said, "I don't have to. All you have to do is look at me. Just give me an opportunity. If I fail, I fail because Jimmy Huger did not measure up, not because Jimmy Huger, the black man, failed."

The second time I ran black people began to vote for me. By then we had started moving people onto paved streets where they had good lawns and flowers growing. One man who had spoken of me as "Jimmy Huger, the traitor," was now my supporter. The third time worked out even better. So I thought, this is it, and ran for mayor. But Daytona Beach was not prepared to have a black mayor, so I didn't get elected. I made a promise—one that lasted a year and a half—not to run for public office ever again.

Then a seat opened up on the Volusia County Council. Richard Moore, the president of Bethune-Cookman, said to me, "This is our chance. We've never had a black person on the County Council and you're the only one who can make it. We're going to break this barrier and open the door for other black people, and you're going to do it." I got elected and two years later I was chairman of the council.

Meanwhile, I resigned from Bethune-Cookman and began organizing Carter's campaign in the Daytona Beach area. Also, I had taken a job with Miami-Dade County. I was to set up a personnel classification system, a training program, and handle labor negotiations. After three days, the city manager of Daytona Beach called to offer me the position of director of Community Development.

What was your focus as director of Community Development?

The city commission and County Council had tried to do something about a place named Madison Heights, an enclave that belonged to [Volusia] County. It was dilapidated; people lived in the most horrible situations. When it rained, the septic tanks would back up. I said to the mayor, "Let's work this through community development." I got the people who lived there to agree to be annexed to the city of Daytona Beach. We promised those people that we would make Madison Heights a first-class community. Today, it is one of the finest areas that you will find anywhere.

We still had the same problems we had had under Urban Renewal. We had not put in sidewalks, lights, and drainage; and people were still living in dilapidated housing. These were our priorities and we were going to upgrade the entire community.

In one instance, a man named Mr. Cottle had started a housing development. His idea was to build some of the finest homes that black people could have. He built half the number planned, died, and his estate took over. His lawyers called me one day to say that there were liens on the land and they didn't know what to do. I thought that if we could pay the liens, we could get the land. I sat down with the my people; we knew that community development couldn't build houses, but we could get a nonprofit organization, the Central Florida

Housing Partnership, to set up a consortium of bankers and real estate people to set up a program. People would have go though the program to qualify for a house, then the banks would carry out the mortgages. That area became a fine neighborhood.

After improving the infrastructure, did you move on to other program activities?

We had a black high school on Campo Street that was abandoned after integration. It just sat there. We made it into a one-stop service center for the community. We did the whole building over—put in a gymnasium, converted the cafeteria into an activity building, put in handball courts and an Olympic-sized swimming pool, and made a park. We had offices for Social Security, Legal Services and the National Association for the Advancement of Colored People (NAACP). We had a representative for the city, and we had a library.

Quite a few places in Daytona Beach are named after you.

Every once in awhile someone asks, "Are you the man they named the park after?" One man added, "They don't do that until people die.'
I said, "Well, I damn sure ain't dead yet."

James Huger lives in Daytona Beach, Florida. He is retired but remains active in community development.

Martha Brown Hicks
Executive Director, Skid Row Development Corporation, Los Angeles, California

"I had a very wholesome upbringing," said Martha Brown Hicks of her youth in St. Louis, Missouri, during the 1930s and 1940s. Her father, a minister, and her mother, a teacher, let their children know that "college was supposed to happen."

In the segregated black schools, as Hicks recalls, teachers prepared students "for the day when the doors would open. [We] went to the same elementary school, the same high school, and the same poor black churches. Our children will never understand what this meant to us. It is an important part of our fiber."

After graduating from high school, Hicks pursued her education and at one point attended Howard University in Washington, D.C. Later, she returned to St. Louis where she worked as a secretary for the president of a major department store until moving to Los Angeles, California—an aunt had convinced her that job opportunities were better there. Soon, she was working as secretary to the first black superintendent of schools for the Willow Brook School District. In 1965, the year of the Watts riots, Hicks began working for the city of Compton. Fortunately she had listed Howard University on her resume.

Hicks had made a perfect score on the clerk's exam and, on top of that, typed 80 words per minute. Yet on the hiring list, she had been ranked below white women who were less qualified. Doris Davis, a black woman who later became mayor of Compton, saw the entry for Howard University on Hicks' resume and assumed that she was black. Ms. Davis sought her out, interviewed her, and convinced her that she should take a cut in pay in order to become the first black Civil Service employee in the city of Compton. Hicks advanced rapidly. After becoming city manager for Compton, she soon left to work for the city of Santa Monica and, eventually, for the city of Los Angeles.

Plucky Lady

During the course of dispensing zoning information across the counter, I decided that urban planning was a good field, so I went to the University of California at Irvine. My first professional position was as a planning aide [in Compton]. Within a year, I became the coordinator of Research, Planning, and Evaluation for the Compton Model Cities Program (Compton MCP). When Harreld Adams, [who] was director of the program, became assistant city manager for Community Development, I replaced him as director.

Under Planned Variations, the entire city [had been] designated a Model City. We wanted changes in housing, in recreational activities—we built a park with a man-made lake. While we promised citizen participation, I frankly don't believe that a lot of it went on. People yelled and screamed about what they wanted. We listened to them; but we made the decisions because we were professionals . . . and because a lot of corruption and graft was starting to go on.

Why did you resign after you had been assistant city manager for six months?

I didn't feel qualified to be a city manager at that juncture. Also, I thought that some people were going to go to jail, which they did. I went to work for the city of Santa Monica as director of Grants and Community Services and took a substantial cut in pay to become the [city's] first black department head.

It was in Santa Monica that I said to the city manager, "If you want me to raise money, we have to join the National Community Development Association (NCDA)." As a result of that membership, I learned how to get grants for federal money and to go out and tap private sector funds . . . and taught the social service agencies how to do the same thing.

Tell me about the Skid Row Development Corporation.

While I was working for the city of Santa Monica [but living in Los Angeles], I was appointed to the Citizens' Advisory Committee to develop the Redevelopment Plan for downtown Los Angeles. That committee determined that skid row affected other parts of the revitalization of downtown Los Angeles such as the flower market, the jewelry market, and little Tokyo.

You know how your mother tells you to be on your good behavior because you don't know who's watching. Frank Rice, a member of the Board of Directors for the Skid Row Development Corporation had seen me on that committee. He said to Jim Bonner, who was also on the board, "I've seen this woman in action. You are going to want to hire her."

I went to Skid Row in December of 1978. The corporation had been in existence for six weeks and needed money. [So] I went to Washington to talk to the NCDA. I knew I could get money from HUD to do a shelter—this was during the Carter administration—but there had to be an economic development component. I was to meet George Karras, [deputy assistant secretary of Operations at the Commerce Department, which includes the Economic Development Administration (EDA)], at a reception that night. I had my little brochure . . . the story is that I pinned Karras to the wall for 30 minutes until he signaled [a mutual friend from NCDA] and said, "If you will tell this lovely young woman to shut-up, I will send her a million dollars." And he did. The $1 million built the first Commercial Industrial Center.

What was your plan for Skid Row?

Before I went to Washington, I called together all the social service agencies. I said, "We have got to do something that is not being done. Tell me what is missing." They told me that the missions don't sleep women and there is no long-term care—three or four days and you're out on the streets.

I envisioned a shelter that would keep people four to six weeks; start to process them; and, if they were employable, help them get into jobs. If people were not employable and didn't even know what services were available to them, we would route them to the social service agencies so that they could obtain a benefit. To us, that was a success . . . as much as getting a job and moving into independent housing. The long-term shelter, named Transition House, opened in 1983 and would receive a number of awards, including the International Shelter Award from HUD.

What did you do for economic development?

I realized that if we were going to revitalize skid row, we could do a [second] commercial industrial center as a rehab [and] generate jobs. For $1, the city acquired the old Air Quality Management District Building and turned it over to us. I went to George Karras [at the Commerce Department], who gave us $2 million for a second center, a six-story building named Renaissance Building.

George Karras always said, "You bet on people."

By law, we had to promise to hire a percentage of local residents and lease to companies that would agree to hire a certain number of people in entrance-level jobs. We had a contract with the Federal Reserve; they gave us bags that would normally have been thrown away, and we recycled them and sold them back to the banks for $1. Next, we got some money from Neighborhood Self-help to do Justice Bakery. A former airline pilot started the bakery, which employed all skid row workers . . . the bakery still exists today.

We needed another kind of housing for people leaving Transition House. We bought and renovated a skid-row hotel with a Section Eight subsidy . . . it has 59-units and is still going.

The first year the [Los Angeles] Community Redevelopment Agency (CRA) funded us, we [had] a $95,000 budget and, by the end of that year, we had $3 million in the bank. The CRA had thought that we wouldn't go anywhere and they could then say, "Well, we tried." But the Skid Row Development Corporation survived. When I left, we had $12 million in assets and had bed and sheltered over 20,000 people in Transition House.

The most difficult thing I faced in later years was getting private money. Private-sector foundations would say they were interested in "women and children" . . . or that they would prefer to give their money to disadvantaged minority youth. How can you compete with that? Although the Community Redevelopment Agency continued to fund us, money was dwindling and so were federal resources.

What was the importance of the Model Cities Program?

Model Cities provided a lot of young professionals with an opportunity to grow. I have a wonderful story. I was in San Juan [Puerto Rico] for my first National League of Cities (NLC) meeting. I was in a curio shop looking at Haitian carvings when an elderly white man came over to me. I don't think he was flirting; he just wanted conversation. We were both wearing the same NLC badge. He said, "What does your husband do?"

I said, "I don't have a husband."

"Then you're a city clerk."

I said, "No, I'm a city manager."

"You can't be," he said. "City managers are tired old men."

And I said, "That's why cities are in trouble."

Martha Brown Hicks died in 2001.

Dwight Robinson
A Field Perspective in Public Housing

Every night, before Dwight Robinson's father left for work, he would ask, "Boy, have you got your lessons done?" If Robinson answered, "I don't have any tonight," he knew his father would reply with the directive, "Well, get in there and read that encyclopedia." According to Robinson, the nightly ritual, in addition to providing him with an array of A-Z facts, taught him to value education.

Robinson's parents were among the many African Americans who had migrated to the cities of the industrialized North after World War II. They settled in the North End section of Flint, Michigan, where Robinson was born on July 4, 1953. From age 10 on, he was never without a job—delivering newspapers, peddling ice cream door-to-door, or selling shoes and shirts at the mall.

The Flint Model Cities Program (Flint MCP), which began in 1968, was centered in Robinson's neighborhood. Chester Simmons, the director of the program, lived just up the street. Robinson recalls that "people went to his house to talk about things they wanted corrected and how to use the money that would be available to the neighborhood . . . about planting flowers on nearby Detroit Street, making sure that derelict houses were torn down, getting street lights fixed, and potholes repaired. The idea that impressed me most was that we had some say in how the money would be used. It was the first time I came across African Americans who were in charge . . . I never saw so many black people with suits on, and it wasn't even Sunday."

One major issue dominated their discussions: the planned route for Interstate Highway 475 (later renamed the UAW Freeway). Despite help from the Flint MCP, the North End's fight for a sensible route that would not isolate and damage the neighborhood's economic viability was lost. The neighborhood, as described by Robinson, was "pinned between the freeway and the railroad tracks with no stores, no fire station, no school and no services," and the Robinson house, which was originally slated for clearance, was somehow left intact . . . with "an economic value of $0."

Not long afterwards, Robinson chose urban planning as his major at Michigan State University. He listened to lectures on the merits of curved versus linear streets, and where to put the park. He said, "I argued with my professors in urban planning that none of the things they taught were about community. I had different issues that were germane to the time." When he began work in public housing in Ann Arbor, Michigan, his focus was a small community of people who worked in the houses of the affluent. Of them, said Robinson, "They lived in plain sight, but nobody saw them."

Our Man from Flint

I never disassociated myself from the experience of growing up in the North End of Flint. We never thought of public housing as having negative connotations.

Most people didn't pay the rent. Hell, I couldn't blame them. I was to figure out a way to collect rent and recertify people. One thing I did . . . I established a one-on-one relationship with people rather than being the guy in the suit that came to the door. At the time I had a Chevy Vega hatchback. I'd get a big tub of ice and put it in the Vega, get a case of beer and put it in the ice, and then drive into the projects and park under a tree. Of course I was an idealistic, twenty-something kid so what did I know? People came by. We'd have a beer together. I'd ask, "How about some rent?"

They'd say, "Mr. Robinson, I'm going to give you something on the rent." I didn't know all the HUD rules, but I figured that some rent was better than no rent.

The Community Development Block Grant Program had just started. I remember the city making applications for CDBG grants and using the people of public housing to establish need and to help make its case. It became clear to me that the city was not interested in helping these people . . . and had no intention of spending any money on public housing. I got frustrated with the process. Nobody seemed to feel any urgency to get things done.

Then I heard about the Michigan State Housing Development Authority (MSHDA). I was hired at the lowest possible rung and became the number-two man in the authority. I learned the ins and outs of housing finance. It was obvious; if people had money, they could make things better.

We had three notable accomplishments. One, we recognized people, particularly minority people for the work they were doing and established an intern program that gave people opportunities. Two, we expanded the focus of state financing within the inner city. And three, in the 1970s, we financed what, I believe, is a model of mixed-income housing in my hometown of Flint. The complex was the first new housing within city limits following a 20-year period.

Sr. Vice President of Corporate Relations: Freddie Mac

I came to Freddie Mac in 1991, in the aftermath of the Savings and Loan scandal. Checks and balances over government's response to enterprises were needed because of the government's potential liability. [Freddie Mac is a Government Sponsored Enterprise (GSE).] There were two expectations: there would be a safety regulation, and there would be a regulation referencing the requirements for low- and moderate-income housing. As a result Freddie Mac and Fannie Mae decided to make explicit efforts to increase affordable-housing availability. I was hired to begin that process for Freddie Mac.

We began developing affordable housing, community development, low-income housing tax credits—programs, beginning in the early 1990s, that laid the groundwork for housing and that both agencies, Freddie Mac and Fannie Mae, were financing . . . today both agencies routinely purchase low, down-payment mortgages—as low as three percent. That was unthinkable when I first came to Freddie Mac.

In 1993, after your confirmation by the Senate, you became president of Ginnie Mae and given two major responsibilities.

The first was to manage the agency on an ongoing basis. The second was to create what's known as a multiclass securities program for Ginnie Mae—a housing financing program that was common at Freddie Mac and Fannie Mae in 1993, but not at Ginnie Mae.

At the request of Henry Cisneros, secretary of HUD under the Clinton administration, this became our top priority. We developed the Real Estate Mortgage Investment Conduit (REMIC) Program in 1994. It's very simple: Ginnie Mae guarantees pools of Federal Housing Administration (FHA) insured mortgages, which are sold to investors. By statistically determining streams of income—some mortgages will pay off in the short term with a lesser premium, some will pay off in the middle term, and some will pay off in the long term with a higher premium—Ginnie Mae can then sell those streams of income. This is what is known as a REMIC Security. In this way streams are tailored to the needs of particular investors. An example would be a pension fund that needs to match its stream of income to the average age of its insured employees, in effect, to match [income] to the time when people will need it.

We accomplished our agenda and impressed Secretary Cisneros. Soon after, Terry Duvernay, [deputy secretary of HUD], decided to go into the private sector and I was nominated to be his successor. I would be the hands-on mechanism making the department run.

I served in the Clinton administration for about five years. Soon after Andrew Cuomo became secretary of HUD I was offered the opportunity to rejoin Freddie Mac as vice president of Industry Relations. Eight months later I became senior vice president of Corporate Relations. Here was an opportunity for me to build on work begun at Freddie Mac in the early 1990s, and to do it at the level of a senior officer.

Although everyone cannot be a homeowner, a high ownership rate is one of the real lynch pins of the American success story. Freddie Mac agreed with

HUD: 50 percent of all the mortgages that Freddie Mac—and Fannie Mae—
purchase should meet an affordable housing goal requirement. About 67 percent
of the households in the United States are homeowners. The benefits include
equity and satisfaction for the individual owner; home ownership also creates a
stable community with needs and objectives. The homeowner buys into those
needs and objectives.

What Freddie Mac does is provide liquidity to the mortgage market. In the
movie, *It's a Wonderful Life;* the issue that faced Jimmy Stewart, in running the
family's savings and loan business, was that the number of loans outstanding
was based on deposits. When the deposits dried up, no money was available to
make more loans.

Today, banks sell the loans they make almost immediately to Freddie and
Fannie thereby replenishing the availability of mortgage dollars to their deposits.
Dollars are available because we have a national perspective. Freddie and Fannie standardized the terms—the rules are the same; the availability of mortgage
dollars is the same. Because we buy such a huge percentage of all the mortgages
in the country, we have been able to create an enormous data bank. The ability
to understand how housing works—what is important in the lending process and
what is not—is better understood. We don't credit ourselves for all the home
ownership opportunities out there . . . but Freddie Mac and Fannie Mae have
played a major part.

*Dwight Robinson lives in Herndon, Virginia. He is senior vice president of cor-
porate relations at Freddie Mac.*

Diane Voneida
Director of Community Development: Gulfport, Mississippi

After graduating from Dickinson College in Pennsylvania, Diane Voneida
left the tradition of family-owned businesses—a farm, a grocery store, and a
machine shop—to accompany her husband on a series of work-related sojourns
across the United States. From the rural Susquehanna River Valley they traveled
to South Dakota, then back to Pennsylvania, and next to New Orleans. When her
husband announced that he would be transferred to Midland, Texas, Voneida
had had enough and decided to remain in New Orleans.

While thinking about her next step, she began doing temporary work for the
city. One assignment, named the Pride Package, was a campaign initiated by
Mayor Moon Landrieu. Its purpose was to help residents of the city distinguish
which amendments, among the many being proposed annually to upgrade an
out-of-date state constitution, would benefit the city. Before long, she was working full time for the city researching zoning petitions. To understand what she

was "supposed to be doing," as Voneida put it, she decided to pursue a master's degree in urban studies. By 1976, she had established her own business as a consultant on land use and transportation planning and was about to become director of Community Development in Gulfport, Mississippi.

The Economics of First Impressions

Gulfport was a small city with a population of 40,000. But because it was a central city within a county, it was eligible for funding. [The city] had had one year's allocation from its Community Development Block Grant Program (CDBG). To administer the program, it had set up a commission—a separate office whose application of funds was fragmented—directed mostly at public improvements such as streets. When I read the regulations, I didn't see how that usage could help low-income people or make viable communities. So, I urged the commission to devote a major share of the program's resources to housing rehabilitation in the most challenged neighborhoods. Considering that I was a female Yankee carpetbagger, I was amazed when they agreed. In fact, the commission never said "No" to me.

Our initial concern was with existing homeowners . . . and *doing that* was something new for Gulfport. The five commission members—one black man and four white men—were doing the right thing. We had discussions . . . but citizen participation wasn't volatile. The process was straightforward and concentrated on the needs of the community.

I found vacuums and filled them . . . and because of that, Gulfport Community Development became the agency that issued bonds for housing. We were the Certified Development Corporation for the Small Business Administration. The fees from that service allowed our agency to administer the CDBG funds without taking so much of the program's money for administrative costs.

The legacy of the program was allowing people to live in a safe environment. And with downtown redevelopment, we actually negotiated the sale of land from a railroad—[one] that never sold land—and left that land in the public trust. That was a coup.

Director of Community Development, Rockford, Illinois

[The Rock River] divides the city in two—really two towns put together. One side was settled by the Italians and eventually became the place where African Americans settled. The other side was Swedish. The two sides didn't talk. Despite this divisive behavior, my major confrontation was getting the Community Development Block Grant Program targeted—not at people but on areas of the community.

Rockford had 14 different wards; CDBG money was spread out over the city without any effort to target. The housing program, concerned with moderate rehabilitation, allowed for minor repairs primarily. The city had recently consolidated the Community Development Department so that all activity having anything to do with development was under the same umbrella. The ability to influence was there . . . from beginning to end. To have more impact, the City Council decided to target 60 percent of the funds.

Citizen participation was good but not representative. However, the aldermen, [who] were very involved in their respective wards, listened to people and had input into the community. Within the department, three of the four divisions were dysfunctional. Money was spent citywide on housing, streets, and public works . . . but not on community services, and the housing program did not address the problems of rental housing.

What was your strategy to get the program to work?

After the staff and the citizen participation committee had reviewed all the neighborhoods in the community, we decided to target three neighborhoods. We put the aldermen, many of whom had never been west of the river, on a bus and took them to see the areas in question. These visibly, seriously challenged neighborhoods were the western and southern entryways to the city . . . [and] what people saw, coming into Rockford for the first time. The aldermen, because it was clear that a major turnaround was necessary, agreed to invest funds in those areas for multiple years to come.

We elected to do a three-year plan. To make sure that all elements of the neighborhood were included, housing programs ran the gamut from rehab, to acquisition demolition, to acquisition rehab for homesteading. We upgraded rental properties, got rid of vacant dilapidated structures, and put up new housing. We had an economic development program that successfully attracted the return of small businesses to two of the three neighborhoods. In those two neighborhoods, all the businesses were within a two to four block area—a critical mass opportunity—so that customers for one business contributed to a pool of customers for the other businesses.

What comes to mind when you reflect on your experience in Gulfport and Rockford?

I worked with three mayors who . . . listened, learned, and took an interest. I never had to fight them and they never had to fight me. In later years, politics did come into play, and in the last few years, people have become less civil to one another. However, without the Community Development Block Grant Program, the two neighborhoods that have prospered would have been devastated.

Diane Voneida lives in Rockford, Illinois. She owns and directs Voneida and Associates, a consulting firm focused on affordable housing and strategic planning.

Carlyle Cox
City Manager, Gainesville, Georgia

"Rubik's Cube"

What I have observed, is that the bureaucracy of the [Community Development Block Grant] Program tends to squeeze all the life-breath out of it. For example, back in the 1980s, in the last year of the "Hold Harmless" policy, we had a Jobs Program. If you could create jobs, you got a big chunk of money. We did one program with a Mexican company that had gone under. We propped it up, hired 100 people—many were handicapped. It was a hell of a success. The state handled the money, about $500,000. After we paid it all back, we started loaning money

Through the 1990s, the economy was good so there wasn't as much need for loans. The state said, 'Loan the money out or you're going to have to give it back to us." I thought, to hell with that. It's technically not legal, but, we'd like to loan this money to our downtown redevelopment authority for downtown business and building owners to update their facilities through joint bank loans . . . instantly. I asked if we could do this on demonstration?

The state said, "Yes."

That was 16 months ago. Three months ago the state came out with a new program: revolving loan money could now be used for downtown redevelopment. They piggybacked our program!

The point is you've got to go to the people who have the money and make them creative . . . or throw them out. It's the old Rubik's Cube. You've got to turn the sucker a dozen ways until it fits. That's what's needed within our local governments if they are to continue to deal with the tough issues out there.

Chapter 12

Reflections and Implications for Future Policy

Mark Tigan

Reflections on the public policy successes and failures of President John-son's "Great Society's" should provide some guidance going forward in the era of "New Federalism." Although the interviews in *A Little Noticed Revolution* are wide ranging in topics, common themes can be identified that not only assist in the formation of future public policy but may also explain how local government progressed to the present state. What follows is a discussion of the most substantive themes.

Community Development Corporations

Practitioners of Model Cities recall the utility of involving the nonprofit sector in both formulating and carrying out Model Cities' activities. In the classic article, "A Ladder of Citizen Participation" published by the APA, Sherri Arnstein suggested that community controlled nonprofits are near or at the top rung of the community participation ladder.[1] The perspective of many Model Cities practitioners is that the capacity of the program was enhanced by the inclusion of the nonprofit sector. Citizens were not only afforded the opportunity of program and budget control but also the civic and fiduciary responsibility to implement project activities when nonprofit Community Development Corporations (CDC) contracted with the Model Cities agencies.

Especially in its early stages, the nonprofit community was generally representative of most Model Cities neighborhoods because its board was comprised of residents. The devolution of decision making along with implementation tasks was an attractive alternative to both the citizenry and local government. To a great degree, the explosion of community development corporations grew out of this era of a symbiotic, give-and-take relationship between Model Cities and nonprofits. This created an environment in which Model Cities' successor, the Community Development Block Grant Program, could begin with a substantial amount of subcontracting from city to nonprofits, which pleased the Nixon regime. As they interpreted it, this was one form of "privatization." Support for privatization efforts came from both the political top and grassroots bottom, leading to the rapid growth of the CDC sector. However, over time, there is some evidence that the pluralist grassroots participation in CDCs is waning if board representation is used as one indicator.[2] Boards are gradually becoming more elite as the fund raising and networking becomes more crucial to CDC survival. This phenomenon should be the subject of further study.

Citizen Participation

According to Edgar Chan and Barry Passett, Model Cities "broadened the scope of the [participatory] examination until the definition and understanding of citizen participation has achieved recognition as an issue of paramount importance."[3] A few pundits, often from academia, tend to criticize the community participation component of the Model Cities Program as a failure—a failure in both effectiveness and efficiency. The goal of "widespread participation" may have been underachieved. In comparison to subsequent—or then current— federal programs Model Cities' citizen involvement was exemplary. Analysts observe that "federal officials as well as the general public grossly overestimated what could be achieved and . . . underestimated the difficulties involved in a comprehensive community development effort. The program was thus a

---

[1]Sherry Arnstein, "A Ladder of Citizen Participation," *Journal of the American Institute of Planners,* 1988.

[2]Mark Tigan, Ph.D. Dissertation (forthcoming).

[3]Edgar S. Chan and Barry A. Passett, eds., *Citizen Participation: Effecting Community Change* (N.Y.: Praeger Publishers, 1971).

victim of unrealistic expectations." Other evaluators, though fewer in number, cite Model Cities as a "revolutionary change in community participation."[4] Schorr says, "The widespread belief that the antipoverty initiatives of the Great Society were a failure was more than a misreading of the numbers."[5]

Practitioners of Model Cities recall community participation as one of the program's chief benefits—a genuine empowerment of neighborhood residents. Model Cities agencies were willing to endure planning delays—attributable, in part, to inefficient and contentious public process—as a tradeoff for ultimate program creativity and effectiveness. Conversely, HUD deadlines often led to a truncated process near the end of planning periods. Timeframes and funding levels insufficient to meet real needs caused citizen frustration.

Furthermore, observers recall that the Model Cities community participation policy was paradoxical. HUD had intentionally crafted rules to permit maximum local flexibility when designing the participatory process. This effort was intended to balance federally required citizen controls with City Hall responsibility while trying to avoid the alienating hyper-participation that had resulted from earlier Office of Economic Opportunity (OEO) programs.

Mayors, in turn, demanded more direction from HUD on levels of community participation but resisted other regulatory infringement on their program options. Similarly, HUD became more prescriptive in community participation methods while simultaneously encouraging local flexibility. This two-way stream of conflicting messages created opportunities for experimentation by Model Cities directors but also fomented local political problems. As Model Cities transitioned to CDBG the Nixon administration attempted to provide "for a somewhat more limited role by local citizens in actual decision making on community development activities."[6] Former Model Cities officials argue that citizen participation has gradually decreased under Community Development Block Grant. In the future, if participatory decision making is to be revived, strong federal guidelines will be required.

Minority Advancement

Approximately one-third of this book's contributors are African American. When the percentage is computed using only former local officials the number is much higher. In short, African-American leadership in Model Cities agencies was pervasive because hiring residents representative of minority neighborhoods—including qualified women and other minorities—was politically expe-

---

[4]Lisbeth B. Schorr, *Common Purpose, Strengthening Families and Neighborhoods to Rebuild America* (N.Y.: Anchor Books/Doubleday, 1997), xxii.

[5]*Ibid.,* xxi.

[6]Peter Marris, *Meaning and Action* (London: Routledge 1987), 8-9.

dient and required by federal policy. As reflected in the interviews and supported by the literature, the Model Cities program directly resulted in numerous advancements for many minority residents to higher positions.[7] Atlanta's Model Cities Program, for example, spawned city councilors, school board members, developers, and other community leaders. Of the African Americans participating in the book's interviews, many advanced to highly placed government offices—director of Civil Aeronautics Board, chairman of Fannie Mae, and assistant secretary of HUD. Prior to Model Cities, talented minority residents were often tracked to post office jobs, teachers, and the like.[8]

Sixties legislation (e.g., the Model Cities Program, the Voting Rights Act, the Equal Employment Opportunity Act) released the latent creativity and leadership that often migrated to Model Cities staff and policymaking due in large part to the resident hiring policies of Model Cities. An unintended consequence, as opined by some observers, was that the racially inhibited neighborhood talent "gentrified" leaving today's urban neighborhoods with fewer organizers, fewer leaders and therefore less likely to bootstrap out of poverty. One concern with the CDBG replacement of the Model Cities program was that minorities would suffer a loss of gains made in professional advancement.[9] If current minority participation in the National Community Development Association is an indicator, the forecast for reduced minority participation was correct. A more aggressive effort to hire or involve minorities is called for from both local and federal officials as well as from university planning and public administration programs.

Creativity

The hallmark of the Model Cities program was implicit in its legislative name, The Demonstration Cities Act. One federal purpose of the program was to experiment—think out of the box. In doing so cities learned how to negotiate, how to protect the public interest, and how to blend housing and economic development with social services. Neighborhoods demanded and were granted the right to guide programs that directly affected them. Ideas were conceived and tried. Some worked; some did not. From a mothballed ship serving as neighborhood center to an unimagined cash crop for co-op farming to an innovative, attachable or freestanding sanitation module, ideas were born. Creativity did not lend itself to short-term cost/benefit evaluations; costs have long ago been paid while benefits continue to accrue.

---

[7]Interview with David Gibson, former Model Cities Director, City of Atlanta, Georgia, on June 10, 2004.
[8]Interview with Ronald Gatton, former Director, HUD Field Office, City of Chicago, Illinois, on June 1, 2004.
[9]Marris, 36.

The seeds of Model Cities' innovation have grown and intertwined themselves into today's civic society in a way that can be best appreciated through the rear view mirror of a 30-year chronology. Too often, evaluators using only short-term data collection maligned the Model Cities Program—most literature covering Model Cities was published in the 1970s. When today's historians examine the effect of Model Cities—and probably to an equal degree, OEO programs—on civic organizations and local government approaches to the empowering neighborhoods, two observations are likely to be made.

One: many Model Cities innovations have taken root and have been improved upon for the benefit of low- and moderate-income people.

Two: federal guidance to local government in the period following Model Cities lacked incentives and the authority, creativity, innovation, and, more sadly, resulted in less pluralistic community development decision making.

Model Cities introduced a comprehensive perspective on urban development. This welcome historic event also introduced unprecedented challenges for public administrations regarding the *how* of planning, managing, and implementing complex multi-sector, community improvement efforts. The culture of experimentation was difficult to advance. As, Peter Marris observed, "by the mid-1960s sociologists were questioning the ideal of a value-free social science, but experimental reform still adhered to the systematic institutionalization of scientific impartiality."[10] Urbanists have to again dare to experiment without fear of failure or federal sanctions. The federal government must offer incentives—and funding—for creative urban experimentation. And once again, the long-term cost/benefit ratio is likely to prove favorable.

Civil Unrest

The interviews contain many stories relating the occurrence of civil unrest and how heated advocacy—in some cases, violence—spilled into citizen participation. Guns were present at community participation meetings, and police were used to keep order. As passion subverted orderliness, contentious debates over project and geographic targeting were difficult to control with Roberts Rules of Order. Extended deliberative discussions as time-consuming inefficiencies of participatory planning were a common thread in the historic Model Cities literature. On occasion, neighborhood residents came to meetings prepared to aggressively assert their rights thus putting the well being of docile participants at risk. However, there are only anecdotal stories of actual physical harm. Although such behavior was questionable, one could speculate that community participation offered at least the alternative to street violence, albeit contrary to a civil society.

---

[10]Marris, xi-xxi.

Citizen participation must be conducted with a certain order so as not to discourage representative civic engagement. Although a threat of violence is rare at public meetings, the participatory environment may change if urban unrest reemerges.

Community Development Profession

Among the multitude of urban professional fields, it was most often city planners who were assigned to the local Model Cities Program. According to Professor Nathan Glazer of the Massachusetts Institute of Technology, "the planner was being transformed from prophet and reformer into professional . . . the idea of what the planner was supposed to be underwent kaleidoscopic changes in the urban turmoil of the late 1960s and early 1970s. The central conflicting images of what a planner in the heroic mode might be—Mumford, Jacobs, Moses—were never superseded." Although underreported, the Model Cities era witnessed the growth of a new profession; namely, administrators of community development. These professionals were former planners, urban renewal officials, economic developers, social workers, and in many cases neighborhood residents who had been hired into the program and advanced to lead a city's community development efforts.

The evolution of the professional organization that has represented Model Cities from its inception evidences the growth of the community development profession. In 1968, a national organization was formed named the National Model Cities Directors' Association with an initial membership of 130. In 1974, the name was changed to the National Model Cities and Community Development Directors' Association with a membership 250. And in 1979, the name changed to the National Community Development Association (NCDA) with a membership 450. In 2004, the NCDA membership exceeds 500 cities, counties, and other CDBG "entitlements" jurisdictions.

Today, the field of "community development" is known by governmental practitioners as the comprehensive profession most often charged with the multifunctional responsibilities of planning, citizen participation, grantsmanship, housing, social service delivery/coordination, and economic development. Often this will include other responsibilities for which mayors and city managers cannot find a "home" such as coordinating tax increment districts, building parking structures, special studies, coordinating tourism facilities, and similar activities not clearly "inside" the purview of other line departments. An interesting illustration of this occurred in Hartford, Connecticut, where even rat control was assigned to the agency charged with community development.

However, depending on the bias of a city's leadership, the field of community development has been subordinate to, or a subset of, other more deeply "rooted" professions such as planning and public administration. It is not uncommon for professionals from within each discipline to view theirs as the dominant or, historically, more important one. Each discipline views itself as distinct. Each struggles to keep from being assimilated into another. Until recently, academic programs and professions categorized the municipal government fields as public administration, urban/regional planning, public policy, urban affairs, city management, housing, and economic development.

With increasing numbers of progressive cities such as Santa Monica, California, opting to organize a greater number of functions under community development, academia has begun to recognize community development as an important part of university offerings. A historic dichotomy exists in many urban and regional planning schools between theory and practice. Some theorists posit that community development is a poverty-based program, carried out primarily by the nonprofit sector. Practitioners, on the other hand, would subscribe to the multidiscipline function of community development and recognize it as a major municipal—and often state—department. As younger '60s- and '70s-inspired educators enter the top ranks of academia, traditional terminology is changing. Professor Allan Jacobs, City and Regional Planning, University of California, Berkeley, reported that most of the incoming students want to prepare for the field of "community development." The once subordinate profession of community development apparently has, over the years, become much more dominant at the municipal level.

Fueled by budget constraints and the public's demand for effectiveness and efficiency, i.e., "one stop services," the trend in both small and large cities is for the director of community development to be responsible for planning, economic development, housing, and other divisions. This is in contrast to several years ago, when cities generally had stand-alone operations and distinct functional separations. Planning is, in the opinion of some observers, most closely related to community development. Yet planning is the profession that seemingly struggles the hardest against assimilation due, in part, to its own inability to find a balance between a physical space approach and a social-economic program relevance. Planners can identify the needs with planning methods and depict/forecast clearly with Geographical Information Services (GIS), but they struggle or do not consider within their realm the financing or implementation of the planned solution. In *Planning Support Systems,* Britton Harris writes, "We will define Planning as the premeditation of action, in contrast to management which we see as the direct control of action."[11] Generally, this is the view of planning literature. This definition poses an obvious question: If a planner plans action and management controls action, who executes the action? Often the community development departments at the municipal level have conducted the "action." This practical and results-oriented profession, rooted in participatory

---

[11]Britton Harris and Michael Batty in *Planning Support Systems: Integrating Geographic Information Systems, Models, and Visualization Tools,* ed. Richard K. Brail and Richard Klosterman (Redlands, Calif.: ESRI, 2001).

inclusion first piloted in Model Cities, is a welcome addition to the traditional departments of local government.

Personal commitment to the community and an action-oriented approach form the substance of the Model Cities profiles reported in this book. Irrespective of professional title or level of government the city bureaucracy needed then—and needs now—to be held accountable. More effort needs to be directed toward disenfranchised groups. They need to be more empowered. The multifunctional, comprehensive approaches to community development could provide an incubator to advance that empowerment. As Schorr states: "Antipoverty programs were a noble chapter in our history." Schorr continues, quoting War on Poverty architect Hyman Bookbinder, "'The country as a whole, starting with its president, was saying we will not tolerate a situation where the many who are okay say it's not their business to be concerned about those who are not. And that is probably its most important legacy.' For those of us who were part of the War on Poverty, it represented a shining alternative to social indifference."[12]

---

[12]Schorr, xxii.

Chapter 13

Rethinking Model Cities and Social Policy Innovation: Towards a *Developmental Public Administration*

Madeline Landau
with thanks to Nancy Gilbert for her assistance

I. Understanding the Policy Context: Social Change and Governmental Reform in the Great Society

President Johnson's "Great Society" is associated with a bold expansion of the federal government's role in solving social and urban problems. Americans widely believe that the War on Poverty and Model Cities brought a proliferation of innovative programs on behalf of the poor and racial and ethnic minorities that swelled public expenditures, the federal bureaucracy, legal powers and program commitments.

In fact, this is not an accurate portrait of policy innovation in the late 1960s and early '70s. A systematic initiative to solve poverty would have required major dimensions of redistributive social policy: to equalize urban school finance; to provide health insurance, child care, and affordable housing at scale; and to create jobs and institute labor market protections or income guarantees. The planners of the War on Poverty and other initiatives were constrained by President Johnson's commitment to the tax cut of 1964 and the spiraling cost of the Vietnam War. As a result, a critical opportunity for major action on behalf of the nation's poor was sadly lost. Apart from Medicare, and several significant proposals carried over from the 1950s, "innovative" programs enacted in the 1960s did not substantially enlarge the level of federal spending. (Marmor, Mashaw, and Harvey, 1990). Funding for Model Cities was really quite modest; Maris and Rein (1973: 265) noted, e.g., that the total appropriation for all 151 Model Cities was approximately $500 million—a fraction of the amount that urban areas like New York City spent on public welfare alone.

Contrary to popular image, much policy innovation actually turned on reforming the structure and process of government, itself. (Landau, 1988; Katz 1986; Moynihan, 1969; Sundquist, 1968). In fact, the mid-'60s found a liberal tradition in turmoil. The American policy system confronted the new challenges of an advanced industrial society—including the emergence of intergenerational, geographic, and racially based poverty and unemployment. In the attempt to treat the "paradox of persistent poverty in the midst of plenty," a period of intense experimentation and innovation evolved that challenged traditional ways of doing the business of public policy and public administration. Reforms targeted bureaucratic structure and operational issues, the relationship between national and local government, and the relationship between government and community, including the question of how to treat the multiple roots of complex, deeply embedded social problems.

The new thrust in reformism leveled critiques at key tenets of the public administrative framework that had grown under Progressivism: top-down and apolitical planning, neutral scientific expertise, professional specialization, and individual-based solutions to social problems. These counter-themes were so powerful they rivaled the focus on substantive social and urban problems themselves. Beyond this, public policy turned to scrutinize its own impact on social and economic affairs. The state was seen as more than a remedial instrument; it was, itself, seen as a dynamic causal factor in societal problems. This critical, antibureaucratic current was so influential as to establish patterns of reform that continue to shape liberal social policy to this day.[13]

---

[13]Indeed, much of the bureaucratic and governmental reform credited to the "new public management" of the 1980s and '90s actually began in the '60s, when a focus on such themes as decentralization, antibureaucratic reform, innovation, and citizen demand for empowerment moved to center stage (Landau, 1988; Marris and Rein, 1973; Sundquist, 1968).

With higher levels of funding, Model Cities might have had greater positive impact on urban areas. But the discussion of Model Cities in this volume should be read against the special nature of this policy context—in which substantive promise shifted to governmental reform. It will be seen that Model Cities was an attempt to promote a number of institutional changes for low-income, minority communities. Yet the reform strategies were never clear, resulting in extensive role and goal confusion.

Underlying this confusion was a powerful idea: the need to develop a greater capacity for brokerage and linkage between isolated communities and the maze of public and private institutions that determine economic opportunity. The middle section of this chapter summarizes findings from organization theory, political sociology and the study of institutional development regarding the importance of connective networks, brokers and "intermediate organizations," for supporting coordination and participation in complex policy environments. Informal connections serve as "back channels" between sectors, and portals to government, that can bypass formal barriers and influence needed changes in institutional process. Such boundary spanning abilities have a neglected role to play in effective policy implementation and the social, political, and economic development of excluded groups.

Cross-cutting linkages are one of the greatest assets for the administration of complex initiatives for social change—one that policy planners must learn to value as highly as program substance itself. The last section raises practical implications for how to support a "developmental perspective" in program and administrative design.

The Discovery of Institutional Complexity

The inward-looking policy turn of the '60s had several roots. First, the distinctive intellectual feature of the period arose from a confrontation with the departmentalized approaches of professional specialization that had grown since the Progressive Era: urban and regional planning, social work, criminal justice, public health, education, housing, and so forth. The institutional complexities and interdependencies that had captured advanced industrial society meant that social problems could no longer be assigned to piecemeal, multi-agency program approaches. America's most intractable problems were rooted in multiple causes and reinforced in complicated chains of interinstitutional interaction.

To signal a sharp break with past approaches, "antipoverty" was created as a new policy area; for the first time, the term "poverty" appeared as a program category in the congressional record. An antipoverty policy supplanted the customary dual focus on dependency and cyclical unemployment with the recognition of a persistent poverty, based in the multiple institutional barriers of "structural unemployment." To treat this complex of factors, federal policy planners attempted to weave such traditionally functional categories as health, housing, education, and labor, into a multifrontal "War on Poverty."

As the veterans of urban renewal discuss in Part One, the 1960s was also the period that first conceptualized the problem of "institutionalized discrimination," involving the recognition that racial and gender inequality were as often rooted in unintentional forms of institutional practice as overt discriminatory policies. There was increasing acknowledgment that federal housing and urban development programs failed to treat the interactive effects of slum clearance; without broader social policies, the poor would not benefit from housing construction or other physical improvements. Thereafter, American social policy turned to the need for *comprehensive* approaches.

The new focus on policy holism quickly posed a second dilemma: how should government re-organize itself to effectively treat complex issues— and, of equal importance, what was the most effective relationship between federal and local government? Many issues of institutional design and process arose, but no strategy was clarified.

Reformers sought to address problems along at least three lines. At the simplest level, social policy confronted the fragmentation and inconsistency of public administration at all levels. The Johnson administration created the Department of Housing and Urban Development (HUD) in 1965, largely in response to the unmanageable system of federal urban programs and grants-in-aid that had grown so rapidly in the late 1950s and early '60s.[14] Categorical constraints and bureaucratic confusion among disconnected efforts had created a crisis of implementation. Mayors and other members of the growing intergovernmental and urban lobby demanded relief from the inconsistent rules, delays, lack of funding and application procedures that prevented cities from accessing and implementing federal resources.

Moreover, the bureaucracy needed to be held accountable. Racial minorities and the poor lacked influence and access to political institutions. Thus, *political poverty* was targeted as a problem in its own right. Reformers sought means to pressure federal agencies and City Hall to be more responsive and to spend more resources on behalf of the poor. These themes combined to produce a powerful focus on reforming government bureaucracy—both federal and local.

---

[14]In a 1961 report, the U.S. Advisory Commission on Intergovernmental Relations counted more than 40 separate programs for urban development involving at least 13 different agencies. The number and size of grants-in-aid to state and local governments issued under these programs had also grown rapidly in the late 1950s and early '60s; in the period between 1960 and 1965, alone, funding rose from $7 billion to $11 billion, and the number of new grant authorizations more than doubled (Friedan and Kaplan, 1975: 15-18).

But there was a deeper, more insidious implication as well. Bureaucratic systems were themselves recognized as the cause of significant social inequalities. Policy critics in such areas as urban and regional development increasingly noted a vicious circle wherein the effects of one institutional arena produced unintended consequences in another.[15]

Thus, complexity involved something greater than a mechanical sense of "comprehensive policymaking." Intractable social syndromes—like urban decline, persistent area poverty or institutionalized discrimination—could not be solved by a simple "arithmetic" addition of separate remedies. Rather, the deeper insight concerned the importance of *interactive* effects between a variety of institutional, social, and economic conditions. Accordingly, a multiplicative approach was needed, whereby solutions in one area could boost change in another, so as to create positive, rather than negative, "opportunity structures."

The language of Paul Ylvisaker, one of the architects of the Ford Foundation's early "poverty programs," is evocative of the search for just such a chemistry of reform. He exhorted planners to search for ways to harness the "dynamic complexity of forces," rather than rely on the linear strategies of social engineering. (Sunquist, 1968). Later, Moynihan, serving as Nixon's social policy advisor, spoke of the search for a "bureaucratic jujitsu" (Moynihan, 1969). The reform theories of the period sought a process of creative initiative—an interplay between national and local, public and private, political and professional, self-help and alliance for the poor—all to move systemic change to reduce poverty and racial inequality.

But what would this mean in practice? What is striking is the inchoate nature of the new perspective.

Strategic Uncertainty

The policy theories of the period did not resolve a distinctive perspective on *how* to break into multi-institutional problems of an interlocking nature. The strategic uncertainty can be seen in the flurry of debates over how to design complex policy solutions.

At the federal level, a kaleidoscope of perspectives vied for how to proceed with the puzzles of bureaucratic reform and institutional change described above: to persuade Congress and federal agencies to concentrate resources and get more money to poor urban areas; to make state and local government agen-

---

[15]Policies to aid poor cities or regions were undermined by governmental actions issuing forth under other policy jurisdictions (as when transportation policies provided incentives for urban divestment through the suburban exodus of the residential, commercial, and industrial base).

cies more responsive to minorities and the poor in the cities; to encourage experimentation, innovation and reduce bureaucratic red tape; and to allow for
local flexibility—yet not alienate the existing power structure and defend the
accountability, research, and evaluation base.

At the local level, Model Cities actors, like their OEO predecessors, debated
at least four disparate strategies: to rationalize and coordinate governmental systems serving the poor; to decentralize and devolve the delivery of services; to
organize the poor to strengthen their "voice"; to advocate for, and catalyze
change in, the larger system. Within the empowerment camp alone there was a
major conflict between the ideas of "community control" vs. "institutional
change," as well as tension between those favoring stronger coordination and
increased bureaucratization, and others pushing for innovation through flexible,
responsive organization.

The need for multiple aspects of institutional change does not inherently
produce functional confusion, conflict or stalemate. Such goals as innovation,
coordination, community participation, and broad planning can be complemen-
tary, if there is a clear distinction between them. The issue is not that such goals
are mutually exclusive; but that each requires diverse capacities that no single
entity can possess. Indeed, effective mobilizations for social change demonstrate
a creative "division of organizational labor" and sequencing over time.

From this standpoint, it is clear that the core problem in the conception of
the Model Cities program, and in social policy innovations ever since, has been
the lack of a realistic developmental perspective regarding the complexity of
institutional changes needed to break entrenched cycles of persistent poverty and
racial inequality: to distinguish between different organizational roles, to identify the needed capacities, to match each to appropriate organizational vehicles,
and to weigh them against a realistic time frame and resource scale.

Indeed, sorting out these dimensions would have made clear that most of
the proposed melee of strategies were premature given the modest nature of the
opportunity at hand. It was not really plausible, e.g., that a demonstration program could move powerful, established administrations (whether at the federal
or local level) to systematically restructure objectives, expenditure patterns and
routine activities; established constituencies and professional viewpoints inevi-
tably would resist major change. Nor, could public and nonprofit organizations
realistically serve as the sole source for political organizing and mobilization at
the local level. The notion that Model Cities was an opportunity to decentralize
local government was similarly ungrounded; established local public agencies
would never voluntarily slip their budgets into the orbit of the Model Cities program's control, nor are "neighborhoods" a constitutive unit of government.

Without a concerted plan of attack, confusion in policy theory unleashed
widespread role and goal confusion in program practice. Indeed, the interviews

in this volume illustrate what happens under the weight of strategic disarray when undertaking institutional change and community building.

Confusion and Conflict over Complex Change

Federal planners could have parsed a division of labor and reasonable sequence for advancing multiple goals. Instead, the full weight of strategic confusion was attached to one organizational entity—the new Model Cities program. Trusting neither the federal nor the local bureaucracy to make the needed institutional changes, President Johnson's urban task force followed the model of administrative innovation set by OEO and Community Action. They established a new parallel coordinating body at the federal level (the Model Cities Administration, organized as a separate division within the newly established, cabinet-level Department of Housing and Urban Development), with counterpart administrations established at the local level (the City Demonstration Agencies).[16] Although Model Cities legislation firmly placed the CDAs under the control of City Hall, rather than in neighborhood entities as sometimes occurred under OEO, intergovernmental funding was still channeled through a new and separate programmatic silo.

The unfolding confusion was further heightened by the fact that the new organizational system for Model Cities not only had to handle goals of institutional change; it was also challenged by responsibilities for the administration and delivery of direct service programs. The local City Demonstration Agencies (CDAs) were even required to act as mini foundations, having been allocated funds that were to be granted to novel community programs. These programmatic responsibilities competed with the mission of "external advocate" and coordinator.

Model Cities history might have turned out differently had the grants been substantial enough to give the program a strong fiscal base for pressing local government and private interests in new directions. But again, as noted above

---

[16]A further set of parallel entities designed to support the Model Cities program, similarly saddled with multiple responsibilities, also had to struggle to establish themselves. Entirely new layers of federal interagency and intergovernmental mechanisms were introduced to urge cooperation and coordination: the Washington Interagency Review Committee, chaired by HUD, and designed to facilitate cooperation on Model Cities from the Departments of Labor (DOL), Health, Education and Welfare (HEW), and OEO; Regional and Local Interagency Working Groups intended to coordinate technical assistance and operational programs; and a HUD "lead man" assigned to each location to provide liaison between the localities and the federal agencies, and to monitor progress (Frieden and Kaplan, 1975).

John Sasso and Priscilla Foley

and notwithstanding grand rhetoric, the direct appropriations for the Model Cities program were quite small.[17]

It bears attention that some veteran community and governmental leaders held a developmental perspective. They tried to sort out the goals, identifying different levels of strategy. As described in Chapter 1, HUD Secretary in charge of Model Cities, H. Ralph Taylor, viewed the resources as, at best, "glue money," and former teacher turned Model Cities director in Little Rock, Nathaniel Hill, recalled that he "encouraged black people working in the program to use it as a stepping stone, a way to get experience and move on to something better." Experienced older African American community leaders, in both Oakland and San Francisco, accurately perceived that the scale of available resources was only sufficient to support brokering with established agencies. Such leaders tried to warn the younger activists that "community control" and major decentralization were not at hand.[18]

But the mixed messages of national policy continued to unleash confusion at the local level. Against President Johnson's promise of the "war to follow," the meager amount of funding available for Model Cities invited uncertainty. In many communities across the country, before the disillusionment created by a shift in resource allocation priorities set in, Model Cities was perceived as a launching pad for major reform—one that would enable communities to create "alternative institutions" to control antipoverty and community development programs, and to bypass and compete with local government. In Oakland, by way of example, a young and active leadership sought to construct their Model Cities program as nothing less than an "alternative City Hall." (May, 1973) Not unexpectedly, such divisions often generated conflict that overshadowed or sidelined desired reforms.

---

[17]The question was never clearly confronted because, as contributions to this volume express, the administration established a false expectation that influenced many at the national and local level. Despite the limits imposed by Kennedy's macroeconomic tax cut —it initially appeared that President Johnson intended a long-term antipoverty commitment. He viewed the Office of Economic Opportunity (OEO), and its attendant Community Action Agencies (CAPs), legislation as only the "first battle in the broader war on poverty" to follow—a view that extended to the inauguration of Model Cities as well. Accordingly, some expected a major expansion of federal spending, while in other minds, increased funding would require a major shift of priorities and allocation patterns under existing program expenditures. Still others did not address the question of resource scale at all, focusing on the search for nonbureaucratic approaches.

[18]See Judith May, "Struggle for Authority: A Comparison of Four Social Change Programs in Oakland, California" (Ph.D. Dissertation, University of California, Berkeley, 1975). These comments are also based on numerous field interviews conducted by Madeline Landau regarding the Model Cities' experience in Oakland and San Francisco, California (1980-82).

Due to the failure to resolve basic parameters, Model Cities programs inherited a fatal uncertainty about their relation to the existing governmental environment: i.e., were they responsible for coordinating and monitoring activities across the maze of local governmental agencies—or only for the planning and allocation of those funds directly administered under their own "sand-box" programs? Were the new units intended to substitute for, supplement, or catalyze change within the established program administrations? These questions were never answered, and the relation between the innovations and the existing institutional environment was left ambiguous.

Not surprisingly, factions embracing one or another of these perspectives characterized both federal and local level operations. The oral histories in Part Two elaborate the local conflicts, while the interviews in Part One bespeak the tensions among various factions at the federal planning level, over such issues as: city government versus neighborhood control; a functional emphasis on social goals or operational administration; reducing the size of federal government vs. ensuring an adequate program capacity; and keeping the number of sites small and concentrating resources vs. dispersing them to build political support. As Model Cities evolved, its participants—both at the local and national levels—continually shifted emphasis in their efforts to define the program.

The experimentation with institutional change as a vital aspect in reducing poverty did not end with Model Cities. It has run as an uninterrupted theme from the earliest deliberations of the CAP and Model Cities, through the Community Development Block Grant (CDBG) "neighborhood district councils" created in the Nixon and Carter years, to the "community governance boards" of the Clinton Administration's Empowerment Zone & Enterprise Communities Initiative. Social policy has continued to call for policy changes that implicate complex, multi-organizational dynamics: from urban development to regional revenue sharing and growth management; from child removal and foster care to family preservation; from service dependency to economic self-sufficiency; from "delinquent careers" to mainstreaming; from bureaucratic modes to participatory and responsive planning. Each effort has been associated with organizational innovations that were straddled with similar functional and role confusions at the federal, intergovernmental and local levels alike.

To this day, social policy reformism remains in limbo: torn between the need for multi-organizational, long-term strategy and the search for what that means in practical terms. Here, taking a deeper look at how Model Cities veterans utilized a modest program helps shed light on ways to close the gap.

II. Model Cities as a Broker Organization: Rethinking the Organizational Continuum for Institutional Change

If small experimental programs like Model Cities could not themselves re-structure government, aggregate political power for the poor, or change the broad direction of social policy—what could they realistically achieve?

Of the many roles imposed on the fledgling Model Cities organization, a practical assessment shows that one was successful: that of institutional catalyst and broker. The histories in this volume identify the value of establishing an organizational "infrastructure" for promoting institutional changes that, in turn, supports the development of longer-term policy change and economic opportunity. A focus on questions of infrastructure is crucial because the usual perspective on institutional change misrepresents the nature of coordination, participation, and access—treating them as "methods" for social change when they, themselves, constitute objectives difficult to achieve in their own right .

Such institutional changes involve a great deal of adjustment, alliance, and re-orientation. They involve reconfiguring routine practices, incentives and interests so as to accommodate excluded groups; or finding ways to redefine diverse interests in mutually beneficial terms. Where interest conflicts prove intractable, outcomes depend upon the capacity for a measure of brokerage and bargaining. Without such operational capacities, even the best policy directives and legal mandates go unenforced. The old adage holds: the capacity to legislate is not the same as the capacity to implement and sustain. Here, the quality of the underlying infrastructure of connective networks, brokers, and organizations is key.

A strong interorganizational infrastructure assists the formulation of effective legal mandates or policy change. The channels for communication, trouble-shooting, and problem identification it provides offer invaluable feedback for targeting policy directives on the important operational bottlenecks, for identifying the relevant pressure points, and for selecting the appropriate "carrots" and "sticks." This kind of sensitive targeting is too frequently missing in the design of formal initiatives.

Building Bridges and Connective Networks

It was in this underappreciated area, which can be referred to as the building of "broker organization," that many Model Cities programs took important steps towards developing a connective infrastructure for long-term change.

It bears repeating that the gulf between poor neighborhoods and local government was wide. Administrative and political systems were fundamentally not oriented to the problems of poor nonwhite urban neighborhoods, while in turn, these communities lacked access to the major political and policy systems that affected them. In this light, many Model Cities activities can be seen as laying the organizational groundwork for closing these gaps. Creating a connective infrastructure entailed many dimensions: establishing institutional allies and policy knowledge for isolated low-income communities; implementing success-ful projects that could earn wider political legitimacy; and creating career lad-ders for talented neighborhood leaders. (Brown and Erie, 1981).

Limited funds were used to leverage interagency resources and build rela-tionships with other departments, to influence new projects on an incremental basis, and to use nonprofit contracts to fill gaps, deliver familiar services in more effective ways, or provide referral services for residents. The local Model Cities programs also served as the community's portal to local government. They operated as conduits for establishing contacts between remote agencies and nonwhite neighborhoods, for training community leadership in governmen-tal affairs, for educating residents about administrative opportunities and con-straints, and for innovating ways for bureaucracies to stretch standard program menus and modify their styles of working with unfamiliar communities.

The Model Cities veterans in this volume speak directly to these functions. They are brokers who read the environment of relations between government and community—and established channels of mutual legitimacy. The interviews reveal a shrewd recognition of different institutional contexts: ranging from cit-ies that lacked any prior tradition of community services to politically crowded cities where politicized community leaders opposed City Hall; from cities with weak ties to the private sector to those with stronger traditions of public-private cooperation; and from cities with prior contacts and experience with federal agencies to those with little or no orientation to national urban policy.

The roles of broker organization, however, are often invisible and under-appreciated by social change activists. It is not widely understood that, in many cities, the development of governmental networks and niches complemented, rather than substituted for, political organizing, as e.g., in Mount Vernon, N.Y. There, Model Cities staff helped African American community leaders gain the policy sophistication needed to advance the electoral influence of a community long controlled by white suburban interests.

In cities such as Newark, San Francisco, Dayton, and Tucson, where com-munities were strongly organized—Model Cities staff moved to translate and negotiate between activists and City Hall. The need for this intermediary role is well recognized in the theory of successful social movements. Lipsky, e.g., has shown the indispensable role of "street level bureaucrats" in translating the de-mands of New York City's rent strikes into feasible bureaucratic responses. (Lipsky, 1970, 1980).

In regions that lacked traditions of policy mobilization such as Des Moines, Gainsville, or Little Rock, Model Cities staff created the first venues for educating the community about the nature of potential opportunity, and the options for directing demands. Here, anthropological studies of Third World development confirm that intermediate organizations and brokers are pivotal in the formation of constituency organization; political and bureaucratic brokers help communities define their "interest" and select appropriate tactics.

Abstracting from these experiences, we see that the functions of *broker organization* cover a wide continuum: "translating" general policies into the practical terms of the established environment and organizing opportunities for cooperation; bypassing the rigidities of the formal process and negotiating unofficial agreements; resolving conflicts and mediating political stalemates; and facilitating a flow of information across the complex urban landscape in ways that enable participants to identify opportunities and mobilize a timely response.

How should such functions be classified within the framework of public policy and administration? Again, they do not quite fall under the familiar headings of program administration or political representation. Indeed, these categories miss the point: the essence of brokerage is the ability to cross the boundaries *between* domains in a myriad of small, facilitating ways. The officials profiled in this collection were brokers at the borders of bureaucracy and community— flying below the radar of either the formal administrative or political process.

But while the language of the period called for a flexible and negotiative capacity, reform discourse did not articulate boundary-crossing and translation as a distinctive territory. This missing of the mark owes to the fact that notions of intermediate organization, infrastructure, brokerage, and "subsystems" were simply not recognized as independent elements in the organizational continuum for institutional and community development.

The following conceptual discussion is offered to help fix these ideas in the practical vocabulary of policy planning and administration.

The Concept of Intermediate Organization

There are concepts and perspectives in organization theory that capture the community and institutional brokerage that occurred under Model Cities and help complete an understanding of the organizational continuum for institutional and community change.

The standard notion of linkage between and among agencies and communities too often reverts back to a mechanical notion of coordination and participation. The ideal is to make all contacts and linkages formal and to "integrate" them within a rationalized, streamlined, and transparent system of public administration. All functions are to be clearly defined, specialized, and brought under one decision-making hierarchy.

All levels of American government have experimented with constructing such "comprehensive" systems of management via merged delivery districts, super-agencies, policy czars, and interdepartmental governance bodies. Their objective is to ensure that all information flows upward, enabling executive authorities to plan consistent, comprehensive programs. Following Model Cities, many cities have, for example, created super-agencies for community development, merging various departmental functions under a single authority. Some reorganized service delivery by establishing "neighborhood service districts," and geographically based interagency teams. In theory, such entities might produce increased agency coordination and open feedback channels between staff and neighborhoods. But in practice, such reorganizations are rarely completed: independent districts, special projects and/or politically powerful administrations resist merger, and a great deal of time, energy and resources are expended on an unrealistic ideal. Invariably, important functions fall outside the designated jurisdiction. Of equal importance, reorganizations frequently disrupt the valuable networks that have informally evolved to work the system. Effective brokers exit the system when they can no longer operate, forcing planners to re-invent lost linkages.

For these and other reasons, the use of "integrated systems" models has not proven to be an effective method for producing coordination in complex interorganizational fields. Calls for interagency mergers and regional government, e.g., have proven to be politically and institutionally unrealistic (Chisholm, 1989; U.S. GAO, 1992). As Franklin Raines notes, the Model Cities experience taught at least some veteran planners *not* to build "monolithic systems." Alternatively, social science research has found that a great deal of informal coordination occurs through systems of trusted brokers or voluntary, person to person ties. These act as auxiliary channels to official decision making and action— offering "back channels" for innovative practice, negotiation, and mutual adjustment.[19]

One of the most effectively coordinated systems of public administration is found in the formally decentralized, fragmented, and competitive set of independent public transit agencies in the San Francisco Bay Area. There, a set of cross-agency brokers, informally referred to as "portals," evolved dozens of operational protocols regarding such problems as overcrowding, mechanical breakdowns, fires, natural disasters, environmental hazards, and so forth, These unofficial agreements were respected, but not codified, by formal management

---

[19]See, e.g., one of the seminal pieces, Mark Granovettor, "The Strength of Weak Ties" in *American Journal of Sociology*, 1973, 78(6): 1360-80.

systems. Ironically, on all indices, Bay Area transportation system was judged more coordinated than the formally integrated systems in Boston and Washington, D.C. (Landau, Chisholm and Webber, 1980). Studies of economic development report similar findings. The distinctive factor in the relative success of Silicon Valley over Massachusetts's Route 128—two industrial complexes that were structurally equivalent regarding levels of capital investment, technical expertise, and proximity to consumer markets and qualified labor—was the presence of informal networks linking companies to each other, to universities, professional associations, and other relevant institutions (Saxenian, 1996).

These subsystems are known as *intermediate organization* because they lie between relationships that are purely personal and social, and those that are institutionally prescribed, official, and formal. They can be contrasted with formal organizations in that their processes are not fully established, rules are not exact, authority is ambiguous, communication channels are diverse and overlapping. Intermediate organizations also tend to be openly pluralistic, small in size, and permit a flexible social space to their participants.[20]

Intermediate organizations are a broad phenomena: subsystems of person to person cooperative ties may develop within the public, private, or civic sector—and do so within, as well as across, all levels. They are found in many policy settings, as illustrated by such familiar assistance networks as police informant pools, informal juvenile "diversion" networks to schools, parents and churches, informal labor recruitment pools, executive golf buddies, alumni groups, and political support networks. "Street-level bureaucrats" from neighborhood-sited agencies (such as park and recreation staff, branch librarians and schools nurses) formerly operated as powerful connective networks that eased community formation during the great African American urban migrations of the 1920s and '40s.

The informal cooperation these produce suggests a different model of "coordination" known as *loosely coupled* systems. (Chisholm, 1989; Landau, 1971). This mode of coordination does not assume the need for integration, comprehensive planning, or consensus over goals among diverse, and often competitive, organizations (a condition that is politically and economically difficult to attain). To the contrary, as agencies or organizations formally pursue their independent

---

[20]For further theoretical discussion in public administration literature, see Martin Landau, "Linkage Coding and Intermediacy: A Strategy for Institution Building," *Journal of Comparative Administration*, February 1971: 401-29. See also extensive discussion in the anthropological literature regarding the role of linkage and brokerage, in e.g., Eric Wolf "Kinship, Friendship and Patron Client Relations in Complex Society" in Michael Banton (ed.), *The Social Anthropology of Complex Societies*, New York: Tavistock Publications, 1969; J. Clyde Mitchell, *Social Networks in Urban Situations*, New York: Humanities Press, 1969; and S. Schmidt, L. Guasti, C. Landre, and J. Scott, *Friends, Followers and Factions: A Reader in Political Clientelism*, Berkeley: UC Press, 1977.

interests and operations—informal relations, at another level, find points of flexibility, and leverage opportunities for mutual benefit. Loosely coupled systems do not operate on the notion that all organizational action must be aligned; multiple levels of formal and informal action may occur simultaneously. Some exchanges flow directly back and forth between all participants. At other times, unofficial brokers who are widely recognized and respected, yet do not hold formal representative roles, serve as third-party "ambassadors." Such third parties meet with various interests and facilitate negotiations among them when direct ties between parties are lacking.

The connective power of informal brokerage is illustrated by the former director of a park and recreation center in Oakland's African American community (De Fremery Park). For decades, Bill Patterson operated as a consummate community broker who created an extensive loosely coupled system of ties connecting West Oakland residents to a wide array of institutional resources and contacts. Patterson also served as president of the local NAACP chapter. He leveraged these ties to link neighborhood youth and families to local, regional, and even national African American businessmen, elected officials, lawyers, athletes, and civil rights leaders. In summary, the center operated as an extraordinary channel for exposing neighborhood youth to broader educational, occupational, and leadership opportunities. Yet, none of its creative exchanges (of resources, projects, events, and innovative activities) were dictated by the center's official recreation function; they were all informally brokered. Unfortunately, this network was terminated when an "efficiency" conscious city council deemed its extracurricular activities to "duplicate" the role of other departments.[21]

This volume provides many similar examples, indicating that Model Cities Program staff and participants at all governmental levels initiated, cajoled, experimented, and educated across boundaries. In short, they assumed *developmental*, not merely managerial, roles. They dealt with uncertain means, ambiguous contexts, and novel ends. They brokered disputes between agencies and communities, and among factions within each sector—sometimes exercising an "administrative diplomacy" that bridged gaps in unexpected ways.

Whereas formal coordination efforts seek the contractual participation of "direct stakeholders," natural brokers and networks deliberately engage the "missing middle," i.e., neutral overlapping interests who, precisely because they possess common connections to disputing parties, can act as third parties to buffer conflicts. Third parties and crosscutting networks, thus, increase the capacity for negotiation and bargaining. Building in many alternative organiza-

---

[21]Interview with Bill Patterson, former drector of De Fermery Park, and president of Oakland Chapter of the NAACP, May 2003.

tions strengthens the connective infrastructure; if any one pathway breaks down, other *back channels* are available.

Such configurations are a key factor in successful economic development, community development, labor market recruitment, social movement formation, political coalition building—as well as public administration. Organization theory teaches that systems of intermediate organization are critical for implementing both managerial and democratic goals; they are operational systems of error detection, problem solving, conflict identification, negotiation, and whistle blowing.

Specialized Linkages

As reformers recognize the impracticalities of re-organization and rationalization, they have searched for alternative ways to strengthen connections within the existing outlines of the governmental system. But the potential value of informal links and intermediate organizations has not been widely incorporated in the modalities of public design. Instead, emphasis has centered on the creation of a specialized set of formal entities (or procedures) whose sole purpose is to organize connections for a given policy area or program goal. These have taken the form of "collaborative" bodies that bring a cross section of participants into direct contact with each other (such as advisory and review boards, interagency councils, and community governance structures). They also include the creation of specialized brokers and third-party instruments, (such as liaison officers, coordinating agencies, and ombudsmen and "program intermediaries"). Neighborhood-level efforts have been further replicated within and between higher agency levels. Here, too, public administration has experimented with a wide variety of intermediate organizational structures ranging from inter-agency "governance" bodies, through multiservice teams and citizen advisory boards, to consumer advocate councils.

Studies of governmental innovation, however, have shown that when they are effective, specialized mechanisms turn out to reflect and consolidate, rather than generate, traditions of consultation and coalition (Light, 1996 and 1992). Nor has the presence of strong legal provisions (e.g., requiring sign-off of impacted interests or multiple jurisdictions) been shown to be the primary factor in producing positive outcomes. Legal mandates have too often been undercut by costly counter-claims, gridlock, and increased conflict, as, e.g., in cases of environmental impact and other land-use planning legislation that lack prior investment in organizing, negotiation, and coalition building.

Disappointing outcomes arise because the specialized approach misses the essential feature possessed by organizational systems with high linkage capacity: i.e., auxiliary channels and informal connections. The value of loosely coupled systems, brokers and intermediate organizations is precisely that such informal relationships lie outside the formal hierarchy; and are therefore positioned to bypass or escape the rigidities of the formal process.

To advance social equity in institutional opportunity, the most important kinds of loosely coupled systems are those that develop between groups and institutions of unequal power and resources. Such brokerage and linkage is often taken as "dependency" because formal equality is missing. But valuable exchanges between those of higher and lower status (regarding information and assistance) create interdependencies that confer some real bargaining power to those in weaker positions. When the role of informal, discretionary, and personal-based behavior under public office goes too far, however, we speak of corruption, bias, unfairness, and so forth. And we call for "transparency." Thus, the challenge for a multi-ethnic, complex public administration is to achieve a balance between formal and informal ties in situations of inequality.

To this end, we further need to understand that informal subsystems, "intermediate organizations," or "loosely coupled systems," vary in the structure of network participation; and not all variations are positive. Informal ties can be monopolized by certain factions; for example, exclusion from the "old boys network" is a major source of operational inequality for women and minorities. In other cases, factionalized sets of informal ties operate—undermining formal dealings and producing gridlock. We must also contend with policy environments where linkages among agencies and between government, community, and the business sector are virtually undeveloped. And we may also face settings characterized by too many linkages, i.e., where a proliferation of self-proclaimed "intermediaries" operate, linkages are not reinforced, and do not cross-fertilize. These fragmented linkages produce clientelism rather than the civic capacity needed to coordinate collective ends.

For these reasons, it may be worth noting that the popular application of the idea of "social capital" is misleading. It has been associated with an indiscriminate call for building "relationships" and "networks" that ignores crucial differences in structure and capacity.[22] In its popular translation, attention is overfocused on the personal quality of relationships, rather than the conditions under which they perform productive or counterproductive links of exchange.

By understanding these differences, we are moved from questions of administrative structure, alone, to the nature of the auxiliary networks and channels that aid or thwart formal organizational process. The idea of this interaction be-

---

[22]For one of the original formulations of social capital, see, e.g., Robert Putnam's *Making Democracy Work* (1993) Princeton, N.J.: Princeton University Press, which does acknowledge distinctions between exclusionary and boundary crossing networks.

tween the formal and informal is what the '60s quest for a "bureaucratic jujitsu" really sought to capture.

Through the 1960s, strong national and local political parties, large nationally federated civic membership organizations, strong local community and ethnic-based institutions, and stable street-level bureaucrats provided informal avenues of communication, resource exchange, and political support for poor and discriminated groups and communities. Although insufficient for overcoming structural poverty and inequality—such relationships aided community life while supplying the infrastructure for negotiating coalition-building for broader redistributive policies. But we now operate in a period where much, if not most, of this civic base has declined (Skocpol, 2000; Putnam, 2000).

Of course, public administrative and policy design cannot revitalize civic institutions and networks alone. Nonetheless, governmental actions and resources can play a significant role if governmental planners can learn to work with informal and associational capacities—both to reinforce positive connections and to interrupt those that perpetuate inequities.

The next section raises some options for further consideration.

III. Towards a "Developmental Public Administration"

Skeptics may well argue that a focus on linkage building diverts attention from advocacy for the substantive national and state social programs needed to solve poverty. In this view, restructuring policies to offer broad-based benefits is the best way to create cohesive capacity for social policy. A policy context of inclusive benefits—such as national health insurance, a livable minimum wage, and fair housing—would inherently build-in the desired cooperation we seek between groups and institutions.[23] Likewise, the difficult task of weaving metropolitan-suburban agreements for "smart growth" and regional equity could be averted by broad public policies for open space preservation, adequate housing support, public transportation and so forth.[24] Or, barring political support for mounting major policy change—we could regulate, restructure, or give monetary incentives to drive behavioral change within current institutional frame-

---

[23]See, for example, Ira Katznelson, "Was the Great Society a Lost Opportunity?" in Steven Fraser and Gary Gerstle (eds.), *The Rise and Fall of the New Deal Order 1930-1980*, Princeton, N.J.: Princeton University Press, 1989, 185-211; and Alice O'Connor's *Poverty Knowledge: Social Science, Social Policy and the Poor in 20th Century U.S. History,*. Princeton, N.J.: Princeton University Press, 2001.

[24]See, e.g., Robert Gottleib, Mark Vallianatos, Regina Freer, and Peter Dreier, *The Next Los Angeles: The Struggle for a Livable City*, Los Angeles: University of California Press, 2005.

works, (e.g., regulatory requirements for citizen and interagency review, administrative mechanisms such as "Little City Halls," multi-agency governance bodies and consumer councils).

These are, of course, crucial policy goals and progressive agendas should be supported. Such views, however, assume that rational incentives—be they the threat of legal sanctions or the promise of program benefits—are sufficient motivation for groups and institutions to work together. But, as developed throughout this discussion, studies of public administration and policy have, time and again, challenged the theory that formal structure and law are adequate to confer organizational capacity.

Indeed, as noted above, research on bureaucratic change, social change, and social movements confirm that administrative and legal innovations produce desired changes in institutional behavior when they consolidate established political and institutional capacities, rather than create them *de novo*.[25] Building the informal capacity for adjustment and mediation, incubation and innovation, however, is a distinctive task; one that is *developmental*, rather than programmatic, in nature.

Investments in formal and informal capacities are certainly not mutually exclusive approaches. Regulatory and administrative mandates are powerful tools. But formal design ignores the operations of informal organization to the peril of effective policymaking. The tendency for formal initiatives to overshoot or undershoot operational problems is well illustrated by the efforts of a large regional corporation in the Bay Area to equalize opportunities for African American subcontractors. Although the company gave full support to the venture—constructing an executive-level office, and transparent procedures to open the subcontracting process—little progress was made towards redistributing the pattern of opportunity. Closer examination revealed that the negative outcome derived from the fact that most contract decisions were actually made by mid-level managers who, operating informally, utilized the "old boys networks" they had cultivated over time. Progress, therefore, required a pointed intervention that went beyond a blanket procedure: either to carefully craft opportunities for African American contractors to penetrate informal systems—or, to police such referral systems and eliminate them. Thus, at times, interventions targeting the weakest areas of linkage, the most intractable factions, or network monopolies, may be more relevant than uniform applications of legal or administrative reform.

---

[25]See aforementioned research on governmental innovations by Paul Light (1996 and 1992). For a discussion of the interaction between policy opportunity and political organization, see, e.g., collected essays in Jack Goldstone, *States Parties and Social Movements*, New York: Cambridge University Press, 2003.

If the creation of formal rules or specialized structures for coordination, participation, and cooperation is not sufficient for building operational linkage capacity—what is the role of social policy in revitalizing strategic connections—politically and institutionally? How can public policy help isolated communities effectively link to the broader institutional environment? One answer is for administrative and policy design to learn to better harness the interactions between the formal and the informal: specifically, to help cultivate subsystems of intermediate organization where they are weak, interrupt them where they are counterproductive, and reinforce their capacities where they effectively operate. While a full response to these questions is beyond the scope of this discussion, a few comments are offered here.

Administrative Design as Network Strategy

Neither community, private or public sector environments are a blank canvas regarding systems of informal organization; to different degrees, internal niches, networks, and factions are always present; and these present opportunities and obstacles. A *developmental public administration* would therefore invest in building a conceptual vocabulary that distinguishes differences in the structure of social networks and intermediate organizations. If we are to embed program planning and implementation in effective connections, policymakers and administrative designers must gain deeper insight in the operational environment. Linkage reforms so often fall short because they are indiscriminately applied.

Once identified, policy designers and public administrators can develop practical strategies for working with network factors. A few approaches are suggested to help point the way for further work in the field:

In general, linking low-income communities and excluded groups can be moved through the routine practices of public administration as well as through "social change" initiatives. The key idea for a developmental public administration is make decisions that do "double duty," i.e., that balance technical and managerial needs with network development. Many areas of organizational and administrative design have impacts on network formation; and they can be harnessed to enhance linkage capacity. These areas include project selection and siting, choice of program provider and administrative jurisdiction, personnel policy; as well as the criteria for nonprofit and private contracting and evaluation.

The idea is to make design decisions that not only satisfy program needs, but also contribute to the cumulative strength of cross-sector ties in a given community or policy environment. For example, altering personnel rules to favor staff continuity and community contact can incentivize the development of stable cadres of "street level bureaucrats" in line agencies and neighborhood branches. The leadership talent reflected in this volume demonstrates the benefits that can result from such modest alterations in administrative practice: through flexible hiring and contracting rules, Model Cities was able to attract a dynamic mix of community activists, business entrepreneurs, political organizers and academics, and minorities and women who had no prior experience, or aspirations for governmental careers—many of whom are included here.[26]

Moreover, many network opportunities do not even require systematic changes in rules or procedures; they can be moved through sensitive and creation application of existing rules, if administrators and policymakers understand the organizational and political environment. This approach seeks to take advantage of existing networks. Here, policy and program planners can work to "socially embed" new program organizations by mapping implementation decisions onto existing network centers, so as to incorporate their strengths in formal program design.

For example, "the homeless" are generally taken as a homogenous social group. But Paul Bowden, long-time advocate and former director of San Francisco's Coalition for Homelessness, described the presence of several natural subsystems within the "homeless community."[27] Each subgroup had evolved its own "loosely coupled system" linking to a distinctive set of community institutions, public agencies, and bureaucratic brokers. The religious-oriented homeless were concentrated in faith-based networks; homeless families tended to work well with schools and social work agencies; while homeless veterans were associated with less structured organizations that shared a common "veterans" subculture. Bowden's recommendations for effective program design respected, and built upon, this three-track system—resisting popular consolidation models and the bias toward a "seamless system of care." Mapping program resources onto existing "centers of gravity" allows government to extend tendrils into relevant social niches; avoiding the tendency to establish too many linkages, or too few.

Alternatively, where natural linkages are underdeveloped in a given policy arena, planners may be able to "annex" organizations or networks from other policy environments that possess the missing community or administrative ties;

---

[26]In particular, many of the Model Cities leaders who moved on to the higher office possessed backgrounds that involved a cross-over from social movement activism to the public service—a fact that testifies to the value of the cross-cutting networks and skills contributed by their multisectoral experience. Indeed, the participants in this oral history were teachers, coaches and homemakers, activist priests, war veterans, student activists and civil rights organizers for CORE, SCLC, SNCC, and progressive political organizations.

[27]Interview with Paul Bowden, in San Francisco, California, 1998.

i.e., borrowing the "social capital" of one field and applying it to another through creatively engaging unconventional partners in program activities. Although these unexpected combinations may defy the usual flowchart, they constitute preemptive strategies for avoiding the high cost of implementation failures.

These and other ways to do administrative "double-duty," prioritizing social as well as technical capacities in the implementation process, is particularly important for the poor and other excluded groups. When the participation of disadvantaged groups is directed into narrow and segregated channels, they are made dependent on single points of entry. There is little opportunity for leveraging contacts made in one institutional arena for the purposes of another. Specialized linkage strategies for the poor are too vulnerable and easily reversed.

Cultivating Brokers, Back Channels and Third Parties

Another fruitful area for re-orienting policy and administrative design concerns the network effects of the way in which processes for policy consultation and public involvement process are structured. Just as policy designers can learn to consider the particular way in which service delivery links, or fail to links, to community networks—the issue of "network embedding" extends to the design of policy consultation. In a sense, all phases of the administrative process potentially broker or exclude connections for the poor—and thus the particular patterns of linkage that are established between institutions, public programs and excluded communities are critical considerations. These patterns can be as important for long-term institutional change and policy development, as program and policy substance.

A particularly important nexus concerns how the structure of civic participation distorts or enhances the composition and dynamic of participation itself. Increasingly all levels of government have moved from "back room" legislating to requirements for public consultation and open deliberation. But the design of these public involvement processes does not necessarily build organizational capacity for subordinate interests.

Designers can be on the alert for a number of "network pathologies" that can potentially arise: First, the structure of consultative processes can limit participation to only those parties that routinely connect to antipoverty programs: i.e., to the extended policy apparatus of professional consultants, "innovative" soft-money programs, issue advocates, think- tanks, and nonprofit contract providers. Many public hearings and planning councils are dominated by those with material stakes in the policy industry.

Another network pattern concerns the engagement of random and marginal-ized individuals or groups, who bring little or no organizational capacity to the process. It has been observed that representatives of well-connected groups or networks tend not to participate in public consultation venues, communicating their positions through respected intermediaries who operate at higher levels. In effect, public involvement venues sometimes become a substitute channel for those who lack access to the "real" political process. Directing the participation of low-income groups and minorities to marginal arenas, perpetuates their ex-clusion from the contexts in which major political brokerage occurs.

But even when government seeks to avoid these distortions, by promoting civic engagement among significant constituencies and institutional players, the formats that are employed are not conducive to building effective long-term channels. As the policy environment has grown increasingly complex and uncer-tain under the weight of technical knowledge and the proliferation of issue groups—policymakers have recognized the need to invest in civic broker build-ing as a condition of effective policy formulation and implementation. It is rec-ognized that the local, regional, or national policy environment may lack the organizational capacity to broker coherent directions; a predicament that can arise from opposite conditions: (1) where the environment is dominated by nar-row factions, while the majority of interests remain inactive; or (2) where a plethora of shifting and unaccountable claimants, unattached to broad-based constituencies, vie for legitimacy.

In a sense, both scenarios present network pathologies for the policymaker. The first, because domination by factional networks resists mediation, tends to exclude flexible views, and imposes polarized definitions of the policy options; while in the second, too great an ease of entry for participants, that lack shared context and ties, ushers in a myriad of confused views and dilutes the possibility of coherent definition.

In both cases, design strategy can try to bring the "missing middle" back in: i.e., recruiting organized interests, brokers, and networks that contribute a stable base, and frame, for negotiation. Promoting such brokerage and intermediate organization is, of course, not an unfamiliar idea in the governmental repertoire. In the social policy area, local, state, and federal agencies have funded civic and policy roundtables, nonprofit think-tanks and planning councils for purposes of cross-sector deliberation in such areas as antipoverty, quality public education, sustainable health, regionalism, and violence prevention.

But the formation of such bodies is frequently premature. Their mission calls for a rich developmental process—one of public education, institutional reorientation, issue redefinition, and policy incubation, as well as the cultivation of trusted brokers and boundary-spanning leaders. But, once again, such efforts are typically tied to responsibilities for producing short-term policy consensus, legislative recommendations, or other tangible outcomes. These pressures defeat the very purpose of intermediate organizations: there is no time for strategic targeting of the participant networks to occur; nor, for cultivating a reinforcement of ties through overlapping organizational involvements. As a result, the "missing middle" is not incorporated, or incorporated in trivial and episodic ways; inclusion is opportunistic, limited to short-term payoff. Not surprisingly, research has shown, "civic participation" bodies tend to reflect, rather than overcome, the fragmentation of the environment; their networks replicate the sectoral ties that formed them. Few new bridges are built (Walsh, 1997).

Alternative approaches to cultivating effective network development include investments in cosponsored projects that advance real, practical reciprocities between government, communities, and targeted groups and institutions; that intrinsically redefine the way in which institutions perceive their interest and "role."

Second, greater attention can be paid to how policy and administrative design influences patterns of constituency group formation to begin with. (Landau and Gilbert, 2004). Increasingly, both legislative and administrative actions have sought to cultivate representation within constituency groups, on the recognition that many sectors are underorganized or lack leadership with an orientation to public policy cooperation. Investments in "community-building" and "leadership development" for low-income groups, and sector organizing and consensus building are not uncommon. For example, initiatives create or contract nonprofit intermediaries to convene the small business sector, e.g., to unify support for policy initiatives. But here again, if government invents or selects intermediaries with no sense of the network implications they carry (i.e., the network niches they may occupy within their own domains), there is no telling what connective strengths or limitations may accrue.

In contrast, the most effective way to build strategic connections in a given sector involves assessment and targeting—to identify promising individuals, groups, or network clusters; and to find ways to engage their involvement. Moreover, such ways need not emphasize official policy participation or representation: Instead, relationships can be cultivated indirectly, e.g., by cosponsoring concrete projects, or through initiating reciprocity exchanges over matters of practical interest. These grounded approaches avoid the disconnected contexts of "policy visioning." Instead, as noted above, tangible traditions of cooperation are put in place. Such settings offer natural opportunities for talented individuals, within or outside government, to evolve as policy brokers— avoiding the need for invention from the top-down or inside-out.

One reason that design decisions do not experiment with such targeted network strategies is the argument that government should not be in the business of picking winners and losers. In principle, an open process allows transparent participation. But as suggested here, the proceduralist approach to "civic administration" offers a false neutrality: all formal designs exclude certain networks and favor other, as rules interact with the operational subsystems in each domain.

This is the informal implication of formal design that public administration must learn to read, and to find proactive ways to steer in positive directions. Such efforts need not be arbitrary, or unaccountable, if they are undertaken to serve public policy objectives, i.e., to increase equitable outcomes. In other words, a focus on participation is a means to substantive policy outcomes, not merely a procedural end. The goal is to employ the process of public involvement to advance meaningful access and attachment for excluded groups by addressing network barriers and cultivating opportunities.

This is where the idea of building in back channels, third parties, and overlap is so fruitful; nearly any network distortion—factionalism, monopoly, or instability—can be mitigated through incorporating these capacities.

From the standpoint of avoiding negative outcomes, it bears repeating that supplementary channels provide an early warning system for identifying operational problems. Additionally, the development of overlapping networks frees our systems of public administration from a continual need to "innovate" and reorganize boundaries, every time a new connection is warranted.

Such auxiliary capacity can also be located inside a formal bureaucratic organization. For example, when serving as executive director of the Peace Corps, Sargent Shriver introduced a supplementary system of executive reporting within the official administrative structure: a series of roving "field monitors" who reported directly to the national office, and bypassed the official management hierarchy. This provided a back channel for information exchange and conflict resolution in a vast international field.

It doesn't matter whether independent and supplementary channels are built within or outside of the administrative system. The important point is that resources allocated to such entities and processes must be understood and monitored in appropriate terms. For example, in the late 1990s, HUD attempted to build intermediate organizations through its Community Builder program—only to then evaluate the new field operators according to standard program criteria; measures by which, many appeared to fail.[28] Perhaps the Community Building program was not designed to best produce loosely coupled systems in the field. But if so, disappointing outcomes most likely owed, as in Model Cities, to the prevailing confusion between broker roles and substantive program goals, and the failure to honor the differences in organizational strategy that they require.

---

[28]Personal interviews with HUD Region IX Community Builders representatives, Keith Axtell, Natalie Bayton, and Jay Smith, 1999.

Conclusion

For forty or more years, we have recognized that poverty reduction and urban revitalization must tackle structural issues—rooted in global and domestic
capital flows, labor market policies, and land-use patterns. But even the passage
of more equitable labor market, industrial, and land-use policies would not
themselves bridge the gap between institutional operations and excluded groups.
Significant change in social policy poses a challenge that is fundamentally organizational in nature, requiring supportive interactions between complex development processes. What is really at stake is something more than the enactment of powerful laws and policies; deep change requires the institutionalization
of new patterns of interaction within old systems—or the building of new ones.

Cross-cutting linkages are one of the greatest assets of an effective system
of public administration—one that public policy must learn to defend against
misdefinition. The trick for future policy is to learn from the misnomers and
mismatched expectations that strangled Model Cities, and that continue to sty-
mie efforts at "system change" and "community change" today. As a field, public administration must sharpen its understanding of the difference between a
long-term investment in strengthening institutional linkages for excluded
groups, and the short-term implementation of particular program initiatives.
They are not the same; linkage development requires strategic investment in its
own right.

The lack of a long-term orientation to building institutional capacity has led
to a "hyper-innovation" that introduces layers of disconnected linkage mechanisms and organizational innovations for each and every new program initiative
(Landau, 1988), especially those, such as Model Cities, that proclaim "comprehensive solutions," coordination, and citizen participation. As these proliferate,
policy design invariably swings back to "integration" models. Public administration must find ways to reduce these costly cycles. Reduction is such a critical
step because the instability and competition introduced by ever shifting intermediaries and innovations have themselves become one of the biggest obstacles to
nurturing effective linkage.

From a broader perspective, long-term commitments require a re-
legitimization of the role of government itself. The goal of building vibrant,
trusted, flexible, and powerful public institutions must replace the prevailing
climate in which all public discretion and initiative is suspect, deserving of constant scrutiny, subject to continual reform and the distorting criteria of "efficiency" theory.

Currently, two different agendas vie to define the direction of governmental
reform. On the one hand, social policy reformers have searched for innovative
ways to make government work better. While on the other, the avowed purpose

is to radically reduce the role of government in social and economic affairs. These two agendas have frequently blurred in recent cycles of governmental reform: devolution, privatization, budget reduction, "quality circles," "re-invention," "re-engineering." As a result, positive experiments intended to innovate, have been undermined and confused with concurrent attempts to cut public resources and restrict powers. By the time reforms hit the ground, both the public and policymakers alike are frequently uncertain as to the designated problems, solution strategies, or intended objectives.

Nor has the application of so called "business models" to public management helped resolve these confusions or strengthen a coherent approach to reform. This trend actually conceals critically different diagnoses of the cause of administrative weakness: According to the first, there is too *little* managerial control, i.e., too many layers, duplication, administrative "fat," and waste are to be solved through making government "lean and mean," eliminating discretion and tightening up procedures. Whereas the second view locates the problem in too *much* centralized control—a condition to be remedied by "flattening the organization" and incentivizing risk-taking and experimentation.

Moreover, a grab-bag of techniques labeled as "market-based" have been indiscriminately applied to either or both problems.

Without diagnosis, reform becomes an end in itself. And in the effort to manage the steady march of "innovations"—the very reforms intended to "banish bureaucracy" have had the opposite effect: re-introducing and even increasing layering, procedural formalism, regulatory complexity, legalism, and rigidity —at the same time they destabilize existing linkage capacities.

Organization theory, development anthropology, and economic sociology have a great deal to teach public policy about the conditions that support innovation in complex institutional settings—and that avoid the circulation of free-ranging reforms and reorganizations. The value of intermediacy and brokerage is that these elements supply the critical organizational groundwork. As discussed above, this is precisely because they supplement the failures and rigidities of the formal system. Informal, auxiliary networks provide the channel for creative boundary-crossing, feed-back, incubation, adjustment, and "self-correction."

As Martin Landau taught, such supplementary capacities are assigned high value by all fields responsible for "high reliability" (such as the military, nuclear energy, law enforcement, and diplomatic intelligence). In these areas, "back channels" and the space for innovation are cultivated.[29] But in the area of social

---

[29]For applications to other policy areas, see e.g., William Westley, "Informal Organization of the Army: A Sociological Memoire" in H. Becker, B. Greer, D. Riesman, and R. Weiss, *Institutions and the Person*, Chicago: Aldine, 1968; Gene Rochlin, Todd LaPorte, and Karlene Roberts, "The Self-Designing High-Reliability Organization: Air-

policy, the same capacities are still regarded as "waste"; or, subjected to the over-specialized and formalized linkage strategies discussed above.

Thus, this occasion for reflection on the Model Cities era reveals an irony: at the very time when successful development in the private sector has learned to value the role of "slack"—i.e., intermediate organization, connective net-works, and social capital—social policy reform has, too often, worked against informal capacity-building. This is because the prevailing debates in administra-tive reform concentrate on a limited set of factors and offer limited choices.

Regardless of their ultimate theoretical validity, the classic dichotomies in public administration (centralization vs. decentralization; accountability vs. dis-cretion; professionalism vs. market incentives) have diverted attention from the importance of interconnections between sectors in a complex society—and how to strengthen them (Smith, 1983). To facilitate complex linkages, the challenge is to better harness the interaction of the formal and the informal; and to espe-cially do so on behalf of poor and excluded constituencies. Decisions in admin-istrative design afford opportunities to informally build in brokers, leadership and recruitment networks, career ladders, and other ties that support expanded institutional access and coordination for disadvantaged groups.

Sensitivity to questions of infrastructure is not a substitute for public law, public policy, and redistributive spending. However, it is a component for re-storing greater effectiveness to such efforts—a general outcome that, in its turn, will help relegitimate the role of government, as contemplated by Model Cities, in promoting equitable social change.

The reflections in this volume should aid the development of a collective wisdom to serve this end.

***

To further this exploration, the University of California at Berkeley's Insti-tute of Government Studies has assembled a group of leading organization and network analysts to examine how public policy can be used to strengthen institu-tional linkage for low-income communities and other excluded groups. This project will provide a context for exploring and advancing alternative strategies of policy design. The effort seeks to re-engage the expertise of veterans of OEO, Model Cities, CDBG, and civil rights advocacy for the benefit of future genera-tions of policymakers, planners, and community leaders. For further informa-tion, please contact: *The Martin Landau Center on Organization and Social*

---

craft Carrier Flight Operations at Sea" in *Naval War College Review*, Autumn 1987; and Alexander Weiss, "Informal Information Sharing Among Police Agencies" in *National Institute of Justice, Research Preview*, December 1998.

Change, at the Institute of Governmental Studies, University of California at Berkeley.

References

Brown. Michael K. and Steven Erie. 1981. "Blacks and the Legacy of the Great Society," *Public Policy* (3) Summer 1981.

Chisholm, Donald. 1989. Coordination without Hierarchy: Informal Structures in Multi-organizational Systems. Berkeley: University of California Press.

Frieden, Bernard, and Marshall Kaplan. 1975. *The Politics of Neglect*. Cambridge, Mass.: The MIT Press.

Greenstone, J. David, and Paul E. Peterson. 1973. *Race and Authority in Urban Politics: Community Participation and the War on Poverty*. New York: Russell Sage Foundation.

Granovetter, Mark. 1973. "The Strength of Weak Ties." *American Journal of Sociology* 78 No 6 (May): 1360-80.

Katz, Michael. 1986. In the Shadow of the Poorhouse: A Social History of Welfare in America. New York: Basic Books.

Landau, Madeline. 1988. *Race, Poverty & The Cities: Hyperinnovation in Complex Policy Systems*. Berkeley, Calif.: Institute of Governmental Studies, University of California, Berkeley.

Landau, Madeline, and Nancy Gilbert. 2004. "Democratic Inclusion or Bureaucratic Marginalization? The Impact of Governmental Reform and Policy Innovation Upon Civic Engagement for Low-Income Minority Communities." *California Policy Issues Annual* (5). Los Angeles, Calif.: The Edmund G. "Pat" Brown Institute of Public Affairs, California State University, Los Angeles.

_____. 2003. "Strengthening a Community's Social Capital: Methods and Measures for Low Income Community Initiatives," Report commissioned by the U.S. Department of Health and Human Services, Office of Community Services and the City of Oakland, Calif., Community Action Agency. Institute of Governmental Studies, UC Berkeley.

_____. 2002. "From Service Strategies to Group Employment Pathways: An Institution Building Approach to Connecting Low-Income Communities to the Labor Market," report prepared for the Alameda County Social Services Agency. Institute of Governmental Studies, UC Berkeley.

Landau, Martin. 1971. "Linkage Coding and Intermediacy: A Strategy for Institution Building." *Journal of Comparative Administration*, February 1971: 401-29.

Landau, Martin, Donald Chisholm, and Mark Webber. 1980. *Redundancy in Public Transit, Volume I: On the Idea of an Integrated Transit System*. Berkeley, Calif.: University of California, Berkeley, Institute of Urban and Regional Development.

Light, Paul. 1996. "Surviving Innovation: An Overview of the Minnesota Innovation Project" paper prepared for the annual meeting of the Association of Public Policy Analysts and Management, October 31, 1996.

_____. 1992. "Surviving Innovation: Thoughts on the Organizational Roots of Innovation and Change," paper presented at the Conference on Innovation and Change, September 18-21, 1992, University of Minnesota.

Lipsky, Michael. 1980. *Street Level Bureaucracy.* New York: Russell Sage Foundation.

_____. 1970. *Protest in City Politics.* Chicago, Ill.: Rand McNally.

Lowi, Theodore. 1979. *The End of Liberalism.* New York: W. W. Norton.

Marris, Peter, and Martin Rein. 1973. *Dilemmas of Social Reform: Poverty and Community Action in the United States* (2d edition). Chicago: Aldine Publishing Company.

May, Judith. 1973. "Two Model Cities: Negotiations in Oakland," in George Fredrickson, ed., *Neighborhood Control in the 1970s: Politics, Administration and Citizen Participation.* New York.

Marmor, Theodore, Jerry Mashaw, and Philip Harvey. 1990. *America's Misunderstood Welfare State: Persistent Myths, Enduring Realities.* New York: Basic Books.

Moynihan, Daniel Patrick. 1969. *Maximum Feasible Misunderstanding.* New York: The Free Press.

Putnam, Robert. 2000. Bowling Alone: The Collapse and Revival of American Community. New York: Simon & Schuster.

Saxenian, Annalee. 1996. Regional Advantage: Culture and Competition in Silicon Valley and Route 128. Cambridge, Mass.: Harvard University Press.

Skocpol, Theda. 2000. The Missing Middle: Working Families and the Future of American Social Policy. New York: The Century Foundation.

Sundquist, James L. 1968. *On Fighting Poverty.* New York: Basic Books.

U.S. General Accounting Office. 1992. Integrating Human Services: Linking At-Risk Families with Services more Successful than Systems Reform Efforts, Washington, D.C.: U.S. GAO Printing Office.

Walsh, Joan. 1997. *The Eye of the Storm: Ten Years on the Front Lines of New Futures,* report prepared for the Annie E. Casey Foundation. Baltimore, Md.: Annie E. Casey Foundation.

151 Model Cities

Alabama
   Huntsville
   Tuskegee
Alaska
   Juneau
Arkansas
   Little Rock
   Texarkana
Arizona
   Gila River Indian
    Community
   Tucson
California
   Berkeley
   Compton
   Fresno
   Los Angeles City
   Los Angeles
  County
   Oakland
   Pittsburg
   Richmond
   San Diego
   San Francisco
   San Jose
Colorado
   Denver
   Trinidad
Connecticut
   Bridgeport
   Hartford
   New Haven
   New London
   Waterbury
Delaware
   Wilmington
District of Columbia

Florida
   Dade County
   Tampa
Georgia
   Alma
   Athens
   Atlanta
   Gainesville
   Savannah
Hawaii
   Honolulu
Idaho
   Boise
Illinois
   Carbondale
   Chicago
   East St. Louis
   Rock Island
Indiana
   Gary
   Indianapolis
   South Bend
Iowa
   Des Moines
Kansas
   Kansas City
   Wichita
Kentucky
   Bowling Green
   Covington
   Pikeville
Louisiana
   New Orleans
Maine
   Lewiston
   Portland

Maryland
   Baltimore
   Prince Georges
   County
Massachusetts
   Boston
   Cambridge
   Fall River
   Holyoke
   Lowell
   Lynn
   New Bedford
   Springfield
   Worcester
Michigan
   Ann Arbor
   Benton Harbor
   Detroit
   Genesee County
   (Flint)
   Grand Rapids
   Highland Park
   Lansing
   Saginaw
Minnesota
   Duluth
   Minneapolis
   St. Paul
Missouri
   Kansas City
   St. Louis
Montana
   Butte
   Helena
New Hampshire
   Manchester

New Jersey
    East Orange
    Hoboken
    Jersey City
    Newark
    Paterson
    Perth Amboy
    Plainfield
    Trenton
New Mexico
    Albuquerque
    Santa Fe
New York
    Binghamton
    Buffalo
    Cohoes
    Mt. Vernon
    New York City
        Central and East
        Harlem
        South Bronx
        Central Brooklyn
    Poughkeepsie
    Rochester
    Syracuse
North Carolina
    Asheville
    Charlotte
    High Point
    Winston Salem
North Dakota
    Fargo

Ohio
    Akron
    Cincinnati
    Cleveland
    Columbus
    Dayton
    Martins Ferry
    Toledo
    Youngstown
Oklahoma
    Lawton
    McAlester
    Tulsa
Oregon
    Portland
Pennsylvania
    Allegheny County
    Bradford
    Erie
    Lancaster
    Philadelphia
    Pittsburgh
    Reading
    Scranton
    Wilkes Barre
Puerto Rico
    San Juan
Rhode Island
    Pawtucket
    Providence

South Carolina
    Rock Hill
    Spartanburg
Tennessee
    Chattanooga
    Cookeville
    Nashville
    Davidson County
    Smithville
    DeKalb County
Texas
    Austin
    Eagle Pass
    Edinburg
    Houston
    Laredo
    Texarkana
    San Antonio
    Waco
Utah
    Salt Lake County
Vermont
    Winooski
Virginia
    Norfolk
Richmond
Washington
    Tacoma
    Seattle
Wisconsin
    Milwaukee
Wyoming
    Cheyenne

Glossary

AMERICAN PUBLIC HEALTH ASSOCIATION (APHA): a public service association, which developed standards for housing inspection to determine eligibility for clearance as preparation for Urban Renewal projects.

ANNUAL ARRANGEMENT: negotiated arrangement between HUD and cities specifying an amount of funding per year for certain federal programs.

ANNUAL APPROPRIATION: the amount of annual funding appropriated by congress for a federal agency.

AREA REDEVELOPMENT ADMINISTRATION (ARA): established under the Kennedy administration in 1961 to combat chronic unemployment in impoverished cities and rural areas by increasing their levels of economic growth.

BETTER COMMUNITIES ACT: proposed legislation under the Nixon administration in 1973, which was the precursor to the Community Development Block Grant Program.

BLOCK GRANT: a grant given to cities, counties, or states, which allows the recipient the flexibility to choose among a designated group of categorical programs.

CATEGORICAL PROGRAM: A federal program that grants funds to address a specific category of need such as sewers, transportation, roads and parks.

HOUSE COMMITTEE ON BANKING and CURRENCY (Currently, the Committee on Financial Services): jurisdiction includes public and private housing and urban development.

HOUSE SUBCOMMITTEE ON HOUSING AND COMMUNITY DEVELOPMENT (Currently, Housing and Community Opportunity): a subcommittee of the House Committee on Banking and Currency.

HOUSE SUBCOMMITTEE ON HUD-INDEPENDENT AGENCIES (Currently, VA, HUD, and Independent Agencies): a subcommittee of the House Committee on Appropriations.

SENATE SUBCOMMITTEE ON HOUSING AND URBAN AFFAIRS (Currently, Housing and Transportation): a subcommittee of the Senate Committee on Banking, Housing, and Urban Affairs.

SENATE SUBCOMMITTEE ON HOUSING AND URBAN DEVELOPMENT AND INDEPENDENT AGENCIES (Currently, VA/HUD-Independent Agencies): a subcommittee of the Senate Committee on Appropriations.

COMMUNITY ACTION AGENCY (CAA): a non-profit organization established to help community members attain sufficiency and provide a variety of human services programs.

COMMUNITY ACTION PROGRAM (CAP): serves low –to-moderate income residents with programs such as welfare-to-work, energy assistance and home ownership counseling.

COMMUNITY DEVELOPMENT (CD): locally directed effort to coordinate federal, state, and local programs designed to improve neighborhoods.

COMMUNITY DEVELOPMENT BLOCK GRANT (CDBG): a formula-based federal program stemming from the Community Development Act of 1974, which distributes money to communities for improving neighborhoods.

COMPREHENSIVE EMPLOYMENT AND TRAINING ACT (CETA): a federal program funding money to cities and states to afford job opportunities to people of low to moderate income.

CITIZEN PARTICIPATION (CP): the process by which citizens are afforded the opportunity to evaluate and influence policy decisions that affect their neighborhood.

DEMONSTRATION CITIES ACT OF 1966: the initial legislation leading to the Model Cities Program. Because the "demonstration" in Demonstration Cities was considered a politically charged word, the program's name was changed to the more benign Model Cities Program.

ECONOMIC DEVELOPMENT ADMINISTRATION (EDA): established in 1965 to generate employment opportunities and to stimulate industrial and commercial growth in economically distressed areas.

FANNIE MAE or FEDERAL NATIONAL MORTGAGE ASSOCIATION (FNMA), a stockholder owned, government sponsored enterprise, created in 1938, to increase the availability of affordable home mortgages by establishing an efficient secondary home mortgage market. Fannie Mae purchases home mortgage loans not insured by the Federal Housing Administration or guaranteed by the Veterans Administration from their originating financial institutions.

FEDERAL HOUSING ADMINISTRATION (FHA): an agency of the U.S. Department of Housing and Urban Development that insures home mortgage loans originated by approved lenders to borrowers who do not meet conventional underwriting criteria.

FREDDIE MAC or FEDERAL HOME LOAN MORTGAGE CORPORATION (FHLMC): a stockholder owned, Government Sponsored Enterprise, chartered in 1970, whose mission, like Fannie Mae, is to increase the availability of affordable home mortgages.

GENERAL ACCOUNTING OFFICE (GAO): supports Congress in its constitutional responsibilities and helps improve the performance and ensure the accountability of the federal government. The duties of the GAO include investigation of such agencies as Freddie Mac and Fannie Mae.

GENERAL REVENUE SHARING: formula-based funding to cities or towns that is figured by factors such as population and is not targeted to specific needs.

GINNIE MAE or GOVERNMENT NATIONAL MORTGAGE ASSOCIATION (GNMA): an agency in the U.S. Department of Housing and Urban Development, which, like Fannie Mae and Freddie Mac, whose mission is to increase the availability of affordable mortgages by creating a secondary mortgage market by purchase of mortgages issued by the FHA.

GSE: Government Sponsored Enterprise, a quasi-private enterprise that is chartered by the US government with special provisions that assist it in meeting its mandate serving a public purpose.

HHFA: U.S. Housing and Home Finance Agency—reorganized in 1963 as the U.S. Department of Housing and Urban Development (HUD).

HOLD HARMLESS: In the Community Development Block Grant Program, the provision that a city could not receive less than it averaged from all HUD categorical programs for the previous three years in order to prevent extreme funding loss owing to use of a formula.

HUD: U.S. Department of Housing and Urban Development—created in 1963 from the reorganization of the U.S. Housing and Home Finance Agency

INTERAGENCY PROGRAMING: a term referring to the coordination of funding from various agencies in order to concentrate resources in addressing a variety of needs in a designated community

LGP: Loan Guarantee Program, allows communities to use anticipated CDBG funding as collateral for loans from HUD in order to plan and complete projects taking several years.

MAINENANCE OF EFFORT: the concept that new money received from the federal government may not be used to replace funding for already existing city services.

MCP: Model Cities Program, the federally funded, five-year experimental program administered by HUD—initiated by the Demonstration Cities Act of 1966

NAHRO: National Association of Housing and Redevelopment Officials, a professional association that employs lobbyists to affect legislation related to housing.

NCDA: National Community Development Association, a professional association providing information to cities on legislation related to housing.

NEW FEDERALISM: the Nixon administration's effort to increase decision making at the local level which included the concept of grouping government categorical programs together in special revenue sharing block grant programs with limited federal regulations

NLIHC: National Low-Income Housing Coalition, a public coalition that represents the interests of low-income people.

NSA: Neighborhood Strategy Area, as required by HUD, an area within a community that defined and designated for concentrated community effort.

SCP: Small Cities Program: a HUD program for cities with populations under 50,000.

SPECIAL REVENUE SHARING: under the Nixon administration, a proposal for grouping categorical programs into six block grant programs

THREE-YEAR PLAN: a condition of application for federal funding mandates cities to develop a three-year plan.

UDAG: Urban Development Action Grants, discretionary grants awarded to communities by HUD on a competitive basis for major economic development projects

VISTA: Volunteers In Service To America, a domestic program serving the urban poor.

About the Editors and Authors

John A. Sasso is president of the Community Development Training Institute, former executive secretary of the National Community Development Association, and co-creator of the Culture of Peace Project. He served as executive director of the Pawtucket Rhode Island Model Cities Program from 1968 to 1970, and since then has consulted and worked with local, national, and international groups on economic development, community development, and housing and urban energy strategies.

Priscilla Foley worked in public education from 1965 to 1997. In 1992, she contributed to the Educational Testing Service publication, *A Teacher's Guide to Advanced Placement Courses in Studio Art*. Foley holds a BFA from the Rhode Island School of Design and an MA in education from the University of Rhode Island. Since 1998, she has worked with John Sasso on a project to produce an oral history of the Model Cities Program.

Madeline Landau is director of the Program on Community Change & Public Policy at the Institute of Governmental Studies, UC Berkeley. Landau is a political anthropologist with over twenty years experience in ethnographic field research, teaching and consultation regarding policy innovation, administrative reform and community involvement strategies, and their impact on the social and political development of low-income and ethnic communities.

Mark Tigan has over twenty-five years experience in local government as a Model Cities director, city manager, community and economic development director, local community development corporation executive director and codirector of Community Development Training Institute. Over the last ten years Tigan has consulted on major projects funded by Housing and Urban Development (HUD), including Oklahoma City terrorist bombing recovery, state of Connecticut's pilot economic development program, and Boston's World Trade Center hotel. Tigan served as adjunct faculty to University of Rhode Island and University of Massachusetts at Boston. He is now core faculty member of the Community Development and Planning program at Clark University.

Index

252 *John Sasso and Priscilla Foley*

Martin Landau Center on Organization and Social Change, 234